NAZARÉ

LIFE AND DEATH WITH
THE BIG-WAVE SURFERS

Matt Majendie

WELBECK

Published in 2023 by Welbeck
An imprint of Welbeck Non-Fiction Limited
Part of the Welbeck Publishing Group
Offices in: London – 20 Mortimer Street, London W1T 3JW &
Sydney – Level 17, 207 Kent St, Sydney NSW 2000 Australia
www.welbeckpublishing.com

Design and layout © 2023 Welbeck Non-Fiction Ltd
Text © 2023 Matt Majendie

A CIP catalogue record for this book is available from the British Library.

ISBN
Hardback – 978-1-80279-200-3
Trade Paperback – 978-1-80279-580-6

Typeset by seagulls.net
Printed in Great Britain by CPI Books, Chatham, Kent

10 9 8 7 6 5 4 3 2 1

PREFACE

For the process of writing this book, I spent the latter part of 2021 and early 2022 flying to and from Portugal to rub shoulders with the surfers of Nazaré for their big-wave season.

With each visit came ever-changing Covid restrictions and testing requirements, adding a level of bureaucracy beyond simply poring over the cheapest flights in and out of Portugal's capital, Lisbon.

Nevertheless, every time my flight landed at Lisbon Airport and I prepared to drive up to Nazaré, it was always with a mixture of excitement and trepidation.

The antics performed in the waves by the surfers are both awe inspiring and addictive, watching people do something seemingly impossible day after day, often with what looks like remarkable ease.

But always in the back of my mind was that nagging sensation that things could go horribly wrong at any given moment. Surfing waves up to and over 80 feet is understandably precarious, and lives have been lost at big-wave surfing spots around the globe.

Death is, understandably, not a subject the surfing community talk to each other about with any regularity, nor is there exactly an omertà over the subject. Whenever asked about the prospect of tragedy, the surfers are all honest enough to admit it exists in their thinking patterns, all with the realisation that one day it may happen.

All season long, I had a perpetual fear of such a fate befalling those who took to the waters but especially the main characters of this book – Andrew Cotton, Nic von Rupp, Maya Gabeira, Sebastian Steudtner and Sérgio Cosme – who were kind enough to let me into their eye-catching but unusual world.

Undertaking this, there was always the very real concern that tragedy might unfold before my own eyes. At one point relatively early in the season, I genuinely thought I was witnessing the death of one particular surfer only for him and his rescuers to pull off what seemed like the unlikeliest of escapes.

When the 2021–22 season drew to a close, there was almost an anti-climax that my time as a voyeur of these extreme sportsmen and women had drawn to a close. But there was also a palpable sense of relief that, amid all the wipeouts, hospitalisations and inevitable rehabilitations, everyone had ended the season with their lives intact.

Nazaré is a newcomer to the big-wave surfing scene, and one of its great claims – aside from producing some of the most consistent big waves – is the fact that no surfer had ever died in its waters. At the end of the 2021–22 season that was still the case. Tragically, since finishing this book, that is no longer the situation.

Marcio Freire was a 47-year-old Brazilian surfer. He was perhaps best known from the 2016 documentary *Mad Dogs*, which featured him and his fellow surfers Danilo Couto and Yuri Soledade's attempts to paddle surf the big waves at Jaws in Hawaii.

Freire was on a family trip to Portugal when he took to the water on a relatively innocuous January day by Nazaré's standards, the waves topping out at a maximum height of about 20 feet. During his career, he had surfed waves three times that size.

But he came unstuck on one particular wave, which knocked him off his board. He was pounded by three successive waves and under-water for what onlookers believed was about 40 seconds.

By the time he was rescued by his fellow Brazilian Lucas Chumbo, he was no longer breathing. Cardiopulmonary resuscitation (CPR) was performed on him on the beach but he was pronounced dead at the scene.

It resulted in a lost father, a lost son, a lost husband and a lost friend to many in Nazaré and the wider big-wave surfing community.

Tributes have flooded in about the popular Freire ever since. Von Rupp, also in Nazaré's waters on that day, spoke of Freire surfing all day with a smile on his face.

The incident has understandably left those in the water and those watching from the clifftops traumatised by this tragic denouement. And in the days afterwards, many of them gathered in a circle on their jetskis, holding hands in memory of one of their tribe on top of the very waters where he had lost his life.

The exact details of what unfolded will become clear in time, but Nazaré has finally, as many predicted, experienced its first loss of life. Sadly, the reality is that Freire won't be the last, such is the dangerous nature of the waters these surfers choose to enter during the course of the big-wave season.

While Freire was by no means a Nazaré regular, his loss has been keenly felt. And it comes not long after Jorge Leal, one of the key figures in the town's origin story in big-wave surfing, was hospitalised and left unable to speak after a massive stroke just as the 2022–23 season was getting under way.

Leal, often referred to as Jesus on account of his long hair and beard, features in the pages of this book, and was the original cameraman and photographer on the clifftop for the first big waves ever surfed in this spot. Now, the clifftop is littered with those behind a camera lens – amateur and professional – but Leal was very much the forefather of that particular filming movement.

Universally liked within Nazaré's surfing community, he faces a lengthy period of rehabilitation and recovery, the outcome of which is unknown. And such is the tight-knit nature of the big-wave surfers that its best-known names have tried to rally round to raise funds to pay medical bills of €15,000 a month for treatment they estimate could last up to a year.

Freire and Leal remain in many people's daily thoughts but, even amid such awful moments, life in Nazaré goes on. Day after day, they still pull out of the harbour on their jetskis to surf one of the most dangerous stretches of water in the world.

Some have no doubt questioned their own existence in this unique corner of the planet – as they often do when things go wrong – and yet they remain there willing to risk it all.

Safety is a perpetual work in progress in Nazaré and wider big-wave surfing. There will no doubt be lessons learned from this particular tragedy, and further improvements made to ensure such a perilous pastime and profession can be as safe as humanly possible.

For many, Freire's passing will be the defining moment of the 2022–23 season, which in its early part has been relatively quiet in terms of the big swells compared to the season before. The one thing that Nazaré had tried so hard to avoid has finally happened.

CONTENTS

Prologue

A FIGHT FOR SURVIVAL

One minute, Andrew Cotton is reclining in the December sunshine, the next, fighting for his life, a lone black blob teetering in Nazaré's death zone.

Whitewash surrounds him and for two and a half minutes – a time frame that feels infinitely longer for his girlfriend Justine White, friends and teammates watching on the clifftop above – his life hangs in the balance.

Things tend to go wrong quickly in Nazaré. One minute, he is being picked up on the back of a jet ski after riding a latest wave. As his rescuer Alemão de Maresias hits the throttle to surpass the crest of the next wave, the lip of it juts up just that bit higher than either anticipates.

The rescue vehicle lands heavily back on the water's surface. Cotty, as he is better known to everyone, shakes the water from his eyes only to realise, as his vision returns, that his rescuer has been knocked clean off.

He quickly shifts himself into the driver's seat and hits full gas to try to evade the next breaking wave – only to be sideswiped and sent battering towards the rocks on which the Fort of São Miguel Arcanjo stands.

Those looking out for him on the walkie-talkies, the so-called spotters, are unsighted on the clifftop – their view blocked by the fort

– and unable to help. Others on the fort wolf-whistle to the jet skis surrounding the rock as their drivers try to spot him and find a safe passage to rescue. The level of panic from the helpless above to the even more helpless in the water rapidly grows and reaches a crescendo.

Cotton is thrown against the two standalone rocks that jut out of the water's surface between the fort and the open expanse of the Atlantic Ocean. They spit him out perilously close to the jagged caves below the fort, in which certain death awaits. One more big wave and he will be battered and shattered against the cliff face, and will most likely end up dead. One of his peers, the Portuguese surfer Nic von Rupp, later estimates the chance of survival at this stage and in that position is about 10 per cent.

But, momentarily, the size of the waves offers some brief respite. The current whips him out to safety and his marine walk with death is at an end, 150 seconds of mayhem over. Cotton – by this point relatively breathless, battered and bruised – is finally picked up by a jet-ski driver.

For those standing on the clifftop, that two and a half minutes feels markedly longer, and also lengthy enough for Cotton himself to consider a potential endgame.

"I remember thinking, *This is about as bad as it gets*," he says, showered off and changed just hours after the incident. "I thought, *If the next wave gets me, it could be a really horrible, painful and slow death.* There's some gnarly caves, the rocks are super sharp and seaweedy. If you're pushed down there, it would be horrible. Sometimes you watch the waves and they regularly break where I was. This time, for whatever the reason, they didn't. It's the roll of the dice, isn't it?"

Cotton had previously decided not to go out on this particular day. With windy conditions and bumpy waves, it was an unnecessary risk just two days out from a competition.

Now that he is in his forties, there is no longer the burning desire, the aching need to surf every wave, to be immersed in every single swell he once had. But even now, when all his sensibilities say something else, he sometimes just can't help himself.

Cotton's instinct is to sit it out in the coastline home he is renting during the big-wave season in Nazaré. But on days like this, the strength of the villa's location can also be its curse. There is something in the waves that, on such days, drags even a noncommittal surfer in and stokes a fear of missing out, as jet skis bob in and out of the water and surfers catch the occasional clean wave only a few hundred metres in front of him.

Nazaré's big-wave surfers have a propensity to shake off the near disasters – they have to, in order to mentally get themselves back in the water.

The surfer from North Devon is not the first one to find himself stranded in big-wave surfing's no man's land. Others have been in the same watery limbo between life and death.

Garrett McNamara, the first man to surf Nazaré on its big days, ended up there moments after breaking the world record in 2011 for what was then the biggest wave ever surfed – a 78-footer. Such is the speed with which moments of celebration can nearly end in tragedy along this stretch of the Portuguese coast.

Even years later, the Hawaiian McNamara's wife Nicole likes to imagine she can locate a spot in those caves where he can improbably find himself a safe haven and where she could winch down food to him should he ever find himself stuck in there, confident he could see it out safely until the waves have died down. In Nazaré, family-and-friend onlookers tell themselves all manner of things to reassure themselves, as they helplessly stand a couple of hundred metres above and avoid acknowledging that their loved ones might one day meet with tragedy.

Up until this point – the start of the 2021–22 surfing season in the Portuguese fishing village – remarkably, no one has died in its perilous waters. And yet there is a foreboding for all those working in and out of the water of such an eventuality on any given day. This is the nature of the surfers' dangerous undertaking. The reality is it might even happen this season.

For Cotton, his own dice with death is a bad one but, he argues somewhat unbelievably, for those watching, there have been infinitely worse. For his girlfriend, it is her first time witnessing him in real trouble. Turned white, she is virtually muted, her walkie-talkie, normally used to communicate with those in the water, snatched from her by one of the spotters in an initially vain attempt to launch a rescue mission, which is only achieved thanks to the changing current of forgiving seas rather than all manner of safety operations in place on land and sea.

Cotton, Britain's leading big-wave surfer, has broken his back and torn his anterior cruciate ligament (ACL) in Nazaré's stormy seas on previous outings. Of his latest brush with the rocks, he says almost nonchalantly:

"It's not as bad as the back-breaker, and it's more traumatic for anyone watching than for anyone going through it. But there was a moment where I thought, *I've really fucked it here, this is really going to be it.* But I've thought that a few times before. The nightmare is to get pushed into one of those caves – you'd never get out – so I'd definitely put it in my top five worst, maybe higher."

Everyone has their Nazaré stories: knocked unconscious and face down in the water; the elbow dislocated at its socket and the arm pointing in the wrong direction on exiting the water; the handlebars of the jet ski knocking out a pair of front teeth; an earlobe ripped clean off. The list goes on.

And yet they still return, big wave after big wave, swell after swell, near tragedy after near tragedy, for that ultimate adrenaline rush and that perfect wave – if such a thing exists or is capable of quenching their surfing thirst.

1

SURFING'S MOUNT EVEREST

Nazaré is the pinnacle of big-wave surfing – its Mecca, its Mount Everest, its Holy Grail. It is consistently the biggest wave in the world and perhaps its most visually spectacular. While other big-wave spots might have more stunning barrels and blue skies, none can match the backdrop of Nazaré. Stand well back from the clifftop, with the fort and its small red lighthouse on top, and you see its full majesty and ferocity. Photographs from there almost give a false perspective, as though the wave is fronting up entirely facing that fort, ready to batter a stricken surfer into the rock face. Within it, surfers still look like a mere dot as they are towed in by the jet skis and fight to stay on their boards and for survival.

The place has an inexplicable pull. It brings adrenaline junkies from all over the planet. There are the regulars, those that dip in and out during the season, and even those who come for a one-off visit simply to see what all the hype is about and never come back. Others, meanwhile, call it home for the season or even for a lifetime. None are the same but they all share the same vested interest: to surf the biggest wave in history and stay alive while doing so.

Andrew Cotton, a former plumber and one of the first to surf Nazaré, hails from North Devon in the United Kingdom. At times, he acts a little bemused that he is still here – or that he ever made it here at all. He has given much of his life to the place, and it has given him much in return. Despite his 42 years, in a community that skews young, he has no plans to slow down or pack up, the desire still there to surf the big waves, although he does pick his moments now. From October to March – the length of a typical big-wave season in Portugal – Nazaré is predominantly his home. Each year that home can vary, from his current villa overlooking the waves to a camper van or else CAR Surf, a high-performance centre cut out of a forest, with bunk rooms where the surfers can stay. Often the accommodation choice depends on the budget for that season, and the money he has conjured up from various sponsors.

Wherever he rests his head at the end of the day, he's been coming here long enough to earn himself Portuguese citizenship. For six months, it serves as his main base, although he likes to escape the madness of it all on occasion. Nazaré can be exhausting and all-consuming – not just Mother Nature, but the forces of personality with which he vies on a daily basis. So he will dart back to the south-west of England, where his two children live with his ex-wife. Or else he might head to the west coast of Ireland, where he first established himself as a big-wave surfer and which remains a quieter haven to explore his passion, and almost strip it back to the basics. Another home from home is the French Alps, where his girlfriend lives.

In contrast, for Maya Gabeira, who resides here full-time, this is home – and it may always be. A trailblazer for women surfers, the Brazilian was the first female big-wave surfer of note anywhere on the planet. She was battered by the elements and by some of her peers, experiencing sexism and verbal abuse, but found her own pathway through and smashed the door down for future women surfers to come up through the ranks. That the likes of Justine Dupont are matching anything the men can do here today is testament to the trials and tribulations Gabeira went through to get to this point. That she is even alive is no mean feat, having come within a whisker of losing her life in the waters of Nazaré. But rather than be put off, she returned – after years battling with the physical and mental demons of a broken back and brush with death – to tackle it once more. For her, there is almost an inexplicably magical hold that Nazaré has on her, enough to leave her tight-knit family behind in her native Brazil and buy a house – a paradise in the hillside 10 minutes' drive from the harbour where the surfers head out on jet skis to surf the waves. She lives there in relative solitude with her two dogs, two goats and the occasional stray cats, who prefer the trees just outside the gates to her home.

On paper, her long-time partnership in the water with German surfer Sebastian Steudtner shouldn't work, but does. They aren't quite chalk and cheese, but their approaches are entirely different. Gabeira is neither laissez-faire in her approach nor is she quite as methodical as the German, but she is a yin to his yang in the water, and somehow it is a relationship that thrives. They are poles apart in some ways, but have in common a propensity to often operate alone – a shared partnership in having occasionally been outsiders in Nazaré.

The German is the surfing scientist. Whereas for many, it is just surfer and board against the elements, Steudtner leaves no stone unturned in a perpetual quest to improve. He has use of a wind tunnel at one of his sponsors Porsche's headquarters back in his homeland. With help from his technology partner Siemens, he had a full-body cast made to better understand every nuance of his body on top of the board as it was faced with the elements. Hailing from Nuremberg, a landlocked city miles away from any expanse of open water, he is innovative in a way that is different to that of any of his peers – from the cutting-edge science he embraces to employing a military doctor more used to treating patients in a different type of war zone. And Steudtner has done more than any other surfer to improve safety in these Portuguese waters. He won't admit it, but there are surfers alive because of him and the measures he has pushed to improve safety. He is also one of the benchmarks for the big-wave movement, riding some of the biggest waves in the world with the toughest lines. And yet there are times he can occasionally, like Gabeira, seem an alien within this relatively small community.

Nic von Rupp carries the weight of expectation for home hopes. Born and brought up a few miles down the west coast of Portugal, he is one of big-wave surfing's home-grown talents and has marked himself out not just as the best from within the country, but also one of the very best globally. He is fiercely proud of his roots and of putting his country on the map as a big-wave surfing Mecca, working with the country's tourism board to continue to promote Portugal and lure more people to watch him and his peers in action. Originally a paddle surfer – those who simply paddle themselves into big waves – he initially fought against embracing tow-in surfing, which has enabled big-wave surfers to tackle the really monstrous waves. He likens the difference in styles between paddle and tow-in surfing to doing the Tour de France on a bicycle and on a motorbike.

Nowadays, he switches between the two, paddling on the smaller days, and towing in and out on the bigger days – with the acceptance that the truly monstrous, record-breaking waves are only possible to catch with a jet ski to drag you in. It is an unbroken record that pushes him on, he and his rivals driven by the mythical 100-foot wave which no one believes has ever been surfed, and yet is both the aim and expectation for the season ahead. Cameras follow his moves, along with those of Cotton and others, for the HBO documentary of the same name, *100 Foot Wave*, based around the first man to surf

Nazaré on the big days but, going from one season to the next, focusing on other athletes' roles within the big-wave surfing movement, Von Rupp included.

In Nazaré, surfers work in teams. To get into a really big wave, paddling face down on a surfboard becomes an impossibility after a certain height, so jet skis become a necessary evil. It brings additional danger to the water, with so many heavy vehicles and engines churning away underneath the surface, dodging both the big waves and the surfers immersed in them. Working together, surfers and drivers chop and change, taking turns to tow each other into the waves with a tow rope attached to the back and then taking their turn to surf. Von Rupp's ever-present partner in that regard is Sérgio Cosme. At times, they can bicker and bristle but others have learned to accept that this is just their way, and there is a respect and brotherly love between the pair.

Cosme is Portuguese and surfs big waves too – although to a lesser degree these days, partly because of injury, partly because his other skill is the most sought-after within this band of brothers. These days, he is better known as one of the best jet-ski drivers in Nazaré, both in terms of towing in surfers like Von Rupp and also in rescuing their lives when things go awry. As with Steudtner, there are many that owe their lives to him as the guardian angel of Nazaré's waters, and he knows it. But the prospect of tragedy is one that constantly hangs over him, the thought that one day he might not be able to swoop in to save the life of one of his motley crew. And yet he approaches each day with an optimism that is infectious, an adrenaline junkie as happy riding his array of motorbikes as he is with altogether different horsepower under him in the water.

My own gateway into Nazaré's big waves begins with Von Rupp. We met while I was on a family holiday in a rented house that sat in the grounds of his parents' Portuguese home. It was Von Rupp who drove me to witness the monster waves for the first time and introduced me to some of the sport's leading characters. It is a community with an open-door policy. For all their own commitments, everyone is willing to take the time to talk about a passion and pastime that looks like madness to most but, at the same time, has a sort of magnetic pull over even its spectators. For the 2021–22 season, I had the good fortune to be one – welcomed into that community, driven out on a jet ski into the big waves, allowed into their homes and often wined and dined by them – to try to understand what makes them all tick.

The quintet I followed over a single season in Nazaré are but five stars in a town with many – albeit ones all at the heartbeat of a community trying to stay afloat, literally and financially, and, more crucially, stay alive from one day to the next. Their lives intertwine throughout the season, both good and bad.

2

WELCOME TO NAZARÉ

A simple black sign hangs over a crumbling tarmac road, closed off from most traffic by a small red and white automatic barrier. In white text, it bears the Portuguese greeting "Bem-vindo às maiores ondas do mundo" – simply translated, "Welcome to the biggest waves in the world".

On both sides of the barrier, from first light until last, people of all nationalities – from 120 countries, according to the last count from the visitors' book at the fort – amble to the landmark fort, which has stood in the same spot since 1577, built by King Sebastian I to protect the town's fishing and shipbuilding enterprises from rising pirate attacks.

The sense of excitement for day trippers is palpable, as they hope to catch a glimpse of the thrill-seekers below who are daring enough to brave the waves on those big days. The volume of footfall makes any newcomer to the town quickly realise this is the right spot.

For those who have taken this same walk hundreds of times during the course of the season, it sometimes feels like the place and the people are almost caught in a loop of the exact same moment in time. Claudio Teixeira, better known by his performing name Zuko Nature, is usually there playing out his slightly haunting melodies, with echoes of the sea in the background, from his grassy stage at the top of the road. The same few sellers and their stalls offer surfboard key rings, Nazaré T-shirts and jewellery to the tourists day after day.

Just 100 metres further up the road, a homeless man is enthusi-
astically directing traffic into the few parking spaces available, in the
hope of some loose change from the visiting tourists. Around him,
women in the traditional seven skirts are selling nuts from the stalls
of Sitio da Nazaré's main square, trying to catch the attention of
passers-by. Surrounding these women on the cobblestone square are
the paint-eroded walls of the buildings, impacted by the relentless
nature of the salty sea air.

Each hour, on the hour, the bell tolls at Santuário de Nossa
Senhora da Nazaré, the Catholic church which was built in the four-
teenth century at the behest of another Portuguese king, Ferdinand,
as part of a pilgrimage.

But while the everyday sights and sounds are familiar in the
walk down to the lighthouse, what awaits in the water below is
never the same.

On the calm days – when the lines of people still venture up and
down, unaware of the lack of action in the water – it is impossible to
think the big waves that have put Nazaré on the map could even exist,
the sun glinting off the still blue waters of Praia do Norte, the town's
north beach.

And just as the sea can be utterly calm on some days, on others
it brews up an unimaginable storm which acts as the perfect marine
adventure playground to a small but ever-increasing number of surfers
from around the globe – from Portugal to Brazil and from the North
Devon coast to the northern shores of Hawaii.

As an onlooker, every part of the experience emanates a feel of
organised chaos. Either side of the tarmac road – up and down which
a tuk-tuk service now takes the less active day trippers – are the red
clay clifftops. There is no designated seating and no viewing platform, bar the roof of the fort. Instead, there is an increasingly eroded

clifftop which, on the big days, becomes littered with people. The rudimentary nature of the set-up is perhaps in keeping with the natural phenomenon of the waves taking place in the waterscape below. In fact, simplicity permeates Nazaré, a town that bizarrely – particularly given the hordes of cars that flock here in the hot summer months and, more recently, its wintry water explorers – does not contain a single traffic light. And well behind the crumbling clifftop stand wind turbines harvesting the often blistering gales on nearly the most western point of Europe.

In the water, act after virtual act is performed as a sort of ballet between surfer and jet-ski driver as they mirror each other's moves through the waves, the jet ski acting as a tow-in and then rescue, all of this dance choreographed by a spotter on a radio further along the clifftop from the spectators. There is an order of sorts. The surfers, clothed in a wetsuit with an inflatable vest, a hood and boots to deal with the cold climate of the Atlantic, and jet-ski drivers bob up and down at the back of the wave queuing for their turn.

Inexplicably, the waves drag everyone in – literally, in the case of the surfers, and visibly, for those watching time and again. With each visit, there is a feeling of excitement to be returning, an uncertainty of what that day might bring, and a sense of awe at this natural phenomenon – and at the motley crew gathering from around the world to indulge in a collective obsession.

There is a pantomime element to it too: great cheers as a big wave is caught; "ooh"s and "ahh"s at the waves gone wrong, the moments the surfers are enveloped by the monstrous white water; and cheers when they finally remerge and are rescued. In the 2021–22 season, the surfers have taken to gathering below the clifftop to wave their goodbyes at the end of a session and offer thanks to those watching the water, much like modern-day gladiators.

Some surfers make it back to the safety of the harbour on a jet ski, while others are driven away in an ambulance to hospital and yet others get spat out on the big expanse of sand on the north beach, all too often an eventual safe haven for the breathless surfers devoured and thrown out by the big waves.

On the big days, it is incomprehensible that they perform this daily dance. On dry land, the ground shakes as in the midst of a small earthquake, the roar of the water audible around much of Nazaré, the spray of water powerful enough to batter you in the face even well away from the edge.

Welcome to Nazaré.

3

THE DANGERS OF THE OCEAN

Before the surfers came here, the only men of the sea in Nazaré were its fishermen. A proud collective remains, patrolling its waters with their trawlers today. The first records in Nazaré's history of fishing date back to 1643. Where much of the town of Nazaré stands, along the main beach, was once coastal sand dunes on which the population eventually settled. There are reminders of the importance of the sea dotted all over town, from its various statues to the restaurants and the many murals across town. On the main beach stand a row of colourful old fishing vessels. Throughout the twentieth century, fishing was the livelihood of almost all residents within the town, despite its inherent dangers. Where once, workers would drag their fishing vessels in and out of the water on to beach – in often inclement conditions and at great personal risk – the creation of a harbour in the 1980s has given them a safer haven and a heavily diminished risk of death.

But the harbour was a necessity for the economy too. Without it, profitability was low and fishermen would often relocate to another coastal town – some a few miles along the coast to Peniche, others much further afield to Canada for the potential riches offered by the cod fishing of Newfoundland. For those who stayed behind, it was a struggle both to make money and to stay alive.

Even today, there is a nod to the past dangers faced by the Nazarene population. Some of the older women of the town still dress head to toe in black, as a way of mourning a husband or son lost to the perilous seas. And on the beach, some of the refurbished boats look back at tragedy. One vessel, *Sol da Vida*, was donated by the family of José Manuel Limpinho Salsinha to the town hall. Born in 1946, he joined, at a young age, the ranks of those fishing for cod before branching out to other fish. Some would call him "the king of sea bass". But he lost his life in 2011 at the age of 64 when another ship he was on, *Bruna*, turned over out at sea. Next to *Sol da Vida* stand the lifeboats. Perhaps the most famous is *Our Lady of the Desperate,* which served the town for 65 years from 1912. When 21 fishermen were stranded at sea in 1914, thanks to the lifeboat's crew just two of them died. On the promenade, just in front of the lifeboats, is a statue of Mãe Nazarena (Mother of Nazaré). She holds one child in her arms while another leans at her side; on her head is a physical representation of the cliffs and town. It is a nod to her role looking over both the sea and the town's children.

The fishermen would dress in tartan shirts and trousers with a black waistband. On festival occasions, that traditional dress occasionally reappears. The traditional dress for women was known as the seven skirts, a series of petticoats covered with one heavily embroidered outer layer. It it still worn by those at their stalls in Sitio or else on the main beach. The story of how the seven skirts became a part of Nazaré's traditions is muddled. Some say it marks the colours of the rainbow, the days of the week, or even seven big waves at Nazaré before the flat water arrived. The skirts were also supposedly designed to keep them warm in the inclement winter fishing weather and to cover them modestly while their husbands were away at sea.

Fish is the culinary lifeblood of Nazaré. On sunny days, all year round, sun-dried fish lie on wooden-framed metal grills: sardines and mackerel, in particular. This traditional delicacy gives off a pungent aroma and is typically sold by the older women of the town, who are usually in traditional dress. The sun-drying process involves several steps now carried out on the beach and previously done in the neighbouring fish market, which has since been transformed into a museum. Fresh fish is gutted and washed in salt water before being cut in half. It is then placed in brine for varying times. The fish are then laid out on racks to dry in the sun, some for just three hours and others for three days. Traditionally, this was a process carried out by the women of the town and passed down from one generation to the next.

Inside the many restaurants on the main beach waterfront and the meandering streets of the town, there are all manner of traditional fish dishes on offer. Most common perhaps is *caldeirada* (a fish stew), or a fish soup with noodles known as *massada de peixe*. Whole grilled fish caught in the neighbouring waters are commonplace on most menus, so too is shellfish rice (*arroz de marisco*) and monkfish rice (*arroz de tamboril*).

The number of fishermen is dwindling in Portugal. In 2010, it stood as high as 16,920, but by 2019, it had dropped to 14,617. Nazaré has felt the effects too. Joaquim Zarro is one of those still standing – or sitting, in fact, inside garage No. 86 at the harbour, fishermen and surfers acting as neighbours in the warehouses on either side of him. With the sardine season over for this year, he is tending to his nets with members of his crew, including his adopted son Joshua.

The radio plays in the background inside a workplace stacked high with netting. On the walls hang a series of pictures: of Zarro's mother and father (himself a fisherman), Jesus at the Last Supper and the other thing Zarro worships (for his sins), Benfica football team.

An ebullient man, he once appeared on a Gordon Ramsay television show, *Uncharted*, taking the British chef out to fish and subsequently cooking their catch.

The names of the two boats Zarro owns, *Companheiro de Deus* (*Companion of God*) and *Deus e Pesca* (*God and Fishing*), which rest quietly in the harbour a mere 50 metres away, are in keeping with the rest of the boats in the harbour, highlighting the importance of religion to the fishing community in Nazaré. He jokes that all the fishermen are Catholic as "they have to believe in something" to go out in the stormy seas day after day.

Despite the name and the Portuguese look, Zarro speaks near-perfect English with an unlikely, thick Bolton accent, a nod to his time in the north-west of England, running pubs including the Lever Arms. His life has always been synonymous with the sea. Fishing is in his blood. His great-grandfather died at sea, an all too common occurrence in Nazaré before its harbour was built. But Zarro left his home town for a different marine adventure with Princess Cruises, the company for which he worked for five and a half years. "I did everything from cleaning the toilets," he recalls proudly, "to being a waiter."

It was there that he met, as he calls her, "a girl, a bartender from Bolton", Andrea, and the two immediately hit it off. They did three cruises together before deciding to open a bar and settle in Portugal. When that didn't work, he thought, *Oh crap, what do I do now?* "We were in the middle of the town and I go to the girl, look, I'm up for a challenge. Let's go to England." Andrea's response was: "Are you crazy?" His first trip to England was going to be for 10 days, to see what it was like and whether he might be able to settle there. Within two days, he informed his girlfriend he was returning home, the primary problem being the accent.

"I always listened to Americans in the movies and they speak very clearly – and then I came to Bolton," he says, wide-eyed, amused and chuckling at the recollection. "I said, 'I'm going back to Portugal tomorrow.' I'd said I'd stay 10 days, but that was before I'd heard them talking! So, she had to speak to her family and ask them 'Can you please speak proper English?' Now, I speak the same way!" he says, laughing even more loudly.

In the pub trade, Zarro's job was sort of as a problem-solver for four of Tetley's watering holes. But the call of Nazaré's waters, which has a hypnotic effect on so many, once again dragged him back home, where he and Andrea set up a pub-restaurant. But being close to and serving the fare from the sea wasn't quite enough, and he found himself being lured back to being a fisherman – "It's in my blood, all my family are fishermen." The couple talked excitedly about his ambition to buy a fishing boat.

Barely a few months into their time in Nazaré, they were walking along the town's main beach in the early hours of a Sunday morning when a freak wave swept Andrea out to sea. He dived in to save her.

"She loved the sea and the sand, and that time, the sea was just like this," he points to the ground, suggesting it was innocuous and flat. "But it came from nowhere, lifted up and the sea took her off. There's a saying in Portugal that anything the sea wants, the sea will get, no matter what." He tried, in vain, to rescue her. Her body washed up 10 days later, 15 miles down the coast towards Peniche, another well-known surf spot.

"That changed me," Zarro says, with tears welling up in his eyes. "The restaurant was ours. I'd spent a fortune, so then lost a fortune by closing down, but I thought, *I don't care anymore*. At the time, I was already thinking about buying a fishing boat. One morning soon afterwards, I woke up and bought a boat."

Today, he has a crew of 12 working for him, ranging in age from Joshua, aged 21, to a 73-year-old who fell overboard last year and has since understandably ended his seafaring fishing career after the close shave, and now only works on dry land.

Sardines, mackerel and anchovies are Zarro's staples from the sea, and he feels the burden of catching enough to pay the families of his crew members. The financial spoils are shared out between the 12 of them at the end of the fishing week.

Despite the pressures and obvious perils, he says, "I do love it. Not many people say this, but I love my work. I do. And it's not just being the captain – I love to be at sea. It's the same with my son. If he could make a house on the sea, he'd do it right now!

"But it's hard. Sometimes people will look at the fish on their plate and say 'wow', but they don't realise the trouble it has given the fisherman. It's the same with the waves. That guy McNamara, I take my hat off to him because he was the first one to do it when the waves had been there a long time. He's made it here, he's playing and it's scary. I have respect for him. I'm not scared of the sea but I have respect."

Joe, as Zarro was known back in Bolton, insists fishermen like him and surfers like McNamara get on well. Often their interaction is little more than saying a cursory hello or briefly lending out some tools for a quick jet-ski repair. And yet there is an element of disbelief in what they do, in a town that has seen more than its fair share of tragedy in the water.

"We all – surfers and fishermen – have got to respect the sea. It can be calm, it can be rough, but the sea is the sea and it always needs respect. I know what the sea can do. These guys are mental, because they go and play with the waves. You can fall and break your neck or your spine – and they don't care."

Joshua once swapped places with a surfer – trading his nets for a surfboard for a one-off coffee advert in Portugal. Asked if he would be tempted to head out in the waves again, his answer is an unequivocal shake of the head.

But the Zarro family's story of tragedy is just one of a countless number from Nazaré's seas. Generations have lost loved ones to these ferocious tides, be that the fishermen or the hordes of holidaymakers in the summer months. Countless families in the town have been affected by marine tragedy.

4

THE BIRTH OF NAZARÉ

No one ever used to surf Nazaré on its monstrous days. Local surfers and bodyboarders knew where the tipping point was for dicing with death. They would still walk down the road to the lighthouse on those days and look at the feral nature of the water. But bar the fishermen further out to sea, the waters stayed empty on such occasions. Being out there was unthinkable, the risk simply too great.

Big-wave surfing spots have long been on the map. There is Mavericks, off the north California coast, where the break is caused by the formation of the rocks under the water's surface. Its name is taken from Maverick, a pet German Shepherd owned by surfer Alex Matienzo's roommate. The dog tried to swim out to join Matienzo and his friends as they attempted to surf the spot in the late 1960s. Jeff Clark put it on the map in 1975 when, aged 17, he surfed waves of nearly 25 feet. It was also at Mavericks two days before Christmas in 1994 that Mark Foo lost his life. His body was found two hours later. He had a small injury to his head, and the popular belief is he drowned when the leash attaching his foot to the board got caught on the reef.

There is Pe'ahi, off the north shore of Maui, Hawaii, better known in surfing circles as Jaws – so named by a group of surfers in 1975, the same year the Steven Spielberg film about a man-eating shark came out. They likened the speed with which the wave changed to a shark attack. Pe'ahi is the scene of some the biggest and most picturesque waves in history. Also in Hawaii stands Waimea Bay, first surfed on its bigger days as far back as 1957.

In Tahiti, French Polynesia, the standout surfing spot has long been Teahupo'o, which has attracted surfers globally since the 1960s. Teahupo'o literally means "pile of heads". Its name supposedly comes from the son of a murdered Polynesian king, who ate the brain of the man responsible for killing his father. It is seen by many as having the heaviest wave in the world. It is also the competition location selected by organisers of the 2024 Paris Olympics for only the second iteration of surfing at the Games.

In contrast, big-wave surfing is still in its infancy in Nazaré, dating back to just 2010. Back then, the area was deemed something of an upstart, frowned upon by the traditional surf crews of California, Hawaii and Tahiti. In its initial years, its fledgling community had to fight for both recognition and acceptance.

The first man to surf the monsters here was the Hawaiian-based Garrett McNamara. The shortened version of the story often told in articles is that McNamara was sent a picture of the wave via email by local surfer and town hall worker Dino Casmiro, and immediately packed up to come and surf Nazaré. He then went on to break the world record there. As with most good stories, its truth is a bit more nuanced and long-winded in its path to fruition, and involves infinitely more characters.

McNamara remains the father of the wave, as the first man bold enough to go out in such conditions. Today, he is the town's No. 1 celebrity. Spend any time in his company walking around town, and you will see he is usually accosted – by the local elderly women, in particular. He is undeniably the central act in putting Nazaré on the map, his early exploits key in making it a year-round destination and, in doing so, boosting the economy of a once poor fishing community. But he also owes his place in big-wave surfing folklore, as does the town, to a group of Portuguese friends, who had stumbled over ways to put Nazaré on the map – and make it a tourist attraction beyond simply a picturesque summer holiday destination.

At the start, in and around the water, the team assembled to achieve that goal was a small, close-knit group originating from within the town hall, all with a shared goal and a formulated plan to get Nazaré and its waves known by the wider world. They were given the thumbs-up by then-Mayor Jorge Barroso to somehow use the waves to make a name for Nazaré, as long as it didn't involve dipping into the town hall coffers. There were the two Paulos. Paulo Caldeira was the ideas man, brought in as an expert with a major events company in Porto. Paulo Salvador, whom McNamara nicknamed "Pitbull" early on (which has stuck within the surf community), was responsible for sport at the town hall and remains the official safety officer on the bigger days. There was the aforementioned Dino Casmiro, who had set up a local surf club with Pitbull, and was in charge of forecasting for the event. Adding his skills to the group was Jorge Leal, the photographer and cameraman who ensured the necessary footage – still and moving – was captured for all eternity.

It was as a teenage bodyboarder that Caldeira first heard of the "fucking crazy waves" of Nazaré. The first time he pulled up, aged 18, at a deserted lighthouse, so inclement were the conditions on land and sea that he was too nervous to even get out of the car. Only on the smaller days would he go out in the water. But long before Caldeira and his friends joined forces, Nazaré as a competition locale made its first small ripples in a European bodyboarding contest in 2001, and two years later six bodyboarders were invited to compete at a one-off event in Nazaré, Bodyboard Special Edition. Caldeira later worked on subsequent editions of the event in 2005, 2007 and 2009. The problem was that bodyboarding didn't resonate with the wider public in Portugal, making few splashes outside of its own community. Sponsors were hard to come by. To put Nazaré centre stage, a new approach was needed.

Gradually, the finalised team to do that was assembled. Pedro Pisco, already employed by the town hall, was the last to come on board. Surfing and event management were not initially his thing, but he believed in a vision that would shine a spotlight on Nazaré. Come 2009, the group put on a national surfing event, but again it failed to properly ignite. They got a Brazilian sponsor as a backer, but the story goes that, even well over a decade on, they still haven't received a penny in sponsorship money. However, the American bodyboarder Mike Stewart accepted an invitation to come to Nazaré that same year for a month which, in turn, sparked a fresh wave of thinking.

Casmiro, the son of a fisherman who leaves on a Sunday and only returns on the Saturday once the boat is overladen with fish, was adamant he would always pursue a different water passion to his ancestors. He had sent an initial email out to the surfing community with a picture-perfect shot of the Nazaré wave taken from Sitio with the lighthouse in the foreground five years earlier. McNamara was not the only big-wave surfer recipient of the email, others included Laird Hamilton, one of the founding fathers of tow-in surfing. But the difference was McNamara was the only one to ever show a true interest. In the intervening time, Caldeira and Pisco designed the logo for the Praia do Norte tourism brand, which still exists today and can be seen on billboards and merchandise.

As the ideas man, Caldeira realised a big event was no longer the way forward. He was adamant that the only way for Nazaré to properly make its mark was to bring just one guy to the town to surf the big waves, film and photograph it when he did, and share it with the world. The events company he worked for went bust in 2009 but Caldeira was determined to carry on with the Nazaré surf project, and decided to work on it full-time. It marked the birth of what would become known as the North Canyon Shore project. Pisco dealt with the politics of town hall, with the logistics and sponsors.

There is a slight resentment from those behind the origins story that they do not get the attention they deserve. As Casmiro puts it, "I think the connection of four really good friends is the really important part here," the quartet working around the clock, from dawn into the early hours each day to make the project a reality. They readily admit they are somewhat responsible for the ongoing circulation of the origin story, as they created it early on – the idea that McNamara came to Nazaré on the whim of just a solitary email picture.

"It's not that Garrett arrived here and found this," explains Caldeira. "I know it's not great to kill a good story with the truth but, in fact, it was not what really happened. We already had the vision and passion. Of course, we were never going to surf that big wave. Garrett has all the merits, but he was maybe lucky that he replied to Dino's email. He was also interested because he's an animal – that guy, in the water, is just a machine."

A big part of surfing – especially big waves – is to find your "spot". McNamara was perpetually searching for that, and found it in Nazaré. As he described it, "I was really looking for adventure at this time in my life." After a litany of emails and calls between the surfer and the team in Nazaré, his reply to those in Portugal was clear: if they find the means to make it happen – the jet skis, the logistics, the hotel – he would get in the water.

So everything was arranged, flights were booked, and the latest attempt to put the town on the world's radar was underway. While waiting at Lisbon Airport for his arrival, Pitbull received a text message from McNamara to say he was no longer coming; he'd had a change of heart. For a few moments, the team were left wondering what to do next. It felt like going back to the drawing board. McNamara left it a few minutes longer to tell them he was pulling their leg – his connecting flight had been delayed in Frankfurt and he would be with them shortly. That simply set the tone for how the group operated.

On that first day in the harbour at the end of October 2010, the small Nazaré town hall team met with the American to proudly show him the equipment they had for their first day on the water. Unknown to McNamara, they had switched over the jet skis, replacing them with watercraft with burnt-out engines – to much laughter when the surfer despairingly first lifted the lid on them. Pitbull recalls: "In those days, it was always like that. Just a lot of laughs." Everyone just clicked. Years on, Caldeira likens it to that "first vacation with your wife – it's just perfect. The first time with Garrett was a dream come true." The North Canyon Shore project was under way.

McNamara thinks a lot about that first day on the clifftop and the one in the water a few days later. After our initial meeting in 2019, dissatisfied with one particular answer of his recollection of the early days, he sent a lengthy follow-up message. He wrote:

"It gave me chicken skin, explaining the feeling of first being up there. It got me thinking about your question of how it felt to be there, and this is how I wished I answered it. I'm beyond proud of what has happened to Portugal since.

I'm so honoured and grateful that Nazaré and I found each other. It's a fairy tale – literally a love story. I feel blessed that I had the intuition to see Nazaré for the majestic massive mystery that she is when no other surfers did and that I had an incredible team to support me while I got to know her and learn her different moods.

I remember so many days when I was out there completely by myself. No ski, no surfer, not one single person on the cliff – literally no one, just the wild ocean and myself. It's been a dream the past years, and it makes my heart swell with happiness when I see all these people from all these countries enjoying the ocean and nature, and when I see what the discovery of this wave has done for Nazaré, and Portugal as a whole."

5

RECORD-BREAKERS

There were those who doubted the group's attempt to put Nazaré's waves on the map; they believed that it would never reach fruition. But those people were mere outsiders. Ask the Paulos, Dino and Pedro, and they say they always believed it would achieve a successful end point, even in those years of earlier failures. The inception story was told over two films, *North Canyon* and *Zon North Canyon* (the latter a nod to a sponsor who was involved with the project), which are still available to watch today on YouTube. Seeing it back, the fondness for each other and the tight-knit nature of the group are clear to see. Many are still close friends today; they even organised a reunion during the course of the 2021–22 season.

The day before he surfed it for the first time, McNamara went underwater to see – and partly understand – the workings of the canyon, afterwards singing the lyrics to a Madonna song: "like a virgin, touched for the very first time". The next day, he had his maiden surf in the waters. He recalls this experience as "Puerto Escondido on steroids", a nod to another surf spot in Mexico. In another breath, he called it "one of the eight wonders of the world".

In that first winter, he would train by running up the track of the town's funicular railway, which, in summer, took tourists from town to the raised Sitio. It's a lung-busting jog that is no longer possible these days, with the railway running almost every day year-round, such is the tourism demand.

That first time in the water, it was just him and local surfer José Gregorio, not just the best Portuguese big-wave surfer at the time but virtually the only one back then. The waves were perfect, but Gregorio did not have the tow-in experience McNamara had grown accustomed to at home in Hawaii with his regular partner Keali'i Mamala. That first day, there was a point where McNamara was left stranded, too close to the rocks. He quickly decided he needed somebody else.

This realisation coincided with McNamara getting an email from Ireland, where Al Mennie and Andrew Cotton were surfing the island nation's big waves. They invited him over to join them; his response was to instead lure the duo over to Portugal just a few weeks into his stint there, with the promise of a big swell looming. Mennie and Cotton packed their bags immediately and began the journey south. They made an unlikely double act in many ways. Mennie is known as Big Red in his native Northern Ireland, a giant of a man with a large red beard. In contrast, Cotton has the bleach-blond hair of a typical surfer. But they had a shared ambition and thirst for big waves. Neither was prepared for Nazaré. The three of them sounded like the start to a bad joke: "An Englishman, an Irishman and an American ...", but they clicked from the outset, feeding off McNamara's experience and the other two with a willingness to take risks and learn.

They arrived at Lisbon Airport at 10 p.m. and were told, on being picked up, that the incoming swell was so big it would come to the shops in town. Mennie's reaction was that something must have been lost in translation – until he went out the following morning to see it with his own eyes. And as the day dragged on, the waves went over the newly created breakwater in town.

The group pulled up at the lighthouse for the first time one morning at 6 a.m., while it was still dark. They gradually got a perspective of the scale despite the lack of light or people in the water. What made Mennie realise the place was different was the looks he received from the locals. "You saw it in their eyes that they thought this was very dangerous," he recalls. There had been countless fishermen whose lives were lost in the same water. McNamara was concerned too. He stressed to both Mennie and Cotton that they had to be here because they wanted to be.

Greeting them at the harbour were the carcasses of two jet skis, which had clearly been demolished by the sea. Mennie and Cotton looked at each other. Mennie remembers thinking, *Why are they destroyed?! That's not the best sight to greet me.* While aboard newer, functioning jet skis, and before leaving the harbour, they huddled together in the water and hugged. As they headed diagonally right out from the harbour and got closer to the fort and its lighthouse, they could see the waves breaking, spray going high up into the air. Mennie remembers: "I was pretty experienced at this point in my life, but those waves were like nothing I'd ever experienced."

Within minutes, McNamara was shouting at Big Red to get on the tow rope at the back of the jet ski, to be dragged into a wave. He duly obliged, but rather than carrying on in the same direction to which he'd been towed, he turned right into the far riskier direction of the rocks. It rapidly dawned on him how wrong this might go if he got in trouble, pounded perilously close to rocks in waters unknown to him. But as the wave came to an end he was safely spat out into deeper water away from the rocks and scooped up by McNamara seconds later. It was that day, he believes, that provided the "turning point in how Nazaré became successful". That day, all three chopped and changed from driving to surfing to rescuing each other, and, crucially, all came back safe. Mennie remembers thinking at the end of that opening day that it was here that he could ride the biggest wave in the world; all of them thought the same thing.

Mennie did three seasons in all. Now, he prefers to surf in Ireland, away from the crowds. He has always kept himself to himself. Doing so in the Nazaré of today is impossible. Growing up, he had a VHS tape called *Monster Mavericks* and remembers, aged 13, being hooked. He told his brother he would surf the big waves one day. At age 22, in the last conversation they had before his father died, Mennie told him he was heading to Mavericks that winter. He did it, and transferred back home what he had learned in California. He pored over rock formations in Ireland that were similar to Mavericks; he had bought a boat and become, in his own words, obsessed. And then, for a brief spell, Nazaré was the obsession.

For Mennie, there are parallels between what he does and the motorcyclists who travel at breathtaking speeds at road races like the Isle of Man TT. Where he hails from in Northern Ireland is home to the Dunlop family, the two-wheeled dynasty that have enjoyed glory and tragedy almost in equal measure. He remains good friends with Michael Dunlop, having taken him out surfing and then been a passenger on the back of Dunlop's motorbike. "I think motorcycling on the road is more dangerous than big-wave surfing," comments Mennie. "Michael said to me, 'When you're going at 200 mph and approaching the corner, the thing in your head is "You have to want to die."' I rode on the back with him; he said if he was going too fast to squeeze him. But I was putting my trust in him. With tow surfing, you're also putting your trust in somebody else." Even now, there are points he misses Nazaré – but the Nazaré of then, not now.

For McNamara, he had found his natural playground on the west coast of Portugal and, despite calling Hawaii home, has never really left. He has always felt more comfortable in the water than on land, however rough the seas. Unlike a lot of big-wave surfers, he has always rather relished the poundings from the elements. His philosophy was that nothing was ever too big or dangerous; he'd surf anything. Now well into his fifties, he has mellowed – but only marginally. Back then, he had an insatiable appetite to surf wave after wave, day after day. The most pivotal of these was in his second Nazaré season, on 1 November 2011 (or "11 a.m. on the eleventh month of the eleventh", as he puts it), the day he surfed that 78-foot wave changed the fortunes of the entire place. There was a nervous anticipation the night before; a monstrous swell was looming large off the coast of Portugal and was due to hit that night. Together with the town hall team, and Cotton and Mennie, he craned over a computer screen to look at the latest swell forecasts.

Back in town for his second main stint, Mennie was struggling to sleep where he was staying, his 6-foot 5-inch frame too big for the small bed he had been given. On top of that was the noise. As his mind turned over the potential events of the day ahead, he became irritated by an occasional rattle. At first, he thought it was him moving in his bed. The rattling got louder and more persistent. He realised it was coming from the bedroom door – and also the bedside table – the waves were hitting the shore so hard that it caused rattle after rattle. "This was my second season in Nazaré and I'd never heard this before. You think, *What's coming tomorrow?* I didn't sleep after that." That's often the way for big-wave chasers, exhausting themselves thinking of all the possibilities and scenarios – and then thriving on adrenaline the following day.

The surfers should have already been exhausted that night, as during the day things had not gone entirely to plan. McNamara had come to scoop Mennie up from one wave. He went full throttle towards the shore as another wave chased them down. Caught between two rapidly breaking waves, the American tried to find a means of escape but the lip of the second wave caught the ski, sending both men spinning into the water. Mennie briefly panicked that the tow rope was going to get tangled round his neck as he and the ski went, as he put it, "up and over the falls, like Niagara". His surfing boots were sucked halfway off his feet. As Cotton came to the rescue, Mennie let McNamara be scooped out to safety first, Mennie taking a few more waves on his head before he too was rescued.

It could have been any of them that broke the world record the following day. All were capable enough. It is just the vagaries of big-wave surfing, the luck sometimes based on if it's your turn on the wave – although you need the skill and bravery to stay on it. Towed in by Cotton, McNamara did just that. Over the radio, Nicole, McNamara's then girlfriend (now wife), gave the call from the lighthouse that three giant waves were coming.

Coolly, with Cotton moved into position, McNamara went from two hands on the rope to just one and then released himself on to the wave that would change his life. His board bounced up and down throughout the few seconds on the water, but he never seemed troubled. As he headed left, a surge of white water chased him, which he looked like he was attempting to swat away with his bare hands before eventually, riding out of the wave. On the radio in the aftermath, he declared it both beautiful and "kind of big".

Back on the hilltop, Jorge Leal had filmed and photographed it. While others celebrated, Leal rushed back to ensure the images captured – both moving and still – were safely downloaded. And while it took time for it to be officially measured at 78 feet – bigger than any wave surfed in history – interest in it (whatever its eventual official size) instantaneously took off.

The moment might never have happened. Initially, the team had not necessarily intended to surf that day. But when Cotton and Mennie looked out on the water at first light, they immediately went to wake McNamara from his slumber. Pisco missed it because he was sleeping and laughs at the version of the story that has it playing out at 11 a.m. In fact, it was infinitely earlier that morning. Whatever the exact timings, the project team, after searching for years, had finally found its eureka moment.

As the only ones aware of what had happened, the small team held on to the footage for a week before the likes of Pisco sent out the pictures and footage to the Big Wave Awards (although the record wasn't officially ratified until May the next year), and also to broadcasters around the world for free. As Pisco recalls, "We were almost completely unknown in the surfing industry", but on a budget of €15,000 for that first season, they had cracked it. They were shown across every global network from the BBC to CNN, while the American TV presenter Anderson Cooper came out to film an episode of *60 Minutes* about McNamara. For the Hawaiian surfer, it was all about timing. Just a year earlier, Instagram had launched. For him, it provided the perfect platform.

Where McNamara's Nazaré home for the winter season now stands, he has a perpetual view of the waves, the visual equivalent of a siren song. During our conversation, he still looks at it in wonder, as though seeing it for the first time. The passing years have not diminished his love for the place. Does he ever think where he'd be if it were not for Nazaré? "Sure, probably still searching for another 100-foot wave. I'm grateful we found this, as we'd still probably be living out of a suitcase trying to find my wave."

Now there is no longer the same overriding ambition to surf every big swell. For one, the body is not quite up to it. There have been major injuries that have meant periods of time out of the water recovering. Sometimes, he just doesn't feel it, so instead walks down to the clifftop to watch with the spotters. Other times, he merely rides the jet ski – getting pleasure from putting friends on big waves rather than surfing them himself, he says. And there are very occasional days when he will still go big on the surfboard. In the early days, he was insatiable, chasing big wave after big wave – whatever the country. "If I missed a big swell when I had the means and money to get there, I'd be so depressed, I'd literally be on suicide watch. Now, since injuries, it's kind of freed me. I had this big-wave monkey on my back that finally jumped off. I had to be everywhere, every swell; I'd pay my last penny and sell surfboards to get out there. It was just my passion. I loved it and, back then, it didn't seem unhealthy at all. Idiot, hey?" he says, and trails off with laughter.

What is it about Nazaré that still appeals? The question comes up while we're sitting at breakfast on the main beach, the morning sun hitting the left-hand side of the lighthouse, the north beach hidden behind on the other side. "What's not to love, man?" he says. He has a point. "This place has so many big days; you don't have to go searching around. It's just there. There are more perfect waves and more playful waves. This wave is very challenging, which keeps it interesting. People say it looks impossible – and it does. But riding it's OK. When the waves are glassy [flat and shimmering like a pane of glass], which is rare here, it's like cutting butter with a hot knife, and it's the best feeling in the world. There's just nothing – and nowhere – like it."

For McNamara and Nicole, who met in Puerto Rico and were both married to other people at the time, the place has been transformative. First, it was the ideal fresh start, a chance to explore a new adventure together. He was the instinctive, impulsive one, she the calm-headed one – with a practical approach that was needed.

That hasn't really shifted. For Nicole, who travels between Hawaii and Nazaré with her husband and the couple's three children, it is home. It was also here, on top of the lighthouse, that the couple tied the knot. "It definitely changed our life completely. I don't know what we'd be doing. It's our home. It's where we made our life, got married here, had kids here. Barrel was made here," she says, mentioning their son, who is named after the barrel shape made by waves. In this moment, Garrett McNamara calls his wife "the mother of the wave", a fitting moniker given her husband's founding-father role in Nazaré's big-wave surfing inception story.

Mennie, now watching from afar, would like other players in the story to get more adulation. "All the guys like Pedro and Paulo, they are the ones that have made it successful – the men that pioneered the whole structure."

For Caldeira, he would simply like a small plaque recognising those pioneers placed inside the four walls of the lighthouse and take its place alongside the surfboards signed by the many surfers to have tackled Nazaré over the years. As a result, for him, the whole experience is *"agridulce"*, or bittersweet. "This is not just about me, but the group. This started with just four people. If we were not here, it would not have happened like it did. If I didn't put my passion, my time, my money, my white hair into it. It's not only me, but the group behind. Everyone should get recognition."

Immaterial of the story that is now legend, they all know their part in it and the transformative effect it wrought. In considering the contrast between then and now, Pisco said: "This is now a place of joy. It's one of the things I'm most proud of. It's a goldmine for Nazaré. We gave a means for people to make money. There are now restaurants that do better in the winter than the summer."

6

THE SURFING PLUMBER

Andrew Cotton

Just like in those early days, Nazaré keeps spitting out Andrew Cotton, yet he keeps coming back, year after year. It is the one place that has defined him above all others, both for the good moments and the bad.

It was here that he broke his back in 2017, here that he spent the Covid lockdown over the 2020–21 season alone in a camper van on the clifftop, away from his two children. Now he is back again, 12 years on from his debut. But it was also here that he turned his back on life as a plumber and gained notoriety for riding some of the biggest waves in history. It's also the place where he's most feared for his life.

For all his past experiences here – in fact, perhaps because of them – he carries with him uncertainty for the season, for his future life after the big waves and even for his own ability, despite the fact he has the respect of his entire peer group. In addition, he is universally liked – a rarity in this often high-testosterone, competitive, ego-driven world.

"Everybody loves Cotty," says Garrett McNamara, with a warmth that typifies his affection for the Devon surfer. Cotton is easy to like. With his sun- and sea-bleached hair and laid-back demeanour, he looks like a stereotypical surfer. And he's good company – generous with his time, constantly thinking and self-assessing, far more interesting than he seems to think and funny to boot.

43

On the long drive across continental Europe for the season start with his girlfriend Justine White, a ski instructor, the urge hits him to stop to surf along the way in Peniche, another surf spot 40 miles south, but with waves a fraction of the size of those in Nazaré. It is a session that does not go particularly well. Some days, it just doesn't click in the water, however experienced you might be and however diminutive the waves in comparison to what you normally surf.

Later, in the afternoon, he pulls into the Red Bull garage at the harbour first, before even making it to his home to unpack his laden car. There, he warmly hugs McNamara; they are old friends reunited after an off season apart, McNamara primarily in Hawaii, and Cotton back on the UK's south-west coast.

Before twilight on day one in Nazaré for the 2021–22 season, they are back in the water, and entirely on their own. Most have yet to set up camp here for the coming season. This is how it was back in the day – Cotton and McNamara – before Nazaré became the surf Mecca it has since been transformed into.

There's old footage of Cotton from back in those early days, describing himself while laughing nervously as a "pretty average surfer with pretty big ambitions". Even now, he doesn't particularly like watching clips of himself, be that surfing or talking. But he is very much one of this place's mainstays, as well as one of its early pioneers. And the Devon accent hasn't diminished in the intervening years spent away from home.

Had it not been for a jet-ski wipeout, he and Al Mennie might never have been contacted by McNamara. Back in 2006, Mennie had become a feature in Mullaghmore, off the coast of Donegal, in Ireland, while Cotton had already tackled big waves in Hawaii and Ireland but remained a jet-ski novice. You can watch footage back of his misdemeanour – on YouTube, it's labelled the "Worst Jet-Ski

Wipeout Ever!". Cotton attempts to tow Mennie into a wave, only to get himself totally out of position, bailing on the jet ski and diving into the sea as the watercraft turns over.

Cotton was able to get himself back on board but, despite his best efforts, could not restart the machine. So, he decided to jump overboard (again) and backstroke himself and the jet ski into the harbour at Mullaghmore. He laughs at the ridiculousness of the plan in retrospect. For 10 to 15 minutes, he pounded his way back with all his might, only to turn back and find the current had taken him further out than where he started from. So he eyed another spot at which to hopefully land further up the coast, but this also backfired.

After some more time thrashing about in the water, a helicopter began hovering overhead, and down came a winch. Someone landed on his jet ski and offered to lift him out. Determined that he could rescue the jet ski singlehandedly, he turned down the offer of help, despite being warned there were neither rescue boats nor fishing boats out in the water to help him. Freezing cold by this point, he continued on his fruitless voyage before the helicopter flew overhead again. Down came the winch once more and he was advised a little more forcefully to jump in or else allow himself to take his chances in eventually being washed up in the United States. So it was that the jet ski was left to float away on the ocean, as a devastated Cotton looked on mournfully.

It coincided with a time when online surfing forums were taking off, and he got slated. The remarks were essentially along the lines of "he doesn't know what he's doing" and Cotton readily admits they had a point. To be a big-wave surfer, you essentially need to be able to master the waves both on a surfboard and a jet ski. Cotton felt he had the mastery of neither and the easy choice would have been to give up big-wave surfing altogether. Had it been his choice, he might well have taken that option. Looking back, he says: "Without Al, I probably would have given up."

Instead, he went on a K38 Water Safety course to learn, in particular, how to ride a jet ski in the big waves. When the email from McNamara dropped for Cotton and Mennie, they jumped at the chance, despite Cotton admitting more than a decade on, "I was still very much inexperienced, but I had the certificate. I couldn't really do it at all, but I knew it was an opportunity – so I blagged it and said I could do it!" Without that initial contact from McNamara, he has no idea whether he would have cracked the big waves and made it as a professional surfer.

From day one, Cotton and McNamara hit it off, despite their markedly different personalities. McNamara can be intense and wild, although the elder statesman of Nazaré is a much more mellow character nowadays. In contrast, the Briton has always been the laid-back, perhaps archetypal, surfer. They are united by their love of the sea and the desire not just to surf it themselves but also to tow each other into the biggest waves of their life. Cotton feels perpetually indebted to his long-time partner in crime:

"I'd never have been able to do it and spend the hours I did doing it if this opportunity hadn't come up. If not for Garrett, no one would be here. Maybe someone else would have done it later on, but he persevered. There's not a whole heap of people in the world that have done that. He's taught me what's humanly possible: how to survive, surf big waves, goal-setting, focus. Not wanting to brown-nose him too much but, without Garrett and meeting him, I'd probably still be plumbing in Barnstaple. I knew what my dream was, but I didn't think it achievable."

In those early days, everything was paid for by the town hall as part of the North Canyon Project, aimed at getting Nazaré recognition (it has to be said, years on, this was done rather successfully). For Cotton, he couldn't have afforded either the jet ski or the daily cost of petrol. This support meant that – with his Mullaghmore partner in crime, Mennie – they could surf all day. "I'd never have had the time or money to learn. To be the best, you need to be the guys spending the hours out there to get better. It's hard work – but that gave me my big break."

Within a few years of his precarious jet-ski wipeout, he would be towing McNamara into what was, at the time, the biggest wave ever surfed. Cotton has been the only British surfer to be at Nazaré throughout its nascent time in the big-wave surfing scene. This year, he has the perfect spot for the season – a rented house whose veranda stares tantalisingly out to Praia do Norte. When not surfing, he spends much of his time just looking out at the water – his playground and workplace.

During any conversation, sitting there with his feet up on the fencing that surrounds the veranda, he can spend almost the entirety of it talking while staring at the waves, whose caps catch the reflection of the sun. Even as he looks out, he can still feel the fear, acutely aware of the dangers the waters bring. But this rented property has the perfect angle with which to look at the ocean's prospects.

"Any wave is intimidating, but every angle you look at it from in Nazaré is different: bigger, smaller, scarier. And I think this is the least intimidating angle," he says of waves which, to the less trained eye, still look terrifying. "On the beach, it looks giant; if you're at the lighthouse, it looks fat. The worst place is to check it from low down on the beach in the morning and you're like, 'Oh my God.' That's what it was like when I was in the van. You look at it and think, *How is this even doable? How are we going to do this?*" He gestures again at the view from the veranda: "But mentally, this is the best place to look at it."

In this moment, his life feels pretty perfect. It's the season's start; the Portuguese climate is still warm enough to be sitting outside in a T-shirt. Surrounding him on the decking is a laid-out yoga mat on which he has just done his morning exercises. Behind him sits a deserted water park, temporarily closed down because of the impact of Covid. In seasons past, it has produced a buzz of noise and activity, it now stands silent. His girlfriend briefly joins him for a salad and sparkling water.

Although he's a decade younger than McNamara, Andrew Cotton is still one of the older surfers plying his trade here. And yet it is refreshing to find how strong his love for the big waves still burns.

7

AN UNLUCKY BREAK

Sebastian Steudtner

It's in the water where Sebastian Steudtner feels safest but, diametrically, also where he takes the greatest risks. His family like to tell the story of how, when he had just learned to walk, he tottered to the edge of the family swimming pool and promptly threw himself in.

Chaos ensued: his older sister screaming out for help, his father running from inside and jumping in the pool to scoop him to safety. Years on, he remembers the story more from recollection than reality, his mother retelling at family gatherings how, when he was brought back inside and told he couldn't do that again, he freaked out, as an enraged toddler does. All he wanted to do was thrash around in the water, however unsafely. From day one, there was this attraction to water, in his mind like a siren's call. It's not a feeling that has abated in the years since.

His father travelled extensively for work and would bring home small metallic Lufthansa toy planes purchased on his flight and chuck them into the pool. Sebastian, by this time a little older and only marginally more capable in the water than he was upon his first foray, would dive in to get them. Even then, he couldn't swim properly. Instead, he likened himself to a small dog caught in a perpetual game of fetch with his father, repeatedly throwing himself to the bottom, scrambling breathlessly to the water's edge and handing the metal plane back. On and on it went, until he was finally called inside, usually for a meal.

To this day, he says he cannot think of a single moment where he hasn't wanted to be in the water, despite the obvious perils of his day job. That he should feel such a connection to the water is perhaps down to the lack of vast expanses of it in his youth. He hails from Nuremberg, one of the European cities that is furthest away from the ocean. But as an impressionable child, water was the one place where he could live his life without instruction. At school, the teachers would coax and cajole him to pay greater attention in class and focus on his studies; but he wasn't stupid, just bored. At home, his mother would repeatedly warn her young son, who already had a penchant for putting himself in harm's way, to be careful. In the water, he was oblivious and impervious to any direction from anyone else.

"For me, water's just been fun," he says. "I think my connection to water was built on the fact that it's the one place no one could tell me anything. Until I went into the water, I'd have my mum saying 'Be careful; don't do this.' But if I wanted to dive, I did. If I wanted to swim across the lake, I'd do that. In the water, I remember thinking, *This is where I feel safe, this is where I'm in control. This is my place.*"

Steudtner has a measured approach to the waves. In many ways, he is Nazaré's surfing boffin, poring over every technological advance imaginable to improve his performance in the water. On the big days, he is meticulous in his preparation but, despite all that, his control is not always absolute. The solid cast currently on his left leg, in place before many of his peers have even arrived for the season, tells its own story of a session and a season already gone wrong.

Entering Nazaré's waves for the very first time in the season, he was feeling fitter and better prepared than ever. So methodical is he, that each season starts with a new plan, this time to get "barrelled" – essentially being enveloped and inside the wave as it pitches forward and breaks. A wrong move in that position has consequences.

On the day in question, the waves were relatively manageable by Nazaré standards, 25 feet at most, and he implemented his summer practice of adjusting his line to get barrelled. The wave initially opened up perfectly, then changed abruptly – Nazaré has the propensity to do that, such is its unpredictability – closing in on him and pounding him on the back. The first issue after being rescued and finding himself on the back of the rescue jet ski was losing feeling in his right arm. It wasn't until he put his foot down stepping off his jet ski at the harbour that he realised there was a problem with his foot, although he was still able to walk. His assumption was that, at worse, he had a small fracture. But as the specialist studied the X-ray, he grimaced when he spotted a grainy area that he said "looked weird". Steudtner's understandable internal response was: *I don't want to hear "weird"*. He had broken his foot, damaging it in three places: towards the top of the foot, a broken metatarsal and ligament damage to the side of the foot. The severity of the injury was grave enough that surgery was the only option.

The initial prognosis from the October break is that February looks like the earliest potential return date, which means this season is in danger of being over before it has even begun. Outside one of Nazaré's multitude of waterfront restaurants overlooking the main south beach – Taverna do 8 ó 80 – he pulls up in an electric Porsche, the trappings of a sponsorship deal with the German manufacturer. The car typifies the material success he has had because of his achievements in the water in seasons past. As he hoists himself out of the car and on to crutches, restaurant staff who are quick to offer assistance – he says he's OK on his own – gather around and ask animatedly about the injury.

Steudtner is both happy to talk about and also resigned to the implications of it. And, in a bizarre way, he is also relieved by his plight. "For me, it's not so bad, it takes away the stress," he says. The expectation of a season, of keeping fit, preparing the equipment and team around him, of being primed to risk it for every big-wave session imaginable. But now he has a purpose: to prove the doctors wrong, move his comeback date forward and throw himself headlong into his rehabilitation programme. From dawn to dusk, he is now fully focused on ensuring he can win the race to be up to full form and fitness before the season draws to a close and he returns to Austria, which the German now calls home.

Everything is geared towards recovery and keeping in shape. The dietary plan predetermined by his nutritionist is in place and already under way. When ordering *picanha*, a type of Brazilian steak from the top of the rump, he replaces the restaurant's recommendation of chips with brown rice and cooked vegetables, accompanied by a bottle of sparkling water. Today is his first day back in Portugal after a return home to see a specialist, his attention shifting from the waves to the home he is having built up in the hills surrounding the town. Steudtner already has an apartment where he stays whenever he's here, which will act as base for the early part of the season, while the construction is ongoing.

His "mountain place", as he likes to call it, is a modern, square, glass-fronted villa in the middle of a nature reserve, with every single room looking straight out towards the waves. The house had been abandoned years ago and seemingly no one could track down its previous owner. But such is Steudtner's tenacity when he locks on to an idea that he managed to locate the owner and bought the house and the land back in 2020. It has been, as he puts it, "a long process" – but he loves construction, likening it to meditation.

He pores over pictures of the site on his phone, and the swimming pool being installed to help meet his persistent fix for the water, like a proud parent.

The irony that someone should be building him a pool is not lost on him. In a life defined by water, his first job was building swimming pools in Hawaii at the age of 16. The previous year, he had quit school against his parents' wishes. The last two years of education just hadn't worked for him.

"I was a troubled kid," he says. "I had ADD [attention-deficit disorder]. I was in a lot of fights. I didn't have a career path in anything. I had little interest in the normal stuff. I wasn't interested in school – but not because it was hard; it was boring. It was way cooler to go into the forest, chop some trees down and pretend I'm hunting. My parents couldn't do anything about me leaving school. I was like, 'I'm done.' There's something in me that when I'm sure, I'm sure. I believe 100 per cent in what I'm doing and take any risk to do it. I don't know where that confidence comes from."

Despite their reservations, his parents gave him the all-clear to pack up and move 7,500 miles to Hawaii to pursue his dreams in the waves there, first windsurfing and latterly surfing. The mountaintop home and the state-of-the-art Porsche sitting outside the restaurant would suggest it was a leap of faith that has proved warranted, although there has not exactly been a shortage of hiccups along the way.

To earn money, for six years he worked in construction – building swimming pools, of all things. The first guy he built one for was a millionaire American car salesman, who introduced himself by his nickname, "the Snake". Weeks later, with the job complete, "the Snake" duly walked off without paying for the pool and sold the house. Steudtner laughs at the recollection, and at a lesson learned. "DMX, the rapper, said, 'Always trust everyone to be themselves.'

So, a snake is a snake, a liar is a liar, a thief is a thief. You have to recognise who you are."

The teenage German had no official training for building pools, but found he had an immediate aptitude for it, and relished it. "There's nothing I love more than building stuff." He was like that as a kid too. His approach to the big waves is the total antithesis. While he strives for perfection in the bigger body of water, it is unattainable, as he has come to understand. "There's something rewarding about a pool," he says. "You have grass, you cut that grass and know where the pool is going to be. You accomplish that first. There are times in sport where you win or get somewhere, but you can never close the chapter. You always could have done this or that. With a swimming pool, you say, 'This wall has to be a metre' – and it's a metre, it's perfect. It's not perfect in the waves."

Because his expertise in pool-building is allied with his perfectionism, he has been a thorn in the side of his own builders in ensuring his infinity pool is absolutely spot on at its completion. His specifications for the main house itself have been no less demanding.

Despite the magnitude of the building project, the primary focus remains on getting back, fit and in the water. It is, after all, his livelihood; he has sponsors relying on him to keep his position surfing the biggest waves. He is anxious to get the rehabilitation going. For the initial weeks, he is consigned to merely wiggling his toes.

Steudtner is an interesting mix. He is unbelievably – perhaps unhealthily – driven in his pursuits. This ambition brings with it an intensity that some of the more laid-back surfers shy away from, but the drive and dedication is admirable and alluring. And being out of action enables him to turn his attention to his surfing life out of the water.

That morning, he is up early, just after sunrise, driving a Porsche for a photo shoot arranged by the car manufacturer. He does this on the road from the lighthouse, which is usually closed to all traffic, before the crowds begin to gather for the day. After a day spent on his rehabilitation and dealing with Portuguese builders, by dinner the next night, he's the most captivating of audiences: not remotely guarded, covering every subject imaginable and talking virtually non-stop for two and a half hours. Once someone is invited into his inner circle, he immediately gives them and anyone else within it a sense of belonging. No ask is too much, and he's always contactable (and if not in that exact moment, he gets back in touch as soon as he can). In many ways, his relationships are all or nothing. "I never have shallow relationships," he says. "If someone is my friend, then he's my brother."

The broken foot is giving him time to take stock of the last 12 years in Nazaré, the perpetual inner desire to push the boundaries with every season – in fact, with every wave. Sitting back in his restaurant chair, Steudtner says the lay-off has given him a different perspective. "It's actually a nice break not to go into the season crazy, like a psychopath on top," he says of the singular focus required to be an elite big-wave surfer in Nazaré – before conjecturing his new-found outlook may yet alter his approach in the future, and become a part of his surfing life. But in the same breath, he knows it is not entirely convincing because of the mentality he employs and, in fact, needs to adapt when he enters the water on the big days. In reality, he knows he'll be swept up in his old ways as soon as the foot allows and the opportunity to do so again arises.

There is an almost a split personality to him, perhaps to all the big-wave surfers. On dry land, they seem perfectly normal, laid-back, engaging, intelligent and rational human beings but, in the water, they are totally willing to risk their lives in a way that seems unthinkable to most. When it comes to the surfing, there is another personality to

Steudtner as well. He uses the example of Mike Tyson – the German often turns to boxing – the former undisputed heavyweight boxing world champion, who was about the most menacing of opponents outside the ring, but speaks in his own podcast of being riddled by self-doubt until he entered the ring and it was fight time.

"I see a lot of what he says in me," admits Steudtner. "It's like you have two different characters living in you. One is like, 'You're a god!' and the other is, 'You're a nobody, you're not good enough.' Mike Tyson described it as being very scared of his opponent, worried of being humiliated, not winning, not living up to expectations and [being] worth nothing. But as soon as he comes into the ring, he becomes God. When he's in the ring, he's putting his mouthpiece in, hitting his knuckles, getting ready to kill the guy – and knowing he's already broken the guy just by looking at him. In a similar way, I don't know why I'm so confident in the big waves, but I am. That's the 'I'm God' card, I guess. I have that. I know I'm going to do that, even if I die doing it."

But surely he is not willing to genuinely risk dying just for the bravado of surfing one single, giant wave? "You need to have that psychopath in you, and I definitely have that. Not everyone has that. If you're in a tunnel, and if your brain tells you you're going to die to reach this, you're either going to reach this or die reaching this, everything depends on this – and that makes you different. You have a different commitment, you have a different approach, you have more discipline, you have more drive, you have more energy."

He realises, at the same time, that this "psychopathic" approach and drive could prove his eventual undoing and, in the worst-case scenario, cause him to lose his life in the water, his workplace. But he has done everything within his capabilities to ensure it never comes to that, primarily for himself but also for his peers.

The broken foot aside, he can rattle off the different moments he has carried on surfing when all sensibilities, not to mention his body, have suggested it is clearly time to pack up for the day.

The season before, after one particular pounding in a heavy surfing session, he had liquid on his lungs. He went to shore to recover and promptly vomited blood on the sand at his feet. As the lifeguard approached, with the recovered board, to check on his well-being, the surfer covered up the blood, knowing the lifeguard (with Steudtner's health in mind) would have questioned him and tried to ensure he did not return to the water. Within minutes, he was back out there and catching what was without doubt his best wave of the day.

8

THE SEASON'S FIRST BIG SWELL

Nic von Rupp

Early meteorology reports suggest winds approaching 80 mph are already circulating in the mid-Atlantic. Fifteen hundred miles away, the first excited whispers of the storm and its predicted effect when it hits mainland Europe are being talked about: WhatsApp messages exchanged, predictions made of the first swell of the big-wave surf season that will batter the continent, and any previous plans put on hold or rescheduled. As night falls, rain lashes the restaurants along the beachfront, while around the corner of the lighthouse – originally in place to protect its fishermen – winds are already whipping up into a frenzy.

In Nazaré's nearby port, the security guards that rotate shifts have grown accustomed to late-night and early-morning comings and goings to the site. Most faces are recognised with a simple nod, the security barrier raised aloft for mercurial late-night visitors to the otherwise deserted warehouses.

The arrivals come from two groups, both obsessed with the neighbouring waters off Nazaré, which are rich in sea bass, dorada, yellowfin tuna and shark. Outside dozens of warehouses, fishing nets hang loosely alongside stacks of fish cages for shellfish, and fishermen gather near to their moored boats.

The inhabitants of the other warehouses opposite are of a different breed linked to the seas. Blasting out from a black Opel estate stacked with surf gear, dents littered around its four corners, are the words of Roddy Ricch, the 24-year-old American rapper from Los Angeles' renowned Compton neighbourhood; the opening line "I ain't tryna die young" pertinent lyrics for the vehicle's owner. This is Nic von Rupp's car.

The logo of the energy drink Monster is emblazoned on the warehouse he shares with his team. Some individuals boast their own warehouses, some share a space within a team, and yet others belong to big brands like Red Bull. Inside Von Rupp's warehouse stands the central, ever-present member of his big-wave surfing crew: Sérgio Cosme. Cosme is diminutive, with a wide-eyed stare and high-pitched giggle, strangely reminiscent of Joe Pesci's unhinged character Tommy DeVito in Martin Scorsese's *GoodFellas*, although without the Brooklyn menace. Cosme is part teammate, part confidant. But he's also a jewel in the crown – as the aforementioned "guardian angel" of these waters, a jet-ski rider responsible for towing surfers into the biggest waves imaginable and, more pertinently, plucking them back to the shore and safety after the attempts to tackle such waves go hideously wrong (as they so often do).

Like Cosme, Von Rupp can allow his Latin temperament to spill over, but he can also be laid-back in his approach to everything bar surfing. On a 120-mile drive from Lisbon Airport to his Nazaré base, Von Rupp exchanges repeated phone calls and messages with Cosme, as well as with other fellow surfers and the photographers and cameramen who will shoot their record-breaking attempts the following day. His two repeated mantras are: "It's on" and "It's going to be huge." As he drives along, he nervously tinkers with a gadget that allows him to pass through the motorway tolls without stopping, hinting at the anticipation of what lies ahead in the rough seas the next day, in waters no sane mortal would dare enter.

The clock has struck 10 p.m. when Von Rupp arrives at the warehouse, knowing that an alarm call is coming some seven hours later. But instead of contemplating that, he makes preparations for the morning. Many of them veer on the almost basic, Von Rupp etching the word "OPEL" in marker pen on his surfboard as a nod to one sponsor, while stickers for Monster and his own brand, Brusco – whose products include tail pads, leashes and dry-bag backpacks, among other items – are attached to a board newly made for the first big waves of the season. The surroundings are basic too: a breeze-block facade with wetsuits adorning one wall and surfboards of varying lengths the other, a small bathroom at the back and a fridge stacked with water, energy drinks and beers, depending on the occasion. Upstairs is a small sofa-cum-bed with a table, the faded rug more at home in a student flat than at what has become Europe's home of big-wave surfing. Outside stands the jet ski, just 24 hours before it will be damaged, flipped repeatedly in the monstrous wash before finally being angrily spat out on the golden sands where bemused onlookers watch events unfold.

Von Rupp's restaurant of choice before and after a day in the big waves is often A Celeste, but it closes at 10 p.m. on this particular night; instead, a dinner of steak and chips is taken at Restaurante Adega Oceano. There is a sense tomorrow could be the moment he etches his name in the record books by surfing the first 100-foot wave in history. Meteorologists suggest the weather could be sufficient to produce such a break; the Portuguese are hopeful of being responsible for attaining big-wave surfing's Holy Grail and breaking the (then previous) record – an 80-foot wave – surfed by Rodrigo Koxa just two years ago.

But such record-chasing comes with an inherent risk. As Von Rupp puts it: "If you're under for two waves, it's life or death – that's you under for a solid minute and a half. It doesn't seem like much, but it's hell of lot when you take into consideration that you have the breath knocked out of you before you fall. Tomorrow, I want to ride the biggest wave of my life, but the main goal is just to survive and come out in one piece. There's so much risk, but it's a rush that makes you feel so alive. When you're underwater, the shit really hits the fan and you're just fighting for survival."

Nazaré is notorious for its brutality. Its secret is down to an underwater canyon which goes from 5,000 metres in depth to just 50 by the time it reaches the lighthouse. That rush of energy from such a volume of water has to refract; it goes up the beach and meets slower energy on that shallower shelf. The sudden influx of water creates monstrous waves and brings an increasing number of adrenaline junkies to test themselves against the elements. All the big-wave spots work in a similar way. At Mavericks in California, the depth goes from a deepwater trench to shallow water in an instant. For the most part, the waters surrounding the UK, for example, are shallow from so far out, so the energy is lost early on and therefore, the waves are nowhere near as giant.

Just a matter of metres from where this big swell is beginning to hit – its peak set to be reached at mid-morning the next day – Von Rupp will rest for the night in Zulla Nazaré's Surfing Village, a diminutive motel that's packed out in the summer. Now, Von Rupp is its only attendant, flicking on a small electric heater to warm the ice-cold room before setting the alarm clock for 5 a.m.

Given free rein of the venue with a key to reception, he lets himself in for breakfast the following morning. Aside from the breaking waves, the electronic whirring of the toaster is the only other noise in the Portuguese darkness, the glow of the machine giving off the only heat.

Pieces of toast are layered with cheese and Parma ham, bought late last night from the supermarket, while a kiwi fruit and apple are also digested. It is the last food he will have until he exits the water nearly 12 hours later. Before sunrise breaks, Von Rupp drives the same way he surfs, quickly but measured, cutting through the wet streets towards his warehouse for the final pre-surfing finishing touches. Among his team and the wider community, hugs are exchanged with a genuine warmth among competitors and friends, the nervousness of the night before amplified but shared with the excitement at the prospect that one of them could conceivably be a record-breaker by the end of the day.

These surfers are – and look – different to the surfing stereotypes. Instead of bronzed bodies, their leathered faces tell part of the story of the battering they have taken in the Atlantic Ocean. The suits they wear contain gas canisters to set off their inflatable life vests, which are intended to both dull the impact of thousands of tonnes of water billowing on top of them as well as keep them afloat in the tumultuous wash and the resultant fight for survival. It makes them look akin to superheroes, weather- and water-beaten Marvel characters, that hero status laid bare when they are greeted on the shore at the end of the day by members of the public, who treat their perilous undertaking with both reverence and curiosity.

From their warehouses, they hop onto the back of jet skis and head towards the thundery waters that spill on to Praia do Norte, the backdrop to the biggest waves ever surfed, bigger and more consistent that those of Hawaii. While Hawaii is the traditional birthplace of big-wave surfing when it began some 40 years ago, Nazaré is the upstart – and on the rise, if the numbers both in the water and out are anything to go by.

By 9 a.m., the roof of the fort is already full. In 2014, the fort – owned by the Portuguese military – welcomed 40,000 people during the season. For 2019–20, that number was 350,000 according to town hall figures. The fort's surrounding, eroding clifftops are littered with hundreds of spectators coming and going, and those who choose to go through the front door of the fort pay a single euro per entry.

The sole tourist attraction attached to the fort is a small museum on big-wave surfing and a series of surfboards leaning against its walls, with the words of its owners next to each one. It's like a big-wave surfing wall of fame. Each tells a different story. There is Antonio Silva, who talks of how "Climbers have Everest, surfers have Nazaré. This is our Everest," and Axi Muniain, who hails from the Basque Country and, like Silva, is a regular on the big days. He is known as the enfant terrible of surfing, or else the "wave madman".

The clifftops are muddied and slippery, barely safe for those that crowd on top of them, from the casual observers to the surf crew's spotters who pick out the big waves to surf and relay that via walkie-talkies, and also locate stricken surfers for their rescue crews. The spotters chop and change but are mostly surfers too, from Dino Carmo, the six-time Portuguese national bodyboard champion, to Diogo Pedro, a former handball player who prefers the smaller wash for his own surfing exploits.

The whole ground rumbles like it's in the midst of a fairly sizeable earthquake. The venom of the waves is so strong that spray wets the face some 200 feet above, all while the audio backdrop is the roar of the most ferocious seas. As each wave is caught, a roar of cheers to match that of the waves sounds out; with each wipeout, there is a collective intake of breath, seemingly held until the surfer in question is pulled safely out of the water. But that is not always the case – the wipeouts and resultant injuries are as much a part of the folklore as the big waves surfed.

This day, the anticipated swell is not as monstrous as the hype anticipated, the biggest waves estimated to be in the mere 60- to

70-foot bracket. With that, the 80-foot wave surfed by Rodrigo Koxa in Nazaré remains unbroken for another day.

But the day, like every day, comes with a cost to the crews involved. Jet skis rolled, engines flooded and washed up on the beach. For Von Rupp, his day in the water is particularly costly. As night falls, back at Von Rupp's warehouse, Cosme – who also doubles as an accomplished jet-ski mechanic – is there as always to pore over the stricken machine. Conversations begin of who might pick up the tab for the damage done. As Von Rupp puts it: "You just live to surf, and no one thinks about the cost until the shit hits the fan, and the shit's hit." Already, just one swell into the big-wave surfing season, the cost is being felt, physically and financially.

9

GENDER INEQUALITY

Maya Gabeira

Nazaré came close to acting as a watery grave for Maya Gabeira. Rather than being deterred by her death-defying antics, now she calls it home – the girl from Ipanema who relocated to this corner of Portugal, 5,000 miles from Brazil.

She is a Jekyll and Hyde of sorts. An outgoing and bubbly character on the surface, she also likes to be a recluse in her idyllic Portuguese hilltop hideaway with her two dogs. The building's sleek lines could not be in greater contrast to the tumultuous waves she tackles.

Her home is a 10-minute drive from the harbour. On my first visit there, low clouds envelop the headland on which she lives. Visibility of what later transpires to be a stunning view is limited on the road out of town, along which are littered a number of homes jutting out of the surrounding greenery. When conditions are like this, it almost adds to Nazaré's mystique.

Along the road, a series of disused gun turrets dating back centuries adds a further allure to the vista. Trying to locate her house isn't easy but, once I'm in the vicinity, she pops out from behind an innocuous metal door with a welcoming smile.

Stormy, a protective Australian Shepard with piercing eyes who also doubles as her training partner, repeatedly barks. Gabeira's other dog Naza – both pets' names a nod to her career and surroundings – offers a friendly greeting, in contrast. The canine pair are thick as thieves, companions to her and each other on her various surf trips, both in her adopted hometown and occasionally further afield.

Her home is like an oasis. While there is no view of the sea – that is blocked off by her house and the trees that surround its perimeter fence – on the stormy days, it is clearly audible.

Behind an automatic garage door lies a lush green lawn surrounded by those trees and tall bamboo canes, with a swimming pool in the middle. To the side is her only real addition since buying the house: what looks like a barrel, housing within it a small sauna. A glass-fronted exterior to the house draws you in – a cool, sleek design bringing in light from all angles and posing wooden staircases either end to the upstairs. At the back of the house stands her home gym, with the words "Practice like a champion" spelled out in the room's narrow glass window.

Three of her old surfboards, painted by a Brazilian artist and friend, hang on the walls. Back outside is the garage, in which she chooses not to park her hybrid Ford camper van; instead, the space is taken up with surfboards, of which there are plenty, along with wetsuits and other bits of surfing equipment.

Her intention had never been to buy a place in Nazaré. The listing for the property remained unsold for what seemed like an eternity. And yet she kept on finding herself returning to it on the web and casting her curious eye over it. But each time she was deterred by the fact it was always too far away from the harbour and the waves. On closer inspection, she realised it was actually a relatively short hop from the harbour, and it spiked her curiosity, so she arranged a viewing the next morning. Her reaction when she first stepped foot inside was, "I'm going to buy this." The house needed no work and she had no intention of undertaking a big DIY project. The fit seemed natural. She put an offer in the following day, and it has been home ever since.

Inside its four walls, come the afternoons, Gabeira likes to sleep – her "nanna naps", she calls them – but has foregone today's to talk, her dogs taking to the customary places on the sofa. When she heads to the beach to surf, they come with her, guarding any possessions and doing what they please. "They can sniff, bark, do what they want. If they're bad, when I come back, I pretend they're not mine and then we run!"

Naza, four at the time of our first meeting, came first; Stormy, a year younger, was added to the household a year later, both with contrasting personalities. Naza she calls her "cuddle dog", a pet who doubles as an emotional support, to the extent that Gabeira's psychiatrist gives her a letter enabling her to travel with the dog on her lap. More well travelled than most humans on the planet, Naza the dog has flown to New York, California, São Paulo, Rio de Janeiro and Amsterdam, among other destinations.

In contrast, Stormy almost serves as her owner's personal trainer. If ever Gabeira needs a reminder to work on her fitness training, the Australian Shepherd is on hand to give her a nudge. "He never lets me have a day off. I don't need a trainer – he wants me to run, bike, whatever, he's pawing at me like, 'Let's go, let's go!'" Not that Gabeira is particularly slack when it comes to training – she knows it is a necessity to surf and survive the big waves. She has that home gym, from which she regularly posts morning training pictures, sometimes as early as 5.30 a.m.

There's jealousy between the two dogs for her attention, but they also work as a team, calling to each other if they uncover something on a hilltop walk, or as they sit patiently waiting for her to come out of the water, sometimes for hours at a time.

The Brazilian's love for animals has been instilled in her as long as she can remember. While her older sister Tami had dolls, the younger of the two siblings always insisted on stuffed animals. From about the age of five, she would pester her mother for a horse, having been inspired by one on TV.

Even now, she says she prefers animals to humans – easier to work with, easier to understand. It's partly down to some of the more negative human interactions early in her career. Greater credence is added to this preference by her ongoing side project concerning a group of stray kittens born nearby, who have been harassed by a pack of dogs roaming the same neighbourhood. After seeing one of the kittens attacked by a dog, she took it to the vet, but it died in her car on the way there. Her animal rescue side operation she describes as "another adventure", which amounts to, with a neighbour, building a small wooden home for the cats in a tree just outside the front of her house, to provide a safe haven from their canine hunters.

By her own admission, living alone does have its periods of loneliness, exacerbated in recent seasons by the impact of Covid. Unable to travel back to Brazil for a whole year, her family's visits over to her were also curtailed. Her mother Yamē Reis normally comes for three months a year, but she went well over 12 months without seeing her parents or any wider family – except through a computer screen or mobile phone. During that period, the dogs acted as her crutch, and still do on a day-to-day basis.

She has other friends – among them Ana Catarina, a photographer, and Stephanie Johnes, a documentary film-maker who, for 12 years, has been plotting a film, *Maya and the Wave*, about Gabeira's life in and out of the water.

It is November. The season is in its relative infancy and has started slowly, the weather still warm and the winter storms that help to create the necessary havoc at Nazaré not quite having hit Europe's west coast yet. The waves have finally recently got big enough – up to 40 to 50 feet – for her to bring out the jet ski for tow surfing, thereby enabling her to train for those bigger days. Here, it is all about preparing for when the monster days come – of which there are plenty in store.

If an 80-foot day was to emerge tomorrow, she readily admits she wouldn't quite be ready for it but, after a good week, she is feeling one step closer. Much of each day is spent on preparation: testing jet skis, surfboards, radios, putting in the necessary hours to ensure a slick and safe operation on the big days. Plus, she does two sessions a week at the local pool to work on her breathing. Much of the systems in place are a carry-over from last year, but with one big difference: Sebastian Steudtner.

"It's like the layers you have to put on to get to the biggest swells of the season. I feel this week will be really good to try the boards, try the teams, try the radios. I need to put a lot of hours into the ski and see where I'm at. We have a pretty good system in place from last year. The only different thing is that I won't be with Seb. God's forced me on his plan. I'm like, 'Fuck, it's meant to be.'"

The "Seb" she speaks of is Steudtner, the German athlete who injured himself on his first day of the season and is facing a battle to get back in the water. Pairings are a key facet in the big waves, and usually surfers will work as a set duo during the course of a full season. It isn't always the case, but it generally works as a symbiotic 50–50 split. As a duo out on the water, half the time they'll surf and the other half they'll tow the other into the waves. As a result, with no partner, there is something of an unknown for what lies ahead this season and with whom she will enter the big waves on a given day.

She had chopped and changed her options for the season's start – a regular facet of Nazaré life – before teaming up with Steudtner, with whom she first partnered in the 2015–16 season. In the wake of his injury, her sentiment was, as she puts it, "Shit, now I'm really out of a team." There is uncertainty whether she can compete at all in the upcoming Tow Surfing Challenge, an event sanctioned by the World Surf League (WSL) and arguably the biggest competition here each season, for which she will need an established partner. In short, her 2021–22 ambitions hang in the balance, a cloud of uncertainty looming over the effervescent Brazilian.

But at the same time, out of the depths of adversity, she is often able to prove herself by standing entirely on her own two feet. It was always thus, both for the teenager who left the family home in Brazil to venture to Hawaii, in pursuit of big waves and her dreams, and for the person she is now. Back in the Hawaiian days, from the age of 19, and in her Nazaré infancy – long before she joined forces with Steudtner – she had worked with fellow Brazilian Carlos Burle. Whatever the partnership, she has fielded constant self-doubt, but it has always strengthened both her resolve and her belief.

"It's so interesting when you rely on somebody and achieve success, and you then question yourself – if your success comes from that other person's ability or your own," she said. "I had that with Carlos for so long. When he dumped me at 26 with the drama and trauma and injuries, I wondered how much of the success was because I was with someone so much better than me and so much more experienced, and I had that haunting and that doubt on myself.

"Then when I had my first world record with Eric [Rebiere], I was like maybe … but Seb was there as a part of the team. My second world record was with Seb, and we had some good waves the last few years. It will be interesting if I can put myself in a good position without Seb. It's kind of a good challenge for me."

The initial move to Hawaii as a teenager – just a few years after first picking up a surfboard – was a bold call, as was leaving behind a comfortable life with an affluent family in Rio de Janeiro to test herself among the world's best in the traditional surfing Mecca.

In those days, that seemingly confident teenager, who was also wracked by doubts like most people her age, did not have WhatsApp, FaceTime or Skype to fall back on for family communication. Instead, it was the same phone booth from which she would call home just once a month to talk to her parents. Much like during the full onslaught of the Covid pandemic, she didn't see them for a year and a half, in what was a period both of adversity but also one of learning quickly to fend for herself.

The reality was she needed a support network, but it wasn't there. She laughs now – albeit nervously – at some of the comments that came her way from the masculine surfing fraternity which surrounded her. But they cut deep. From the moment she first paddled and then towed in to the water, the comments were mostly along the lines of being told she couldn't surf, the big waves weren't for her and that she was making the sport look bad for the rest of them … namely, the men.

"A few really stuck to me. The really nasty ones hurt. If I'd been home with Mum and Dad, I might have told them, but I didn't have anyone. It was tough. I was a young girl working. I was met with this attitude of 'Why should this girl come all the way from Brazil if these Hawaiian girls are not doing this?'" If she surfed a good wave, they would call her lucky; if she had a bad wipeout, they'd tell her she was lucky not to have died. "I could never be on the right side. I was, in their eyes, the luckiest girl in the world. It was nasty."

There have never been apologies from those in the big-wave surfing community who verbally abused her as an impressionable teenager and doubted her right to be in the water – although she likes to think some have changed their opinion, given what she has achieved in the decade and a half since.

Both fragile and thick-skinned at the same time, if you can be such a thing, she was like a sponge to each barb, both in and out of the water. "Always being criticised hurts, but you have to absorb it, dig in and find the lessons you can take to better yourself." With the insecurity came the desire to always evolve and try to work out where she could possibly improve and how she could surpass the societal expectation of what she could be as a big-wave surfer. "My limitations were set from the outside and, because I had so many people saying things that would make me insecure, I would have to work extra hard to build up my confidence in order to expose myself in the sport. It's tough to not feel accepted in your group." Today, the acceptance is fully there, but it has been a long time in coming.

She rebuffs the idea that she channelled such adversity for further motivation in the water. "No, I didn't use that. For a long time, it was quite intimidating because I was a woman. That tension was coming from big men, and a lot of men. It was their environment. To be hostile towards a young girl, that makes you feel intimidated. It's not as easy. Maybe a guy would feel very motivated with his ego and testosterone, but for a girl, you're like 'This is so scary.'"

There were times she readily admits she thought about quitting – but never strongly enough for it to become a reality. Her love of the ocean and the Hawaiian waves always outweighed the vitriol that came her way for years.

There was a knock-on effect to those around her, even to the extent that it was hard to get someone to tow her into the waves.

Even her previous confidant, Burle, she says, would get a hard time for towing her when the big swells hit the Hawaiian Islands. And the anger towards her was further exacerbated by the sponsorship deals that understandably came her way as a global trailblazer for women's sport, well ahead of her time.

In her eyes, it wasn't just her gender that created issues. It was her nationality too. Surfing is a territorial sport. Hawaii was often seen as the reserve of the locals and occasionally more widely for Americans as a whole.

"You have to understand that you're Brazilian in those places. We're looked down on. We're a third-world country in some [people's] eyes. We're supposed to be getting the waitressing jobs, the second jobs, the handy jobs – not the top stuff." In that respect, Nazaré has been the polar opposite for Gabeira from the very beginning.

Things in big-wave surfing have changed in Hawaii, and globally, since, thanks in no small part to the crap that she had to endure to ease the way for future generations. She shrugs her shoulders at the suggestion she opened the doors for so many others to follow, among them Justine Dupont, who, along with Gabeira, has gone on to set the benchmark for women's big-wave surfing. The pair of them have vied for the world record for the biggest wave ever surfed by a woman, which Gabeira currently holds.

The pair get on well, but Gabeira makes the point that Dupont and other female surfers like Michelle des Bouillons have not had to endure the same adversity that she was forced to encounter in the early part of her career. "I don't think they're dealing with what I did 13 years ago when I became professional. The #MeToo movement and all those things have created a sense of shame when men come out and are speaking out against women publicly. The movement really has filtered out a lot of what I used to hear, and what people would bluntly put out there with no regrets. There's now a sense of shame in it, so you see a woman treated differently and more accepted. It is challenging to not feel accepted within your group, within the community."

Her hope is that the likes of Dupont and Des Bouillons and others that follow never have to face the struggle she did – that they can feel accepted regardless of their gender and strive to achieve their peak performance without that hostility.

10

THE GUARDIAN ANGEL OF NAZARÉ

Sérgio Cosme

Pulling out of Nazaré harbour on jet skis, teams of surfers, drivers and camera operators temporarily park up by the harbour exit, pausing to indulge in a tradition. The jet skis come together and the characters in question hold hands, heads bowed to briefly pray. Someone always leads the supplication. Each time, the words are different – some religious, others spiritual, yet others purely practical – but however the message is conveyed and whatever the origins of language or faith, the sentiment is still the same: to come back safely and survive to surf another day in one of the most notorious waterways in Europe. For the uninitiated, such a prayer about what lies ahead can seem daunting but it has become tradition, almost always professed – whether the waves are big or small.

Riding on a jet ski out of the harbour at Nazaré, the rules are simple for any passenger, whatever their level of experience: to hold on to the waist of their pilot. The thinking is that, without a firm hold, any sudden change of pace will see the passenger jettisoned off the back and flung into the trailing wake of the vehicle. On what is a relatively calm day, Sérgio Cosme is riding on one jet ski with a novice behind him. On board the other is Nic von Rupp at the controls, with the septuagenarian singer-songwriter Jimmy Buffett riding pillion.

Neither jet-ski pairing is the traditional Nazaré partnership of taking turns between driving and surfing the wave.

The American, Buffett, is a lifelong surfer and has sold in excess of 20 million albums, his island sound of feel-good music made famous by such hits as "Margaritaville" and "It's Five O'Clock Somewhere". He has taken a sidestep from a family holiday in Galicia to cast his eyes over Nazaré's waters for the first time. It is not uncommon for celebrities to make their way into the town's waters. *Game of Thrones* actress Maisie Williams is another relatively recent visitor, while there are whispers all season long that seven-time Formula One world champion Lewis Hamilton, himself a keen surfer, is plotting a visit if and when his racing calendar allows.

Buffett has flown over from the States in his private jet and travelled from Spain to Portugal in a chauffeur-driven car. The town hall has made two jet skis available for his first foray into the water. In return, the crooner poses for photographs on social media: of him in the water by the jet skis and again on a surfboard out in the water, not in the waves but in the flatter water.

To the right as you come out of the harbour is the main beach, while diagonally in front of you sits the fort, jutting out into ocean about a kilometre further away. However experienced a surfer is, there's always that nervous sense of anticipation as the surfers approach this marker. But normality often transfers to chaos as you turn the corner past the fort, into the stretch of water where the notorious big waves make their way to the north beach.

Every single time he's out in the water, Cosme is trying to learn. Before turning the corner, he pulls into Pedra do Guilhim, two protruding rocks that stand apart from the mainland, the connecting land having been eroded by the waves hundreds of years ago. As a surfer, this is the last place you want to be stranded when the sea is restless – the spot where Andrew Cotton would later in the season find himself bobbing breathlessly in and out of the water. Cosme surveys the expanse, trying to work out ways in which to safely get a jet ski in and out around the rocks in rougher times. He looks at it like someone trying to solve a riddle, his eyes darting from one rock to the next, watching the movement of the waves on a stiller day to understand how he might weave his way through it for the most precarious of rescues.

On this day, the waves are 15 feet – child's play for the surfers but gargantuan enough for the novices sitting on the back of a jet ski to feel a tad apprehensive. Cosme plays with the waves, riding just in front of the barrel of a wave and along it, the shadow of the wave acting as a picturesque backdrop on a sunny day.

He reels off stories of some of the times in seasons past where things have gone awry or, alternatively, the great escapes: scooping Von Rupp out of the rocks in time before another wave battered him, or else another audacious rescue, this time of Cotton.

Cosme had timed that particular great escape to perfection, grabbing and pulling Cotton onto the back of the jet ski before being hit by the breaking white water of the wave, sliding and skidding like a car on ice in their attempted escape, but recovering and pulling out of the wave. As Cosme whooped and hollered in celebration, he turned back to share his joy with his partner in crime only to find the float behind him empty, Cotton having decided it was safer to jump ship and take his chances with the waves, seeing that the jet ski seemed to be out of control. By the time they were reunited, Cotton was ashen-faced, having assumed Cosme was lost to the sea. And with that, he laughs, hitting the throttle to head back to the harbour.

It's hard not to feel good in the company of Cosme, a man small in stature but big in laughs, and with his penchant for calling everyone in his company a "legend". Every other sentence comes with a cackle, sometimes a manic one. And his Latin temperament is such that he can lose his good nature when required, which can be relatively regularly due to the stressful nature of his primary role. A big-wave surfer originally, now he is better known as one of the best jet-ski drivers, his rescues of stricken surfers the stuff of folklore. They have earned him that nickname: "The guardian angel of Nazaré". The moniker has clearly touched him.

"It's amazing to hear that name," he admits. "When I saw it, I thought with a title like that, I was like Jesus!" he adds, cracking up. "But truly I was really amazed and grateful for people to call me something like that. There's so many words and names they could call me – much, much worse than that – but 'guardian angel' … I like it. Everyone with a good sense and a good vibe likes to be called an angel. It's such a hard place to be and drive and work, and to have this hobby." To him, that guardian angel tag, in one of the toughest places in the world to surf, shows the trust that his cohabitants on the jet skis and surfboards have in his skills and his work. "It's amazing for me, incredible," he says, his head shaking almost in disbelief at the nickname.

Cosme's Nazaré story begins long before McNamara was first lured to surf those initial waves. Born sandwiched between Nazaré and Lisbon in another smaller-wave surf spot, Santa Cruz, Cosme, from the age of five, would regularly take a family road trip to Nazaré on Sundays for lunch or dinner and a walk along its picturesque promenade, the children often with ice creams in hand. All manner of families in the surrounding areas still do the same today.

He laughs at the idea that his life has somehow come full circle to bring him back here, albeit in different circumstances. "It's funny I've ended up back here in my life," he says. "While the waves were always already here – that's nature – it's nice to understand I was here long ago, before all this started. I never saw the big waves, but then I ended up surfing and driving them."

Growing up, the obsession was with motors, despite it being a passion imparted by neither of his parents. It is, though, a shared love with his cousin Ricardo. The pair were born just 15 days apart in the same year. They were virtually inseparable and would spend time together after school and on weekends, summer vacations, Christmas and Easter; the pair were as thick as thieves.

Introduced to two wheels by his uncle, he first got in the saddle of a motorbike, and was given the controls to steer it, at three or four years old. Within two years, he and his cousin would steal the bike when their parents weren't around and go up and down the street. To this day, he is unsure if the adults ever knew.

Today, Cosme is something of a Mr Fix-it. As well as being a rescue driver, he is regularly called upon to fix and service the various jet skis. He also buys, does up and then sells cars – but more as a hobby than a profession.

One of his passions is still engines – whenever he hears the purr of one, it doesn't matter where or what it is, it spikes his curiosity. And another is the ocean – as long as he can remember he has loved spending time in it – and surfing. As he puts it: "I just always want to be in the water, and those two passions in my life are like one here."

With big-wave surfing, both align and, for him, the parallels between motorbikes and jet skis are closer than you might think, because of the respective bumps and undulations on both land and sea.

When he was taught in a jet-ski course how to tackle a wave, the advice was always to cross it slowly up and down. The first time he saw one of Nazaré's double waves, he tried what he had learned; the second wave hit him full on and nearly took out the jet ski. He thought to himself, *Never again.*

"In motocross, I do a double jump across two jumps [in effect getting enough speed to clear two regular jumps in one go] and I thought, *If I can apply this in surfing, it could be useful*. When I do these kinds of things in training, I do it alone, myself on the jet ski when no one needs me to rescue them."

Where dirt bikes and jet skis diverge: in the latter, the adrenaline never switches off. On two wheels, if he's tired, he merely goes a little bit slower; if he's riding with someone less accomplished than him, he can hold back. The sea is a less forgiving host.

"On dirt bikes, you have 30 seconds of adrenaline. In surfing, you spend hours in adrenaline. Even if it's not your team, it's another team in the water. If something happens, this adrenaline is pure all the time – you go out until you come in. I'm full throttle on both. I like adrenaline, I like speed, I like to hear the roar of the engine. But here, it's a completely different kind of work. The adrenaline when rescuing people is the adrenaline of being scared because of the responsibility to save a life. That's way different to being full throttle and having fun."

While he still likes to refer to himself as a big-wave surfer – although outings on the board in the big water have been limited in recent years – Cosme is well aware he is now better known as being behind the controls of a jet ski on the big days.

A few years ago, McNamara – adept at both surfing and jet-ski driving throughout his Nazaré tenure – took him aside and said to him, "You love to surf but you like to drive. Sérgio, bet on one thing in your life. If you want to show yourself as a surfer, be a surfer. If it's as a driver, be a driver." So he shifted his perspective, knowing that he, in truth, is an even better driver than he is a surfer. And the landscape has altered over the years in that regard, with an increasing number of driver specialists emerging. As he explains, "Five years ago, you didn't have good drivers. That's changed."

The divide between the two has been widened by injury. Going into the 2021–22 season with a body somewhat broken by land and water, Cosme is only capable of being in the saddle, not on a board. In the midst of the preceding season, he was sharing surfing and driving duties with Von Rupp. On one particular February day, the pair were stuck between two waves. He tried to jump over the gap between the waves but, despite his driving skills, misjudged it and crashed the jet ski into the second wave. His mouth smashed into the handlebars of the ski, knocked out his two front teeth as well as some additional bone and left him with a cut lip. As he limped back bloodily to the harbour, with a little more than a shrug of the shoulders, his sentiment was: "Ah, life goes on."

Undeterred, he went out to prove just that and, four days later, got on board his dirt bike with some friends and damaged the anterior cruciate ligament in his knee, for which he had to undergo the surgeon's knife. For the rest of this current season, he is toing and froing to his physiotherapist in Portugal's capital city to get him back to full fitness. He dismisses it all as part of the game he has chosen to play, but the comeback from surgery has been lengthy and, at times, frustrating. At the beginning of this season, at a time when the surfers are all converging on Nazaré, you can still see small threads between his teeth where the latest repairs have been done, the stitches still in place. The teeth look well repaired, but the rehabilitation on his knee remains a work in progress. Surfing could prove to be curtailed for Cosme for the whole season – but, from the outset, he is adamant his injury is repaired enough for him to drive over and around the biggest waves.

Another worry aside from the injury hangs over him: Covid. He lives next to his elderly mother Liliana, who is well into her seventies. The fear – partially a hangover from last season, in the very heart of the pandemic – that he might pick up the virus and pass it on closer to home in Santa Cruz remains very real. So tightly knit is this particular community that if one person gets it, it spreads rapidly. Last season and already in this one, the virus has had a propensity to spread like wildfire through the hub of surfers.

This jet-ski joyride into the sea with Jimmy Buffett is an early coming together for him and Von Rupp, as part of a planned team for the season ahead. The Portuguese pair are blood brothers – like siblings that are increasingly close but also prone to bickering. No row is ever big enough, though, that the issue hasn't been able to be resolved, and their friendship repaired. Since 2018, they have been part of a team, like a surfing Batman and Robin.

One night, long after the day's surfing was over, the pair stood outside a beachfront restaurant where the surfers had all gathered to celebrate the day's antics. Instead, the duo talked heatedly about the events of the day, two rolled jet skis and an uninsured video camera which had been ruined and needed to be paid for. By the end of the night, any fractures had seemingly been resolved.

A friend of the two men likes to joke they are like husband and wife, and Cosme's laughter at that story's retelling suggests it is a marriage of sorts. "Look, like a couple, we fight – sometimes you need to. Sometimes I scream at him and he screams at me, but that's a normal thing. And we laugh, we love. I have a big connection with Nic and we need that connection." Their strong bond is not just important to their friendship but also to their communication in the water – so, too, the screams and shouts. "If I can drive better, I will try to. I want him to say to me, 'Sérgio, let's do this better.'" Towing each other into death-defying situations and then extracting each other creates that indelible union.

Chopping and changing a crew can be hazardous. Having the harmony and an almost sixth sense of a regular pairing makes things infinitely safer – and also makes it more probable that both surfers will catch the biggest waves. For that reason, Cosme and Von Rupp like to stick with the same partnership. Some others have come and gone in their team, such as Rafael Tapia, a Chilean wine importer and big-wave surfer. The South American has dipped in and out of Nazaré over the years and likens it to a drug habit he can't kick. For much of his adult life, he has worked in order to earn the money to surf.

This season, Cosme and Von Rupp's main surfing partner is Pedro Scooby, a wild partygoing Brazilian who is planning to quit Nazaré midway through the season to appear on his country's version of *Celebrity Big Brother*. The other key facet to any assembled team is a spotter, who watches from the clifftop and directs the jet-ski drivers into the right waves and also guides them to the rescue point after a big wave takes down a surfer.

Initially, the dream ticket for their seasonal spotter is Adriano "Strodgy" Cordeiro, who has habitually worked with Brazilian Lucas "Chumbo" Chianca – the Lionel Messi of big-wave surfing – and his crew. With Chianca absent from Nazaré, at least early on in the season, conversations turn to getting Cordeiro on board until Chianca arrives. Such is Cordeiro's loyalty to his surfer that he does not jump ship to join Cosme and Von Rupp even for a single day.

Amid all the moving parts in a team, Cosme and Von Rupp remain the immovables, their understanding fine-tuned to the point that they can often work without speaking. In the water and on the back of the rope ready to be towed into the big waves by Cosme's jet ski, Von Rupp is usually some 10 to 12 metres behind his friend.

With the roar of the jet-ski engines, not to mention the crashing of the monster waves around them, it requires both a shared understanding and a good set of lungs. "Often, we can't hear each other, so we need to scream – so sometimes it looks like I'm a little mad," says Cosme, raising his voice as if to emphasise his point. "I'm screaming and he's like, 'Why are you screaming at me?', but you're just shouting to be heard."

The hard work that goes into their communication, an ever-evolving work in progress, has enabled them to put each other on the right part of the wave however volatile the situation. There are the highs of the waves surfed to what feels like perfection, the moments gone wrong where they work in cahoots to ensure the situation doesn't worsen and those times when either or both lose their rag. At the core of that, argues the guardian angel, is a relationship set firmly in stone in recent years. "Of course, we all catch problems in our lives and days but, if you have a big friendship, it's way easier for anything else to pass."

11

THE VIEW FROM THE SHORE

Spotters, photographers and film-makers

On the surfing days – even the smaller ones – gathered together on the far right of the Nazaré hillside, overlooking the waves, stand a group separated from the rest of the spectators. There are fold-up chairs set up and large umbrellas to protect them from the sun when it's out. From dawn until dusk, from the arrival of the first surfer to the departure of the last, they will stay in their position – a set of bushes behind them acting as a makeshift toilet when required.

Around their necks hang binoculars; in their hands, radios which occasionally crackle to life with news from within the waves. These are the spotters, the lifeline to Nazaré's big-wave surfers.

As their name suggests, they're there to spot anything that goes on in the water – good or bad. They advise which waves the surfers are towed into and, perhaps more crucially, guide the rescue jet skis to where they should come out. The word used above all else is "*esquerdo*" (left), barked down the radio in a fast, rhythmic tempo to guide the jet-ski driver to his left until the moment the surfer has popped out of the wave or been enveloped by it. If the surfer is not seen by their would-be in-situ rescuer amid the white water, it is the spotter's job to locate them and marshal any sort of rescue operation.

Each team has at least one spotter, in some cases paid a daily rate or otherwise employed by a surfer or a team for the duration of the season. Sometimes, the teams will opt for two when the larger waves make their appearance, the spotters' roles akin to that of a Formula One driver's race engineer in a grand prix. Much like over the course of a grand prix, there is prolonged radio silence which, on occasion, is punctured by a transmission. When a surfer is lost, however temporarily, there come panicked voices – usually in Portuguese, sometimes in English, depending on the language of choice in that particular team – as they form a united front to rescue them. Once safe, normal service is resumed, the multitaskers returning to fast talking, joking and eating with their friends.

All are locals trusted with the lives of the surfers. Through their upbringing, they became the most knowledgeable about the way the local waters work. On calmer days, they are often the bodyboarders in the water below. At the epicentre of them is Cordeiro, aka Strodgy. The nickname dates back to his younger days. Having been bullied and called "Monkey" at his previous school, he wanted to drop that nickname when he enrolled in a new one. The change coincided with a programme on Brazilian TV that somehow had subtitles in an Eastern European language. He would mimic the subtitles while watching and repeat them again at school, without knowing a word of what he was saying. And, in the folly of his youth, he pretended he was a refugee. For whatever reason, Strodgy was born, and it stuck – even his mother Tina calls him it in front of his friends.

Cordeiro is a whirlwind of energy. With his mother, he runs a picturesque guesthouse in his grandmother's old apartment in Sitio. Called Casa do Mar, the house has four rooms, all kitted out with aquatic themes and furnished with handcrafted creations by mother and son. The rooms overlook the cobbled streets below, and are just a short walk away from the clifftops where you can watch the surfers. He has earned a cult following on Instagram with his daily surf reports, always beginning with an excitable and loud *"Bom dia, bom dia, bom dia!"* ("good morning") as he scours the waters from the clifftops above for an early-morning surf report. He is often the one who reports what sort of day awaits the big-wave community.

He is the spotter for Lucas Chianca and is generally regarded as one of the best, hence Cosme and Von Rupp having previously sought his help. But his loyalty lies with Chianca; he calls the pair of them brothers, to the extent that they finish each other's sentences, laugh at their jokes before the punchline is reached and have such an under-standing of each other that they keep their talking from clifftop to jet ski to a minimum. In short, Chianca's spotter only speaks when it is absolutely necessary, like a good coach in any sport who knows the right moment to speak up.

The two are mightily similar: both bundles of energy, always laughing and smiling. In Cordeiro's eyes, Chianca is the "Pablo Picasso of big-wave surfing", doing things in the water that others can't. Quite what that makes Cordeiro – the easel or the paint brush, perhaps? – he doesn't know; he simply shrugs his shoulders and laughs at the idea of it all.

He remembers those early days of Garrett McNamara, and the excitement the Hawaiian's arrival brought to a small number of surfers and bodyboarders. Cordeiro would come to the clifftop and watch McNamara and his team surf. One day, he was asked to act as a spotter, given a walkie-talkie that wasn't working properly and told to get to work. Initially, the role of a spotter was more simply for safety; over time, it has become increasingly tactical in terms of knowing what waves to go for and when. It was a steep learning curve, but now Cordeiro knows how Nazaré behaves better than most.

"I'm like a bird – I have an overview," he says of his role. "I just wait. Sometimes we're 30 minutes without talking because there's no new information." The speed with which he converses, and the number of words that spill out, make it is hard to imagine him ever being particularly quiet. "They don't want to have too much talk – at the beginning, I was giving out all the information."

Primarily, the job involves him keeping a cool head in a crisis. In moments of drama in the past, he had been known to scream and shout down the radio. But he has come to the realisation that, however fraught the situation, that is never the way. He and the other spotters have to be the calmest people on the clifftop. His cause is helped by the fact that Chianca barely falls or finds himself in particularly precarious situations. That is predominantly down to his skill as a surfer, but helped by being guided on to the right waves at the right time by his on-land puppeteer. And Chianca's instruction from the sea is always the same: to find him the biggest wave imaginable in any given moment.

The days can be long and the required levels of concentration taxing. But Cordeiro usually comes prepared with food and drink, or else others will help supply it for him during the course of the day. But when he's there, despite being hundreds of metres away from the waves, he imagines he is the one actually in the water. "I feel like I'm surfing, like I'm with him in the water. Sometimes, it's like I'm surfing and [I think], *What do I want to hear? If I was in the water, what kind of information would I want?*"

But for all his apparent delight in – and mastery of – the job, it does not come without its stresses. He has seen enough close calls in his team and those of others to know the dangers involved, how each team is just one freak moment away from a calamity. "I sometimes start worrying, because it is my job to protect. You worry about their lives, and it's super stressful because you can sometimes put them in a bad place." The thought, the worry, perpetually hangs over Nazaré.

The other ever-present voyeurs over the town's waters are those filming and photographing what plays out amid the waves.

A moped is stacked high with equipment, an antique camera tripod sticking out from its driver's protective clutches. Tim Bonython weaves his way down the short drive from the apartment he owns in Sitio, through the barrier that keeps out most other vehicles, and down to the overview of the surfers' paradise. It is barely dawn. He unfolds his tripod and slots his camera – a Red Epic Weapon – into position, embedding it into the red soil beneath his feet, as the first jet skis and surfers arrive in the water for a day's surfing. For much of the season, he is an ever-present figure on the clifftop when there is surf of any kind, filming hours and hours of footage that he edits at the end of a day. The Australian is perpetually upbeat, his videos on social media bigging up the latest swell or waxing lyrical about his latest Nazaré "day in the life" footage.

Each day, the land mass above the waves is awash with cameramen and women, filming and taking still photographs of the biggest waves and those within them. Cameras often fill the top of the lighthouse, which doubles up as a helipad of sorts for the various drones that are piloted out to sea to get an overhead view of the waves. And within the waters themselves, the daredevil camera operators sit atop the back of a jet ski to get the more high-octane footage.

Bonython's pathway to the waves began in the 1980s, much longer ago than most in Nazaré, when he was filming 25- to 30-foot waves at Bells Beach in Australia, aptly the backdrop to the final scene from *Point Break*. Two weeks later, people were queuing round the block to see his footage, what he calls "my ticket to ride". He decided it was a good way to make a living – and Nazaré, which, like most people, he first saw on the internet, has become the latest chapter for him. Some of his iconic film segments have included Rodrigo Koxa's 80-foot world record.

These crews are now central to Nazaré's story, their collective eyes perpetually pointed in the direction of the waves. Without them, there is no footage, no clips to go viral, no record-breaking waves for the scientists to measure and therefore no waves to speak of. Their numbers are increasing, with those in the water similarly on the rise. Often, they are affiliated to one particular surfer or a crew, or otherwise brought in for a particularly big swell. Others, like Bonython, shoot for themselves or for the HBO documentary *100 Foot Wave*.

Back when McNamara first came to tame – or at least tackle – the wave, Jorge Leal was the sole cameraman. It was his original footage and photographs that allowed the Nazaré story to explode. "It's changed a lot since day one," Leal says, like some sort of proud father rather than in any way ruefully. "It was like this ghost village in winter, some fishermen and their families and not much going on."

Originally from Porto, he had worked with Paulo Caldeira – one the key figures in the Nazaré origin story – and was brought on board at his request. Leal had studied at an arts school in Porto, which spawned an interest. He admits he wasn't particularly engrossed in filming, although his father later told stories of him filming family gatherings with his 8mm camera. Caldeira brought him on board to see what was possible to produce with both still and moving images. Instantly, Leal was hooked. "I basically fell in love with Nazaré. There's something going on with it, the beauty of nature. The geography is quite special, with the lighthouse and the cliff and rock in front of it. It has some kind of spell on you." He's been attached ever since and has called the town home for years.

Reflecting on the early days, he readily admits he was learning on the spot – it helped that he was a quick learner. He studied the swell charts and experimented with his position on the clifftop to find the best angle to film. His proudest moment was catching McNamara on his first record-breaking wave, taking stills and video at the same time, with an assistant, To Mané, alongside. It was from there that Nazaré was effectively released to the wider world. He jokes there are now thousands like him shooting when the larger waves come in, but that it still feels "special to be the first one".

Today, he works closely with Gabeira and Steudtner in particular, accruing countless scenes for their respective documentaries – and he opened his own exhibition in town, *Naza10*, to mark the decade anniversary of when it all began. As for the future, his wish is that a stronger surfing community builds from what it is now. "Big-wave surfers have huge egos, like the size of the waves, and it's sometimes tough to build the community with that," he says. "But the truth is that when we come together, we are stronger. That way, it can come an even bigger symbol of the big-wave community."

Everyone has their story for why they got to Nazaré. Pablo Garcia is a Colombian cameraman who now resides in Los Angeles and whose portfolio extends well beyond the waves. His introduction to surfing was watching Keanu Reeves and Patrick Swayze star in the 1991 film *Point Break*. Then, while filming a documentary on a footballer in Portugal, he learned about Nazaré's big waves. He reached out to Maya Gabeira, and the pair made a documentary about her story. In those first days, someone broke into his car, cut out his back seat and stole all the camera equipment in the boot. Others might have been inclined to pack up and leave. Instead, he drove to Lisbon to hire fresh equipment and stayed on for two or three months, filming day after day, and coming back season after season. At the start, he had "no idea, literally I didn't know anything about Nazaré, let alone surfing and surfing forecasts". For him, the lure is the closeness and the access to the wild nature below. Plus, no day is ever the same, providing something new to film each time. His is an addiction to the conditions and the potential for filming.

Despite an infatuation with the water, Garcia has never surfed. In contrast, Laurent Pujol has. He first came to Nazaré from his home in south-west France as a professional surfer rather than a cameraman, hitting the waves of north beach back in 2006, long before McNamara arrived. Even on fairly calm days, Pujol wasn't equipped for Nazaré's waters. He would not surf them for another seven years. And four years ago, he came here properly to film and has been here every season since. It's a precarious business being aboard a jet ski. As he puts it, "all kinds of shit can happen". He can get caught up in a rope or, more seriously, a propeller, or get struck by a wayward jet ski. His is a dangerous occupation. The season before, he face-planted on the housing of his camera, knocked out his two front teeth and one of those teeth cut a hole in his bottom lip. Now, he never really misses a big swell. His is a stressful life when out on the water – what he calls "full on" – but he loves the buzz of it, the burst of adrenaline that courses through his veins in the balance between capturing the best waves surfed and staying afloat. There is also a further role of occasionally acting as safety back-up should things go awry in the water.

The clifftop was understandably far emptier at the height of the Covid pandemic and that 2020-21 season is the only one Bonython has missed since he started coming to Portugal. With normal travel long since having resumed, the Australian acts as a reassuring, friendly presence any time you make the amble down the tarmac track towards the vista to the waves. He is at the heartbeat of this other subset of Nazaré's big-wave community, their part no less important in the global retelling of what goes on.

12

THE SEARCH FOR RECOGNITION

Sebastian Steudtner

The world record for the biggest wave ever surfed is a funny business. Go on to the internet and you will find all manner of videos purporting to be of waves 100 feet or more being surfed – some claimed by the surfers themselves or else their followers – almost all without any scientific evidence to back up the claims. Often, the thinking is that if you say it loud enough, it will be believed. And amid all the hype, Steudtner is confident that even if he doesn't step atop a board again this season, the record will be rightfully his, and that the current 80-foot record surfed by Rodrigo Koxa in Nazaré in 2017 will finally be eclipsed. There are whispers from the initial measuring process hinting it could be as big as 90 feet. But whether there is any validity to such whispers, the answer is not forthcoming anytime soon, despite Steudtner surfing said wave more than a year ago, in October 2020.

It is monstrous on playback, although trying to dissect one giant wave from another in terms of height can be nigh-on impossible to the untrained eye. At its start, it's as if he's almost coming down vertically after being towed in, before adjusting the angle of descent, his knees bent low to absorb the hefty bumps. His body looks tense rather than relaxed on the wave. As if suddenly realising its size, he looks up at the magnitude of the wave and its ferocity catches him off balance, causing him to lift his hands up and down in one quick movement to aid his balance and keep him from tipping off at 82 kmh, the top speed the sensor on his board clocks him travelling at.

As the white water breaks, a first bit of it lashes at the back of the board and his heels, but he stays on. Then another bit of the wave crashes into more of his body before a miniature waterfall effect briefly envelopes him before he reappears to cheers and a single shout in English of "He's out – yeah!" He jumps out over the back of the wave nonchalantly and cranes his head to look for the jet ski to take him out again rather than spend even a minute in celebration. To date, it is approaching half a billion views on the internet, arguably the most-watched wave in history.

But as his season on the sidelines ticks on, Steudtner is still none the wiser whether a fractured season might yet be a cause for celebration as a world record holder. Weeks have passed, then months, and yet still no word from the World Surf League about quite where his wave ranks in the annals of the sport's record books. The wait understandably rankles. Internally, there is a confidence he has comfortably broken the record – he agrees with the whispers that it was around 90 feet in height – but still, doubts remain about whether it will ever be ratified. That hesitation dates back to the times in the past where he feels he has been passed over in the record books and in the awards, notably the discipline's Oscars, the Big Wave Surf Awards, and that he might be yet again with his would-be record.

But the reality is his place in the upper echelons of the sport has long been assured – ever since 2010, when he became the first European to win one of the aforementioned awards, which annually rank the biggest and heaviest waves over the preceding 12 months. In December 2009, he had carved his way through a wave that surprised with both its speed and strength – riding from top to bottom, curving to his right, then left but riding along its length, and flying off the top of it.

By then, Steudtner had already come a long way from the child with that special sense of adventure, when he had first clambered onto a surfboard on a family holiday in Brittany, France, not knowing where it might eventually take him. It was apt his first award-winning wave was caught in the same Maui waters he read about, and subsequently visited, as a teen. It was with board and sail that he could make his first tentative moves in the water in Hawaii, and he got good enough to qualify for the windsurfing World Cup circuit. But it lacked quite the amount of thrill-seeking which he was after.

In time, he came to the realisation that it was surfing that had the greater pull on him, in part because of the increased risk-taking. The German was taken under the wing of Nelson Armitage, who was one of 16 children and a big name within the surfing community in Hawaii. He acted as Steudtner's mentor as well as the surfer who would provide his introduction to the big waves. Meanwhile, a famous tube rider, Dane Kealoha, helped teach the impressionable German teenager how to tow other surfers into the breaks. Unaware initially quite where Kealoha stood in the royalty of Hawaiian surfing – "he was just Uncle Dane to me" – he revelled in the simplicity of life in the ocean. His obsession was just in learning and getting better. That infatuation with the big waves was rewarded with that 2010 win and a life-changing $15,000 prize. Not long afterwards, he returned to his native Germany for a temporary stint in the surfing wilderness as he sought employment outside of the water.

He settled on working as a bouncer and setting up his own security business in Germany. And all the while his mind was elsewhere, the business aimed primarily at earning money to take him back to the big waves at the earliest opportunity. But his surfing Oscar had given him attention back at home for the first time. Fame is not something he has ever pursued – in fact, he shies away from it where possible – but that gong and the footage of his wave going viral on the internet turned him into an acknowledged extreme sports athlete back in Germany.

Years on, his face is still not universally recognised, but his name and his surfing exploits are. It leads to all manner of invites to celebrity functions, many of which he shuns. He is just back from one such opportunity, a trip home to take part in a celebrity charity phone-in on German television appearing with the likes of former heavyweight boxer Wladimir Klitschko, who has become a close friend over the years; they are united by a love of boxing, but also by a shared drive to succeed.

While he was working on his security business, Steudtner still had aspirations to surf the big waves. Although with no sponsorship – and hence little money, bar what his security business brought in – his hopes had to be put on hold until the winter of 2011, when he discovered Ireland. At the time, it had been deemed the place with the best big waves in Europe, and he relocated for the season to Mullaghmore, a tiny village in Ireland which has earned notoriety for its big waves.

One day while alone in the water, Steudtner was returning to the Irish enclave's harbour just as it was turning dark, and bumped into another surfer with a GoPro hanging loosely around his neck; he had just caught a wave and promptly been smashed over the head by it. Steudtner and Tom Butler immediately hit it off and, from there, became big-wave partners. Entirely different characters, at least externally, the Cornishman Butler is in many ways the typical surfer type, talking in a slow Cornish drawl – in contrast to the far greater intensity with which Steudtner approaches his surfing. But in the water, they aligned to become similarly driven. It was while out in Ireland that they saw the early images of Nazaré and decided on a whim to pack up and drive down there.

Rocking up to Nazaré with a Volkswagen camper van full to the brim with surfboards, their gear and a jet ski too weak for the Portuguese swells, they were extremely ill-equipped for the size of the Nazaré waves. But rather than being welcomed into the fold by the town hall team with McNamara as its focal point, the Anglo-German new arrivals were left feeling ostracised.

In a short space of time, they finally got their hands on a jet ski powerful enough to deal with the big waves and were prepared as a huge swell – one Steudtner still considers one of the biggest he has ever witnessed in the town – hit in their early days there. Their plans to go out, though, were scuppered.

Steudtner takes up the story: "We didn't have the little paper permit we needed, apparently. But they'd seen us for months using the same jet ski and suddenly the charts pop up with a big swell and the police were like, 'Excuse me, can we see your papers?' They just basically impounded it for the big swell only." Rather than being put off by the obstruction – which the two surfers decided was akin to kids in the playground saying they couldn't play – they ignited an internal fire instead, and pushed even more than they otherwise might have. And the affable Butler was at the heart of it. As Steudtner remembers it, "Tom might be a gentleman, but he's a great competitor. In competition, he's a killer and so am I. So we just had the same attitude – we're going to beat them."

Steudtner and McNamara haven't always particularly seen eye to eye. There is a respect between them for their achievements, but they are two markedly different personalities. In the German's mind,

McNamara gave off the impression, at least initially, that Nazaré was his place, the spot he had discovered first and that, in the early days, there wasn't room for others outside of his team. Back then, Nazaré was deserted in the winter. The switch to this current season, he says, is like night and day. Even sitting for dinner on a winter's night, the restaurants are bustling with surfers, their crews and tourists, even midweek. Back when he and Butler arrived, many of the restaurants had either entirely shut down for the winter or else didn't even exist, the demand simply not there.

And the change is similarly acute today in terms of his own financial success, since rocking up in that camper van with little money to his name, that rather useless jet ski and virtually no backers. In the midst of the 2021–22 season, it seems hard to believe the business side of things did not always come naturally to him – he is surrounded by global brands such as Porsche, Samsung and Siemens. He would be the first to admit he hated the business aspect of his work, that he wasn't a natural at it and that he could quickly lose interest in it. But over time, that shifted.

First, he came to the realisation that he needed business backing in order to give him the finances to survive and continue to have a career in the sport. In his early days, there was a long line of rejections from various sponsors. Chastened by the experience, at the time he vowed in his head never to work with those sponsors again, even when they came calling again in the future. In that regard, he has mellowed over the years and, in recollection, he laughs at the ridiculousness of that approach. "But everything was personal back then because everything feels so personal in the moment. The main thing I've learned from the last decade has been to detach myself."

At the peak of his career, at 36 years old, he remains one of the major success stories of Nazaré – as highlighted by his homes and car, as well as the brands who have chosen to sponsor him. As a surfer, he's part athlete – in his case, primarily an athlete – and part sales- man. For many of his peers, the biggest selling tool is their Instagram accounts. The most popular posts are footage of their waves and their wipeouts, shot by camera crews on the shore or else by drones that hover overhead. But there are the nods to sponsors, which are plenti- ful, and various insights into their world – from the build-up to a surf session to its aftermath, good and bad. He is one of the less prolific in terms of the sheer volume of posts on social media, but still has in excess of 225,000 Instagram followers. That admittedly pales into insignificance compared to some of the Brazilian contingent: Maya Gabeira and Lucas "Chumbo" Chianca are both edging towards a million, while Pedro Scooby has six million following his stint on *Celebrity Big Brother* back in Brazil. But Instagram is crucial to the Nazaré story, from its infancy to now. There's even a saying among some of the surfers – only partly in jest – that if it isn't on Instagram, it hasn't really happened.

But that surfer versus influencer element of life in Nazaré also bothers Steudtner. Being out of the water because of his injury has given him a different sense of perspective. He's in a reflective mood, sitting at a table at A Tosca, a restaurant on one of the roads leading to the waterfront and aptly next to the hotel where he first stayed on arrival in the town. He readily admits that social media is an important tool for followers and sponsors alike, but his usage is curtailed in comparison to many of his peers – who, it has to be said, are at times relentless with theirs.

"A lot are becoming influencers. From the last time we met to now, I've not been surfing, so I've just been watching and not close to any of the surf. It's just an outside view but it's quite interesting to see the behaviour of everyone and how it's changed with HBO."

That refers to the ongoing filming by the American company HBO on the documentary *100 Foot Wave*. He warns it has now got to a stage where Instagram and being an influencer is, in his eyes, the number-one target for many, even over the sport. With each season, a fresh wave of surfers and influencers make their way to Nazaré, and Steudtner likens it to a "kindergarten class with no teacher" at points. Elements of it, including his frustrations over the past decade that safety improvements have not moved as quickly as he had hoped, eat away at him. It is a frustration bubbling away at the surface, about which he has spoken at length with Klitschko.

Steudtner, a keen boxer and former Muay Thai fighter, has had his own fight to get to this point, and, at times, it has been a lonely one. A recent conversation with Klitschko elicited advice from the so-called "Dr Steelhammer". Klitschko's counsel is twofold: that it is important to adapt to the environment that surrounds him, but also that he has to tread his own path. It is a conversation that has got the surfer thinking, and those thoughts spill out across the table as he goes through his motivations for still being in Nazaré, now that his foot is out of a cast and into a boot.

"I've done everything I can here 10 times over, so why am I still doing it? I'm a private guy, so I'm not triggered by the media attention – the opposite, in fact. I don't like it. If I wanted to make money, I'd do something completely different." This begs the question: why does he still risk it all in the water? In part, there is an addiction to the adrenaline, which is married to that lifetime love of water. But for such an individual sport, surfing does foster team elements. He revels in these, surrounding himself with the right people – be that fellow surfers, jet-ski drivers, doctors, lifeguards or photographers. And then there is the motivation to be the best – but is that summarised by the biggest wave or winning the big titles? "It didn't start with chasing titles, and I'll probably get fucked over five times in a row with awards. My motivation will come back when the goal becomes inside the sport, but outside a title." The frustration isn't helped by his current inability to surf. The foot is improving with each week, but there is still impatience to get back to doing what he loves. For now, that seems a long way off; the record, too.

13

THE HOME-GROWN SURFER

Nic von Rupp

The route down to the house makes you think you've taken a wrong turn – a stony, bumpy dirt track reaches what seems like a dead end but for two houses, both hidden by high hedges. Green electric gates act as the gateway to the one on the left, and slowly open to reveal a beautiful cobblestoned driveway paving the path to what is an oasis. A friendly Alsatian, Leka, lies to the side of it, unbothered by the arrival of a car, as a gardener tends to the perfectly cut lawns and flowerbeds which surround the house. The house was built from scratch for his parents, and the grounds stretch over a wide expanse of land. Attached to it is the original family home – now rented out as a holiday home – where Nic von Rupp grew up with his parents and two brothers.

On the surface, he looks every bit a surfer, the hair bleached by the salty sea and the sun of Portugal and other hot climes where he travels to surf the world's best waves outside of the Nazaré season. He has a year-round tan and boasts the surfer lingo to go with it. But that's just the surface. He speaks five languages faultlessly – English, Portuguese, German, French and Spanish – and has had his own home built on the plot adjacent to his parents'.

His parents are clearly proud of his achievements. His father Roman acted as his manager for a time and still provides advice whenever needed. For him and his wife, Isabel, their middle son's choice of career does not always sit easily. His mother won't even watch video clips of him, and when there's been a particularly monstrous swell, she ensures she only hears about it after the event. His father, meanwhile, recalls one particular swell hitting Nazaré. In the hotel where he was staying, he remembers the shutters rattling, such was the strength of the weather pattern into which his son was planning to throw himself. "The windows were shaking on the land because of the waves crashing down – and in the middle was my son," he says. Now, he prefers to stay away.

Along with Alex Botelho, Von Rupp has marked himself out as the best big-wave Portuguese surfer of his generation. There is something fortuitous in the fact that he was born less than 90 miles away from what has become Europe's headquarters for the big-wave surfing movement. As a child, he had an abject terror of rocks; even now, he has a slight phobia of being underwater.

"Being scared of the waves is normal when you start, but I had a big phobia of the rocks. That's not normal! There wasn't anything else in the world that scared me more than standing on rocks in shallow water. So, the surf teachers gradually took me to the rocks when it was dead flat, but it was a mental barrier that took a long time breaking."

Isabel recalls watching her son, who was on the verge of tears, holding the hands of his instructor as he faced his fear. Yet for three lively young boys, the open water on their doorstep was the obvious choice to burn off their boundless energy. Their home was within walking distance of Praia Grande, which is, as the name suggests, a monstrous beach, and just 45 minutes' drive from the capital, Lisbon. At one end sits an open-air swimming pool; at the other, a series of steep steps down from the cliff above, leading to the pathway to the main road and eventually to the two adjacent Von Rupp homes.

In his home – the one to the right down the bumpy stone lane – he lives with his actress girlfriend Matilde Reymáo Nogueira and their dog Maya. The surfer and the actress make for an attractive couple. Together, they are invited to red-carpet events and occasionally find themselves featured in the Portuguese media. She is currently starring in the Portuguese soap opera *Por Ti*, which tells the story of two rival towns trying to decide in which town a new dam will be built. She plays the character Luísa Melchior, an environmentalist who falls for the guy responsible for having the dam built.

When they first met, she claims: "I wasn't into him to start with – it took like two months," but both laugh in unison, making it hard to know whether this is quite how events happened early in their courtship.

The demands on both of them are high, Reymáo constantly learning her lines and away filming, while Von Rupp is prone to dropping everything at a moment's notice if a big swell hits Nazaré. They have made their different lives work together, and Von Rupp talks and beams proudly about the fact that his partner has just been signed by one of Europe's big talent agencies. There are still moments when their busy, dual lives can be fraught, and their careers temporarily pull them away from each other.

Inevitably, for any loved one of a big-wave surfer, there are those dark days. She was in Nazaré when Alex Botelho, a close friend of Von Rupp's, nearly died the previous year. Even now, Von Rupp's fellow Portuguese surfer has not fully recovered, at least not mentally. The lungs that were heavily damaged are back to normal, but the psychological damage is such that Botelho still struggles to talk about it even now.

Botelho has still not returned to the big waves since the 2020 Tow Surfing Challenge. Riding his last wave of the day, he was scooped up by partner Hugo Vau. But as two waves converged on their jet ski from different sides, the machine was spat into the air, and Botelho landed on his chest, puncturing his lungs on impact. He was knocked unconscious and was out cold in the water for 10 minutes. Doctors, to this day, are amazed he is alive – or, at the very least, not brain damaged. His miraculous, unlikely escape even became part of a Portuguese clinical study as a result. But today, he still struggles to relive it in conversation.

Reymão's primary concern is for her boyfriend, and while she is – as he puts it – "super supportive", there are moments when she finds it a hard watch. "She was there when Alex almost drowned," says Von Rupp, his English coming out fluently but with a multilingual drawl, part English, part Portuguese, part American. "She gets freaked out, but that's how it is here."

Having personal relationships can be hard in Nazaré; it takes an understanding and a thick-skinned other half. The sport is inherently selfish both in terms of the related dangers but also in needing to just up and go when a big swell looms.

"It's a mixture of profession and a passion," says Von Rupp. "My whole life is dedicated to surfing, but it's important to find the balance in life. Having someone solid on your side, your girlfriend or your wider family, helps the performance. But surfing is your best friend and worst enemy. It turns you into a really selfish person. It's you, your wave and that's it." There are a limited few who fully understand this mentality, notably surfing friends and those that share the same passion, a passion that is so deep-rooted it is all too often detrimental to everyday life. "I've missed so many family gatherings, birthdays. Our reality is so different to society's path. I really try to balance it out." When the balance doesn't quite work, he and others tell themselves that it's "now or never", a brief moment to shine in their high-octane choice of workplace. At the same time, Von Rupp can see it isn't entirely healthy: "I don't always want to be that guy. I want to have my time in surfing and then move on."

When the waves are still mild, Nic von Rupp's 2021–22 season begins with a favour for his father – who is friends with the American singer Jimmy Buffett – and that trip out of the harbour into mere 15-foot waves with Sérgio Cosme.

Arranging to meet Von Rupp is, at best, a fluid process. He can suggest midday at the warehouse where he keeps his jet ski, surfboards or other equipment, and the eventual rendezvous can come two and a half hours later. Over the course of the season, one quickly learns to take any of his timings as vague at best – turning up at least an hour later than arranged is usually the best course of action. While it can be an agonising wait at times, his insights into his mentality, and that of his peers, are erudite, and he's able to talk more eloquently than many about the waves, including about their positives and drawbacks. Plus, he wears his heart on his sleeve. With him, the lows can feel like the lowest depths, his highs virtually euphoric. Even when he's somewhere in between, it tends to be captivating.

No one talks through riding a big wave like him – his descriptions take you right into the eye of the storm. My first time witnessing him in the big waves, he ended up crumpled on the beach, with two ruined jet skis and working out with his team how to foot the bill for a €25,000 camera which had also been damaged beyond repair in the chaos of the white water. That's the stuff you can clearly see from the shore, but, discussing the harder-to-view moments from the mainland, his eyes glaze over as he talks of the experience of being enveloped by a wave that's 50 feet or more above him.

"You feel the blood rushing through your veins and going straight to your head. When it's going well, you feel totally invincible, and the feeling of surviving a wave like that is amazing. You've avoided tasting the venom, you haven't tasted what it's like to ...." His voice trails off, his gaze fixed elsewhere in pondering the unthinkable. And yet the moment he actually feels most alive is when the process goes wrong and he is pounded, sometimes left fighting for his life. "It's when I get hit by a huge wave and I survive. It takes you down, you're getting beaten and all of a sudden, you're up, out on a jet ski and you've survived." The euphoria can often be shortlived with the injuries the surfers often sustain. "You're walking on thin ice and that's the moment when you go next-level bad. Then you feel shit, broken."

Watching it go wrong on the clifftop, the speed with which things nosedive is rapid. On a surfboard, it understandably unravels all the more quickly, although Von Rupp can break it down like it all happens in slow motion.

First, his head dips down, shifting him off balance, then the rest of his body follows suit, although being thrown off the surfboard is merely the beginning of what comes next, in an unimaginable torrent. As the monstrous volume of water crashes down upon the stricken surfer, Von Rupp compares it to an explosion, the mind racing through the thought process required in the fight for survival.

"There's so many levels of thoughts going through your mind," he says as he visually takes himself back into the maelstrom. "There's the fear, then the hope; there's the fighting spirit that comes up." It is the full rollercoaster of emotions amid the brutality of it all, and it's a battle not to get fully immersed in the shock mode that immediately takes hold. "It's like, 'Holy shit, it's actually happening.' It's so fast you don't get to fully understand it."

112

He likens it to a heightened sense of stress and anxiety back on dry land – but ratcheted up to the highest level, with the added issue of breathlessness quickly creeping in. "Your lungs start cranking up and you feel that loss of oxygen. That's when you realise you're in deep shit, and your ears start pumping. You open your eyes, and everything around you is black. You go up, you go down, it turns you. You try to keep as calm as possible; you don't know what the hell is going on. It's almost an extension of that feeling when you're hurt as a kid and you're crying to your mum. Your stomach cranks up, it's pure fear in that moment."

Knowing what can happen – he's experienced the moments gone wrong often enough – he still always approaches entering the water with a positive mindset. The same thought pattern is that everything is going to be fine and then, quite suddenly, it isn't. "Then it's like, 'Shit, what now?'" And then, as quickly as it's begun and he is enveloped by the fear, the brutality, the throwback to his childhood, crying for his mum, and the breathlessness, he is out of it all again, scooped from the white water – usually by Cosme – and riding out of danger on the back of a jet ski, gasping for his breath. In that moment, he never feels more alive.

14

MEASURING UP

The waves

In 2004, a multibeam echo sounder found the remains of a Second World War German U-boat on the ocean floor in Nazaré. U-963 was intentionally sunk to a depth of 100 metres on 20 May 1945, where it remains today. Before its sinking, the entire 48-man crew on board was safely brought ashore as prisoners of war. This and other stricken vessels beneath the surface are mere pinpricks in Nazaré's North Canyon, such is the magnitude of the water in which it lies.

The Iberian Abyssal Plain, which leads to the canyon, is the largest underwater canyon in Europe and one of the largest in the world. It spans 140 miles and has a maximum depth of 5,000 metres. The origin of the canyon is still shrouded in mystery because it belongs to a complex geological area. However, researchers believe that it might be related to the Nazaré fault, a fracture zone with movements that can cause earthquakes.

It is here where Nazaré's wave power partly lies. From great depths, the canyon rises, finishing right before the lighthouse. When it meets the shallower shelf, energy starts to focus and dissipate at different rates, creating an enormous surge of water mass and energy. The contrast in depths between the shelf and the canyon cause the wave to refract or bend, and the abruptness of that shift is specific to Nazaré.

It also causes a "shoaling" of the wave, in effect increasing the wave's height gradually on its approach to north beach. Nazaré is one of the best spots in the world in which to see wave refraction in real life.

João Cruz, an expert in wave energy, likens the refraction to a giant rug being pulled from underneath an even more giant slab of concrete. The scholar from Portugal says: "If you think of such a wave as a wall of concrete, because the mass is so enormous – that wall's on top of a rug. It's like someone pulling up that rug." The bottom slows much faster than the top, so the higher the wave is, the faster it will start wanting to come down. "When the wave starts going to shallower depths, the phenomenon of refraction is basically about the speed of the wave. So essentially, the dissipation phenomenon – the drag is dominating and kicks in faster for the bottom of the wave so the bottom of the wave slows down faster than the top of the wave. That eventually will lead to breaking."

Nazaré's canyon exacerbates the effect of a more normal shore break, while the slope up to the canyon's end causes a ramp-up effect to the wave also.

Cruz has watched big-wave surfing in Nazaré and also in Mullaghmore, Ireland, where he lives and often witnesses surfers tackling the biggest waves. With all his expertise, he finds himself dumbfounded that they should throw themselves into such waters, in particular those like Gabeira, who came so close to losing her life in those same waters.

His stupefaction is partly down to the pure science of the wave. Every cubic metre behind a surfer is the equivalent to a tonne – the weight of a traditional Mini car. If that is stretched up 20 metres in height (essentially a 65-foot wave), that's 20 tonnes just for the width of the surfer on a board. Over the course of a single wave, it is an unfathomably monstrous weight of water. As Cruz puts it, "that's a lot of mass".

Above the surface, no one day is ever the same. Depending on conditions, some surfers will come out at the break of dawn and surf until dusk or until the petrol in their jet ski runs out, even carrying food on board with which to refuel in a brief break from the waves.

Certain teams prefer to return to the harbour for a lunch break and a breather, while others might delay their entry into the water until later in the day, or simply tackle it for an hour or two at most. Often, they simply bob up and down in their pairings on a jet ski, waiting for the right wave that never comes, eventually bailing before even riding anything of note.

On the busy days, the water is littered with surfers and jet skis — whether they're the surf crews, rescue drivers, or camera crews trying to get footage in the thick of the action. Trying to recognise one surfer from the next from land is no mean feat. During the course of the season, you begin to identify the colours of their wetsuits and boards, the jet skis they drive or their stance on the board, and the way they hold out their hands for balance. Even after weeks of watching them, you may think you've seen a particular surfer at the time, but later transpires to be someone else entirely.

It looks chaotic within that mêlée; it is a relatively short stretch of water within which the surfers catch the biggest waves, all the action playing out with the fort and its small lighthouse in the background. But the chaos is often far more organised than it appears. While it doesn't take the form of an orderly queue, there is an order of sorts. Everyone gets their turn. When that comes is decided among those in the water.

There are those who gain a reputation for jumping the queue. In the short term, it might get them the best wave in that moment, but the long game is the more sensible approach in Nazaré. In such hostile waters, it doesn't pay to have enemies. The fight for your place in the wave is not always harmonious – but then again, it isn't an exact science. So getting the biggest wave on a given day is as much down to luck of it being your team's turn and you being the one on the board.

Long before Nazaré made its entrée into big-wave surfing, paddling into waves used to be sacrosanct. Over time, some surfers started talking among themselves about using a speedboat, as in waterskiing, to pull each other into the bigger waves which were previously out of their reach with simple paddling. The first known suggestion of that kind dates back as early as the 1960s. There were those who tried it, albeit unsuccessfully, at points from then until the early 1990s, aptly in Hawaii, the birthplace of surfing.

It began with conversations between Laird Hamilton, Buzzy Kerbox and Darrick Doerner, who caused heads to turn as they headed out in a Zodiac (effectively an inflatable boat with an engine) with a rope attached to the back, taking turns to hop on the rope and be pulled into the big waves. In time, the Zodiac boat was replaced by a jet ski. Traditionalists questioned their approach, essentially saying it was against the spirit of surfing.

But it widened the interest of big-wave surfing when, using this innovation, Hamilton surfed a monster wave in Teahupo'o, Tahiti, on 17 August 2000. It became known as the Millennium Wave. His surfing of that particular wave lasted only a few seconds before he was pounded into the reef below, luckily coming away unscathed. The sport gained a whole new set of followers after Hamilton conquered what then was believed to be the biggest wave in history.

Speaking at the 10-year anniversary of that wave, he told the website Surfline: "That was part of it. Riding the unrideable. We'd already done that by towing into other waves, and there was no way that wave could have been ridden without towing in. It was also a barrier-breaking moment. It showed both me and others that waves like that can be ridden, and they have been by a lot of people since then. You have to believe in the unbelievable."

Sebastian Steudtner first learned tow-in surfing back in Hawaii, but it is in Nazaré that he hopes to have shattered the previous record, held by Rodrigo Koxa. But measuring the height of a wave from shore is far from an exact science. So how do you even begin to measure a wave? At Nazaré, no one wave is the same in the way in which it breaks, the height to which it rises and the manner in which a surfer rides it. With surfers of different heights, ranging from Justine Dupont at 5 feet 7 inches to C.J. Macias at 6 feet 5 inches, the disparity is obvious.

As recently as the end of the 2020 season, scientists were locked in lengthy discussions over two waves: one surfed by Dupont in November 2019, the other by her great rival Maya Gabeira three months later. At stake was a new women's world record, eclipsing the 68 feet previously attained by the Brazilian, and also the biggest wave by any surfer – male or female – that season. When the results finally materialised in September 2020, Dupont's wave was measured at 71 feet, Gabeira's at 73.5.

Wave measurement is an emotive business. Some will argue into oblivion that one was bigger than the others. Those who miss out often feel hard done by, though many simply shrug their shoulders at the arbitrary nature of it all. When Dupont missed out, she reacted angrily on social media. She posted a lengthy diatribe about the outcome on Instagram – and she aimed for the World Surf League. At the heart of her complaint was the fact that Gabeira, in Dupont's view, "does not finish the wave", the measuring was questionable and the images used to measure her rival's wave by "a dream team of scientists" were submitted after the deadline date.

The message was clear: Dupont felt, and no doubt still does feel, that she is deserving of the women's big-wave world record, saying she was deeply hurt over a process she branded "totally unfair". In conclusion, she said: "At first, I wanted to scream, then cry but eventually I prefer to keep smiling and my head held high. They won't take away the pride and pleasure I have in surfing those big waves ... I know that I can surf even bigger waves without waiting for any records from them." And yet the record books have it inked in that the women's record belongs to Gabeira rather than Dupont.

To reach that conclusion, and in order to measure the waves as accurately as possible, the World Surf League regularly joins forces with scientists and researchers at the Scripps Institution of Oceanography in San Diego, California, where Professor Falk Feddersen is based. He was among those involved in the measuring project along with others from the University of California, the University of Southern California and the Department of Aerospace and Mechanical Engineering in Los Angeles.

With his long hair and greying beard, Feddersen has the look and sound of a surfer. Born and brought up in St Thomas in the US Virgin Islands before relocating to California, he tried his hand at all manner of watersports, including surfing, but also found he was good at both maths and physics. So, in time, he combined his intellectual interests with his childhood hobbies to become an oceanographer. His expertise is essentially in exactly every facet of how a wave works from half a mile out all the way into shore.

His entry into wave measurement began at the Kelly Slater Wave Company (set up and named after the surfing superstar), during days there specifically put aside to the scientists, after which he was invited to get involved in measuring big waves with the likes of fellow scientists Adam Fincham and Michal Pieszka.

Spotters, photographers and spectators congregate around the Fort of São Miguel Arcanjo and its distinctive red lighthouse for the best view of the breaking waves.

Sebastian Steudtner's world-record wave surfed on 29 October 2020. After nearly 18 months of waiting, and amidst whispers of smashing 90 feet, Steudnter's record was finally ratified on 25 May 2022 at 86ft (26.21m).

Crews can bob up and down for hours waiting to be guided into the perfect wave by the spotters watching from the clifftops. Rows occasionally break out as teams jostle for the best opportunities.

Praia do Norte (left) and Nazaré's main beach (right), separated by the fort and cliffs that provide such a unique viewpoint of the big waves. The sharp drop of the underwater canyon can be seen in front of the main beach.

The rocks beneath the fort and lighthouse form arguably the most precarious spot within Nazaré's waters, and are where Andrew Cotton found himself trapped in one session gone wrong in December 2021.

Nic von Rupp catches a wave in an early swell in October 2021, just as the big-wave season gets under way.

Von Rupp (left) and Pedro Scooby clutch the Most Committed award – after narrowly missing out on the top spot – at the first Tow Surfing Challenge, December 2021.

Maya Gabeira celebrates her first win in a pro competition in the WSL, at the second Tow Surfing Challenge in February 2022.

On 11 February 2020 this 73.5ft (22.4m) wave saw Gabeira beat her own world record set in 2018 for the Largest Wave Surfed by a female.

Sérgio Cosme sits on the back of a jet ski in a break from the waves.

Cosme tries to find a way through the wash, a notoriously difficult exercise when pulling off his plethora of rescues.

A drone captures the dangers and difficulties that the jet ski drivers face in order to find the safest and quickest way to scoop up a surfer in the aftermath of a wave.

Andrew Cotton has been one of Nazaré's surfing mainstays since the first season the big waves were tackled. A plumber from Devon, he quit his job to pursue his passion for the water.

No one day is ever the same on Nazaré's north beach. Often the biggest swells bring inclement weather. Here, Cotton finds himself battling the elements watched by the crowds on the clifftop.

Above, 'surfing scientist' Sebastian Steudtner simulates his body position at the Porsche Development Centre in Weissach, Germany. Steudtner collaborates with the car company's engineers to ensure optimum aerodynamics of board and surfer through tests held in their wind tunnel (below).

Catholic church Santuário de Nossa Senhora da Nazaré in the town's picturesque cobblestone square in Sitio – usually filled with tourists in both the summer months and at the height of the big-wave surfing season.

A reminder of Nazaré's other water pastimes: sardines and mackerel are traditionally sun-dried on wooden-framed metal grills on main beach, soon to be sold at a neighbouring fish market.

Jet skis lie dormant in the harbour at sunset following another day in the big waves for their pilots and passengers.

Of the science of measuring waves, Feddersen says: "It's a difficult thing to do and it's not an exact science. To me, as someone who deals with noisy data a lot, the proof in the pudding is when you apply methods and use that in reconstruction. So if all the sources give you a consistent answer, then it's much more believable. Are there still potential issues? Of course – this is not ideal."

The measurement is done using a variety of input factors, from drone footage to still cameras, to help estimate the crest-to-trough height of the wave from both sea level and the clifftop. Feddersen makes a comparison to archaeology: "That's why it's like archaeology – you're collecting lots of photographic and video footage and you're reconstructing something that you don't have the optimal data that you need to do that. These methodologies are not perfect, but when that was applied in an unbiased fashion, Maya's wave was, on average, three feet bigger than Justine's."

The process is ongoing with Steudtner's wave, for which Feddersen is only on the periphery of the measuring on this occasion. Of that record potential, the German is still unsure whether the outcome will be in his favour. "I was in the running for the world record for almost a decade and just never got it," he says. "So, this would be a big relief for me. [In] the next few weeks, we'll know the measurement, but I have a gut feeling." In contrast to the surfers themselves, caught in the maelstrom of a wave, the cogs can turn leisurely in big-wave surfing. In his case, there will be a further six months to wait, the eventual answer not coming, farcically, until May 2022, more than a year and a half later. For such a high-speed, high-octane sport, things can move painfully slow at times.

15

A BRUSH WITH DEATH

Maya Gabeira

There can be few more precarious workplaces than Nazaré. Its volatility lends itself to a sense of unknown. In Gabeira's case, that sensation is further exacerbated by not having Steudtner by her side for 2021–22. Still in its infancy, the season has the makings of what she calls "a weird one". There are doubts of who might take her into the water on the big days and whether she can compete in events such as the Tow Surfing Challenge. With Steudtner, there had been stability. Long-time friends and cohabitants of the Nazaré waves, they each understand how the other works in and out of the fluctuations of the ocean, and feed off each other's experience.

There are the basics of the relationship: they are both highly capable jet-ski drivers, able to tow each other into the biggest waves and then pull off audacious rescues as required, not to mention their respective long-established surfing skills. There's shared equipment too – jet skis, radios and even surfboards – as well as personnel, from the spotters on the clifftop to the camera operators trying to catch their every move in the water. But they are friends too, confidants and counsel for the obvious pitfalls of a season many miles away from home.

In a bid to fill that void, Gabeira opts for some familiarity in her prospective partner with a phone call to another Nazaré old hand in

Tom Butler, but she is unable to lure him back to Portugal. Butler was one of the first to come to Nazaré after Garrett McNamara, and was an early partner of Steudtner. But having opted for the past two seasons not to come back, he remains focused on life with his wife Emily and the couple's young son Ziggy back in the UK.

Butler has weaned himself off Nazaré and now runs a not-for-profit organisation in his native Cornwall in the UK, helping schoolchildren with disabilities and mental and physical conditions. His attachment to water began in the rock pools of Constantine Bay as a toddler with his parents. Bodyboarding followed, and he was standing up on a surfboard by the age of 11. He surfed Cribbar, Newquay's big wave, at just 16, the same year he travelled to Hawaii. It has been a surfing journey which eventually brought him to Nazaré as a 23-year-old, alongside Steudtner.

"Once you've had ginormous waves, it's so cliché, but the rush and satisfaction from that, you crave it more and more," says the Englishman. "It's for love, that's why I do it."

It's not the difficult moments, of which there have been plenty, that have put him off returning. One time, at the 2016 World Surf League paddling contest, he got in trouble in the water in full view of some of his family. Needing to get on a good wave to make his mark in the competition, he remembers telling himself he would take on the next big wave, in this case a 45-footer – only for it to go horribly wrong. "I remember it all. I was conscious throughout."

As he hit the water, it was like being whiplashed, the wave dragging him down. He heard a massive crack as his surfboard implanted in the side of his head, either the board or the leash attaching his leg to the board ripping his ear lobe off. With blood oozing from the wound and Butler heavily winded – breath that never naturally returned – he remembers someone trying in vain to rescue him before he was washed up on the beach.

His wife and mother were back at home watching on a webcast of the event live and at first had no point of contact to check on his well-being. His brother was on the beach, a helpless onlooker as horror unfolded and his sibling was treated by the on-site medics. In hospital, the Brit had what he describes as a piece of plastic placed in his punctured lung to help it reinflate, what felt at the time "really medieval": two male nurses holding him down as the chest drain was pushed into his body on the painful third attempt. Even now, he recalls "the absolute agony". His wife spent hours ringing around trying to track him down via the various hospitals before hearing on the news that his injuries were serious but not life-threatening.

In a warped way, he almost quite enjoyed even those bad moments, because of the rush of it. But despite her best powers of persuasion over the phone, Gabeira cannot persuade him to come back, not even for part of a season. As he puts it: "I'm a bit over it. I am missing it, but I've done it for the last 10 years. I'll go back at some point." That return doesn't feel imminent with a settled, busy life back at home.

And so, instead of Butler, her attention turns to Eric Rebiere, the French surfer who was formerly competing in the smaller waves on the world tour before making the transition to the bigger waves. He is also regarded as one of the best jet-ski drivers not just in Nazaré but globally.

In any big-wave set-up, the team is central. Much of it is about the individual in terms of training in the gym, the pool sessions, the constant surfing on small days and big, getting the best equipment, ensuring everything is ready. But on those big waves, a surfer is the sum of the parts and people around them. With Rebiere, she says the trust is already established, so renowned are his jet-ski skills.

But while the partnership appears good on paper, it takes time to conjure up a relationship in the water, that pairing as much about their respective skill sets as the amount of time spent in the water together, almost creating a sixth sense. As such, there is no guarantee that she and Rebiere will connect in the water, despite her initial optimism. It is a venture she knows could just as easily fail as succeed.

"I can bring the best driver from Hawaii and he jumps on the ski but he doesn't know any of my signals and I don't know what the hell he's surfing or saying," she explains.

"When you surf a lot with someone on a ski, there's no words anymore. You know what he's thinking when he does something – that he's going for a certain wave around the crowd. You want to know what the driver is doing before he is doing that. You don't want a rough time communicating, as there's wind, waves and people. If you're so connected that you don't need words, it's so much easier. It's so much smoother. You can only achieve that with hours. I've spent endless hours with Seb and Carlos before that. Thankfully, I've spent a lot of hours with Eric too."

Trying to find an initial team for the season and then another so early into it is a stressful business. The surfers talk a lot about this pressure, Gabeira included, of getting fit, of staying alive and of earning a living. But at the same time, they also seem to revel in the stress of it all in an almost masochistic way. She admits as much. "The really good things in life aren't easy," she says, "and if they are, I haven't met them yet. Every goal or world issue to be resolved or to be achieved demands a certain amount of stress and anxiety because, if it's easy, it's not going to be very satisfying."

After a somewhat tumultuous start, Gabeira is now fully at peace with Nazaré, a place that somehow gives her serenity amid the madness of it all.

When she first breezed into town in October 2013, on the surface, she did not have the lack of confidence you might expect from a surfer bullied into submission by her peers, as she almost had been in Hawaii. Instead, the surfers already settled in Nazaré talk of the self-belief – almost bravado – emanating from the arrival of this Brazilian collective, including Gabeira, Carlos Burle and the rest of their entourage. They had all come with the aim of taming the wave they'd heard so much about and yet only seen from the comfort of their computer screens. They, perhaps bullishly on reflection, neither sought the necessary advice from those established there nor did they have quite the safety back-up required for such a dangerous undertaking.

And then, a matter of days later, the horror happened. Gabeira's accident is still talked about, almost in revered whispers, so unlikely was it that she came out of it alive. Even knowing the outcome, watching footage of it back is harrowing. She battles the elements for a full nine minutes and Burle, in particular, tries to find a way to rescue his stricken partner, mostly to no avail, as the clock ticks towards the eventuality of her possible death.

Moments before her fight for life – Burle at the controls of the jet ski, Gabeira towed behind on the rope – an enormous wave headed their way. Gabeira suddenly had doubts, insecure in her ability to tame it, and voiced those fears. But her tow partner reassured her and then talked her into doing it, and she was catapulted on to a wave that would go on to define her for all the wrong reasons. The sudden dawning realisation for her once on it was that, firstly, it was incredibly rapid. She found herself travelling at a speed she couldn't remember quite experiencing before on a surfboard. Plus, in that moment she felt like the wall of water enveloping her was double the size of anything she had surfed in Hawaii or anywhere else in her lifetime.

Once inside it, she rode the first bump, absorbing it with her knees to maintain her balance, so too the second, despite the shockwaves it sent through both body and board. Momentarily, she disappeared from the view of the camera that was filming her every move. At this stage, there was the realisation that the doubts and insecurities had been well founded. The speed of the board over the water seemed to get quicker and quicker, the bumpiness of the water more out of control. She was holding on for dear life, but could almost see the end of the wave and a potential exit from it. Amid the speed of it all, she had the mental aptitude to know that if one minor mistake was made, the consequences would be devastating.

Recalling the trauma, she can't quite remember whether it was the third or fourth big bump in the wave that pitched her off the board and sent her flying into the water. Her ejection was so rapid that, watching it back, it's hard to see exactly what happens in the moment. On impact with the water, she broke her ankle immediately – an injury she wasn't aware she had sustained until visiting a second hospital later that day, such was the severity of the other trauma she sustained – as she ploughed face first into the water with the wave pounding on top of her head.

The violence of the first wave had left her almost breathless, but the subsequent wave was no less ferocious, ripping off her life jacket as it rolled over the top of her. The pounding was so big that she blacked out. As she flickered in and out of consciousness, she would momentarily pop out at the surface, going from pure blackness to a whirlpool of whitewash. She took deep gulps of air in the few milliseconds above the waves before the next pounding, as Burle struggled to spot her and perform the necessary rescue.

The team's cause was not helped by the fact that Burle's radio had broken a little earlier. Going into such waves without radio communication is an oversight that is unthinkable these days. Lessons often have to be learned the hard way in Nazaré. It meant any spotters on the clifftop were unable to guide Burle to his surf partner. Feeling increasingly helpless, Gabeira began to say her internal goodbyes to her loved ones back in Brazil.

"At that point, I knew I was in serious trouble and had to count on instinct." For her, it was, in this moment, a solo fight for survival. Three times her partner came in to attempt a rescue, and three times he was undone by the challenge of the white water. Burle looked to have got to a position to save her but, unfamiliar with the nuances of Nazaré's waterways, he misjudged it and instead hit Gabeira with the sled that hangs off the back of the jet ski, which acts as the rescue platform to any stricken surfer.

The seconds, then minutes ticked on, Gabeira getting increasingly breathless and blacking out. Of her senses, she remembers only her hearing was intact – she was later told it was the last sense to go before death. She recalls thinking, *This is it; I'm going to die.* In those final throes of life, though, she still had the wherewithal to grab the tow rope as Burle circled for another rescue attempt. This time, it got her close enough to the beach that he could scoop her back out of the water.

By the time she was finally dragged on to the beach, she was already unconscious, and CPR was required to bring her back to life. Footage of her chest being aggressively pounded is still easily found on YouTube and makes for hard viewing. While it was never properly diagnosed, she thinks in the aftermath she suffered something similar to post-traumatic stress disorder (PTSD). Watching back the footage was too harrowing initially, and that didn't change for months on end. Now, she almost laughs about it, albeit still a little nervously, all too aware of how close it came to ending her life.

"In the beginning, it was very painful to watch. The first time was extremely painful, very scary and disturbing. I felt all the emotions excessively. Now, I can watch it with a great distance from that. Now I'm really over it, I can see it and not feel all those emotions pop up again." Watching it back, she says, is like having an out-of-body experience years on. "It almost feels like it's not me. I believe I had a good dose of luck that day and sometimes it's not the time for us to go. I had done a lot of training, but there was a lot of luck involved in my survival, and some miracles ... to make me stay alive."

While the mental scars have long since healed, physically, she will always feel it. The broken ankle was a quick enough fix. But a back injury – which required multiple surgeries and needs constant treatment and management, and will do for the rest of her life – remains, the remnants of that brush with death.

Three times she underwent the surgeon's knife to fix her back, a battle not just to rectify her spine but also to enable her to walk again, let alone have aspirations to return to the big waves. The pain was constant. It was a struggle just to sit down or stand up. It meant she was in and out of surgery, and required epidural injections, doses of morphine and other opiates to quell the debilitating pain.

The first surgery failed, as did the second. One and a half years after the accident, she knew a third operation was the only solution. Seven different doctors disagreed before she found an eighth to carry out the operation to fuse her spine. She didn't know it at the time, but it proved the turning point.

"I had this seriously excessive pain, but also the trauma, insecurities and fear of the wave itself. All the media exposure that came with it made me quite insecure about my space there, and question whether I'd ever be able to surf the wave like I wanted to." Her first brief stint in Nazaré had essentially ended in failure. Some publicly criticised her for being there; the overriding message she heard from her hospital bed was "It's not for you, Maya". Such comments took their toll for years afterwards. "It's hard not to let that play in your head when you're not 100 per cent. So for years I was struggling to find my feet physically and emotionally. It was: can I, will I, am I brave enough to overcome that on my mind for four years?"

It wasn't like she could quickly return to the water to heal the mental demons. March 2017 was the first occasion she was officially declared fit and healthy, recovered from her injuries. For the first time in three and a half years, she was able to lift weights, sit down or stay in one position for 15 minutes and walk relatively pain-free. And yet, despite all the damage the place had inflicted on her, there was still no desire to walk away from Nazaré and its big waves, although taking a step back into the swell would take another seven months.

But in those intervening years, she knew the limitations of her body meant there might never be a chance to return, thereby forcing her to think of what she might do if the third surgery was not successful. "I needed an exit plan. That wasn't my choice and it wasn't something I wanted, but it became a very real possibility. So I always tried to ask myself 'What job would I do, what path would I go on, what could I do if it didn't work?'"

But return she did and, since the end of 2017, she has been one of the permanent features of Nazaré, held in high esteem by the locals and international surfers alike. In contrast to Hawaii, where she had been so ill-treated and felt so alien from her male peers, the only hostility encountered in Nazaré was from the water itself.

"It's funny because from the first time back here, it became home right away. I was coming from such a hostile environment where I used to surf, to just have the ocean be hostile to me, that was gold. I'll take that any day, because I'll make peace with her any day. I'll win her over. In contrast to before, in Hawaii, when I first got to the harbour here in Nazaré, I didn't have 20 other guys staring at me. I could just do my own thing. It was so refreshing."

And so, the place that nearly killed her became home, and still is today, more so than Brazil. Five years on from her return, she cannot envisage not living in her coastal mountain home. And at the same time, she realises it is not entirely normal to have settled in a place that came so close to ending her life; yet there is a pull here almost beyond her power, veering on an obsession, which still burns brightly years on.

"I must still love it enough to be in this remote place thousands of miles away from my family – with two dogs and a garage full of surfboards. I could be anywhere in the world doing anything – and it's fucking cold here a lot of the winter, and I'm from Rio! That makes me believe I must still love it." But then there is the other part to it – that this is all she knows and all she has ever wanted to do. Plus, the routine of it all is now such a part of her everyday life.

"I can't break that pattern of wake up, go surf waves, come back, eat, train, nap. After 20 years, you're like, what else do people do? I would have to investigate a lot about what could be a different reality because that's been my reality forever. I don't know what it's like not to look forward to the season, training hard in August and September, the stress, anxiety, anticipation, doubts, surf, surf and surf, and boom – March comes and it's over. I don't see the necessity to change while the passion hasn't faded."

The thought pattern is still the same as that of the 17-year-old girl who first saw the big waves in Hawaii and, there and then, wanted to expose herself to the elements and find out what she could learn about herself in that environment. "For me, it was a bunch of things: the intensity, the magic of the big waves, the fact there was no woman out there – and I thought, *How cool would it be to have a woman in that environment?*"

To her, the guys in the water were heroes, to the extent that she was starstruck by their bravery. But it was something she wanted for herself too. "I felt, if I can do that then I'm brave too, so I wanted that for me." Despite the barbs, it just kept growing from there, and she felt more and more fulfilled by it. "It was not something I envisaged professionally, as there was not one big-wave surfer paid to do that job as a woman. I was the first. It was a progression of falling in love with the sport, a lack of women wanting to be brave." Years later, she ended up in Nazaré, what she imagines will be the final stop in her sporting evolution.

Before finalising that long and painstaking return from injury, she tried to imagine life outside of the waves. She moved into other ventures, including working as a TV presenter and an after-dinner speaker at events. The TV gig, she hated; the speeches, she enjoys occasionally but was of the view that she couldn't be bothered with that as her entire career path. She came to the conclusion pretty quickly in body and mind that she had to figure out how to get back in the water, as nothing else was looking particularly promising. The thought process was always the same, the gnawing sense that "I'm not going to be the best in the world at many things, so let me stick with this one. Let me put my brain here to work, be strategic and see where I get."

And so Nazaré became her life's work, her expertise and her home; all of which was aided by the fact there has always been acceptance, both of her gender and her nationality. The bond between the Portuguese and Brazilians is still tight and goes beyond just a shared language. Partly, that was down to the lack of territorial boundaries, which often plague a good surf spot. Garrett McNamara came relatively late in his career to this area and, while he was the first, he has been more open than territorial about the waters – his push always to share it with the rest of the world.

Gabeira says: "In Portugal, as Brazilians, we're much better received too. Portuguese people have a connection with Brazilians. They like the culture and listen to the music, they watch the soap operas, they speak the same language. They look at Brazilians in a much better light than Americans. I felt straight away I could prosper here. Before, I never felt I could be good enough … as I never had the space to move and thrive there [in Hawaii]."

Though she had to go through hardships and abuse to get to this point, there is not even a modicum of bitterness – just a hope that no one else has to experience that level of vitriol and venom. "I wouldn't want anyone to go through that. I'm not proud that I went through that. It sucked in every way. It was a tough era for women 10 to 15 years ago. I didn't want to break barriers; I wanted to live my life and do my thing. Unfortunately, it was male-dominated. When you're young, you don't realise it. I thought, *It's awesome there's only guys, I'm going to shine.* Then you get in and you're like, *Fuck, no wonder there's only guys.* You're so naïve when you're young."

The tough moments experienced in the past means she wants to shy away from seeing the documentary film that has been made about her life, *Maya and the Wave* (2022). While she has enjoyed the process of its making over nearly a decade, she watched one scene from it prior to the premiere and has wished ever since that she hadn't. But on the wider issue of gender, she would dearly love to see more women in Nazaré and surfing the big waves across the world. Justine Dupont and Michelle des Bouillons are her peers in Portugal, but are in teams with their respective boyfriends: in Dupont's case, Fred David, while Des Bouillons's partner is Ian Cosenza.

The next step for Gabeira is to see women out there on their own – not meant, it has to be said, as a dig at either Dupont or the Franco-Brazilian Des Bouillons and their relationships. Straight-faced, she calls it the "cheating route" before bursting out laughing to highlight the fact she isn't being serious. In the case of Dupont, David is very much a tow-in and rescue driver for his partner rather than a surfer. That makes it a stark contrast to Gabeira, who, when Steudtner is fit, enjoys a 50–50 split of driving and surfing with the German. "If you're willing to team up with Seb, you better be a fucking good driver. Thankfully, I have 14 years on my shoulders for that. The guys on top demand a lot from you. First, they're usually stronger than a woman, they can go for longer hours than a woman." She can recall being in the water for eight hours in 60- to 80-foot swells and, by the end of it, Steudtner's fitness and expectations mean that he is still brimming with energy at that stage.

Comparing her experience to this, Gabeira looks back to those moments of thinking, *"I know if I lose the ski, I certainly die. I'm hungry, I'm tired, I can't see anymore.* Guys do have a different amount of physicality. There's no way around it. Even Serena Williams will probably tell you that. So to make your own path in this sport as a girl, it's tough. Maybe I had to do it for all of us," and she breaks off in peals of laughter. "I had to break the ice and get fucked for 15 years, and then we all get the benefit of no gender in Nazaré!"

She once again stresses she is joking, but there is also a serious element to the laughter. The journey to get the equilibrium her fellow female surfers now enjoy has been arduous. That she has come out the other side intact sometimes surprises her. But it also means the setbacks – be that the daily poundings in Nazaré's waves or else the search for a new surf partner to save her season – are that much easier to bear.

16

THE BACK-BREAKER

Andrew Cotton

Cotton knows his own limitations. This season, he won't be going for wave after wave every day, as he did in his younger days. For one, he needs to preserve his lower back – which was once snapped in two and then temporarily held together only by a back brace. For another, it is about surfing more wisely, picking the right moment and peaking when it matters. "I choose my times now. Maybe I am still gung-ho, but you can't do it anymore in the same way. My body can't go mental every time as physically; it can't take the beatings."

He wasn't always like this. He used to be obsessed with surfing the biggest wave in the world, of being there for each and every swell. Now, he is more thoughtful about how he approaches each session, biding his time to catch the perfect wave. One or two great surfs from hours in the water appeal more than catching wave after wave ad nauseam. And he is also more contemplative in everyday life. On occasion, there can be a haunted quality to him, perhaps a realisation that for a decade and more, this particular wave has had a pull over him that he cannot entirely explain or control.

The season in Nazaré is punctuated with key moments. The Tow Surfing Challenge is one such day, a moveable point on the calendar when global surfing attention is on the town more prominently than usual. In early December 2021, there's conjecture the competition window will be announced imminently, with a big swell hitting the western coast of Europe courtesy of Storm Barra. But conditions initially look better for Ireland, so Cotton undergoes a PCR test – Covid travel restrictions are still in place at the time – in order to travel there from his home in Devon instead. In surfing, there is the constant need to be in the perfect place at the perfect time, driven in many ways by a fear of missing out.

But the predicted conditions change across the Atlantic to Ireland following his negative Covid test result, and so do his plans. It's often that way with big-wave surfing – planned trips flipped at the whim of a swell or a change of wind direction. Throughout the week, he repeatedly scrolls through Magic Seaweed, a website with global surf forecasts, tabbing from Mullaghmore to Nazaré and back again. His girlfriend Justine White makes the point that she, like other normal people, checks the weather forecast once a day. "He does it all the time," and he's looking at it even now, mid-conversation drinking Earl Grey tea and munching on Ritter chocolate at the end of a day in which he has been taking children from a local children's home in Nazaré into the water.

With the contest imminent, and feeling that necessity to preserve a body that has already had its fair share of beatings, he has absolutely no intention of surfing on the eve of the event. This is a bid to keep his fitness for the challenge. Conditions initially look too bumpy, the chance of any clean waves nigh-on impossible. The sensible decision is to sit it out. Partly because of that fear of missing out, partly the sense of adventure and partly because the sensible decision isn't necessarily the right one, he reneges on the promise to himself not to go out. In terms of picking the right moments, he now knows, on reflection, that this wasn't the one.

This December day will be remembered as Cotton's day, for all the wrong reasons. For White, it is particularly harrowing. She refers to it as "the disappearance". Reflecting now on that night after the accident, he is sanguine about it, both amused and bemused about the level of interest it has created. His outlook was exactly the same on the beach in the immediate aftermath.

White's emotive reaction was different: "Fucking twat, we lost you for five minutes." She had raced down to the beach with McNamara, who had walked from his home to the cliff to oversee the session on his first day out after a harsh bout of Covid. It is a heart-stopping experience as a spectator, one she does not want to repeat. But then, she has also spent enough time in Cotton's company and that of the other surfers to know in the back of her mind that there will be other such occasions.

Despite some eye-catching waves caught already this season, the most amount of attention Cotton has got – and arguably will get for the season's duration – is focused on this solitary wipeout and the two-and-a-half-minute battle against the rocks, waves and white water, which has been posted and reposted countless times across social media. For that, he is a little frustrated – the bad often attracting more headlines than the good in Nazaré. Personally, he'd had no intention of posting about it on social media himself because, for him, it is nothing new to have a close shave in such hazardous waters, a mere footnote on another Nazaré day. As he puts it, "This one wasn't a back-breaker," undeniably the worst fate to have befallen him before.

His back-breaker, the one he calls the biggest wipeout of his life, dates back to November 2017. Going out for the day with Garrett McNamara and Hugo Vau, a Portuguese surfer, he had felt fit and pumped for another big day. Within just the first few waves of that day, however, disaster struck. As McNamara pulled him into a monster, the thought entered his head that he might be riding the wave of his life – only for it to alter its shape quite suddenly. His speed then dipped, so he couldn't get high enough to escape the wave over the top and back, and he instead found himself in the most precarious of positions: at the bottom of the wave. He remembers having the wherewithal amid his impending demise to think, *I have nowhere to go.* So he made the do-or-die decision to jump off his board. Again, perhaps another wrong call. If you watch the footage back, you see him time his leap in an attempt to lessen the impact but then he is spat back out violently and then smashed on to the water's surface like a rag doll.

Amazingly, he remembers every single second of it – he was conscious throughout – recalling the impact felt like falling on solid concrete. You can hear the groans of the spectators and those around the camera filming it, realising the severity of what they are witnessing in person. He had the time, even in that moment, amid the violence of it all, to think to himself that he would never surf again – while most of his mind was occupied with being rescued and staying above the surface. But the pain was so bad, he could not even lift his arm for the most vital task of activating his life vest.

And once he was rescued by Vau, each bump of the ride sent such bolts of pain through his body that it became nearly unbearable just staying on board. One bump too many, and he was thrown back into the water. By then, he was near the shoreline, and close enough to be carried up the beach, where he was placed on a spinal board and into the waiting ambulance.

In the midst of it all, he remembers the relief of being able to first wiggle his fingers, then his hands and finally his toes throughout the agonising ride to the hospital. He reassured himself the worst had been avoided – death. The next worst too – paralysis. Instead, he had suffered a compression fracture of his L2 vertebra in his lumbar spine – in essence, a broken back – and he was made to lie still for a day and a half. After that point, he was told by medical staff to attempt to walk in the body brace in which he had been entombed. By this point, he had been reunited with his partners in crime in the water, McNamara and Vau, in his hospital room.

"Those first steps, the pain was just ridiculous," recalls Cotton. "I felt sick and looked up at Garrett. We've had plenty of bad moments together over the years, but that's the first time I've seen him look that worried." So, reflecting the anxiety staring back at him, Cotton started to panic, internally questioning whether he would ever be able to properly walk unaided and without pain again, let alone have realistic aspirations to pursue his near lifelong passion for surfing.

After being flown back to the UK, Cotton began rehabilitation, but the progress was painstaking, the first goal overcoming the sheer agony of it all, then learning to walk and eventually battling the physical and mental demons to make it back into the water. His cause was aided by one his sponsors, Red Bull, who stepped in to run his rehabilitation programme. Much of that time was spent at home in the UK; some at the energy drink company's cutting-edge Athlete Performance Centre at its headquarters in Salzburg, Austria. The recovery process would take seven months in all, but he finally dipped his toe back in the water the following June, first tentatively and then back to his old daredevil self in the ensuing weeks. It was a return that was short-lived.

Not long after his reunion with Nazaré for the early part of the 2018–19 season, he headed to Northern Spain for the Punta Galea Challenge, another big-wave surfing contest. On his first wave, he rode a near-perfect barrel. On his third wave, he looked to be in control before the wave closed on him and he had what looked like a fairly innocuous tumble. But the full force of the fall landed on his back right leg, an impact he likened to being hit by a lorry or having his leg ripped off.

"People can't comprehend what it's like being hit like that, and there's no training you can do to prepare for it. It's what happens when you push the boundaries ... you get the good and the bad." After he was carried away in a lifeboat and then driven to hospital, a scan showed he had ruptured the anterior cruciate ligament in that knee – the third time doing so in his career – which amounted to another nine-month lay-off. Rather than be put off, it only made him more determined to return.

Now, on a sunny December day, his most recent two-and-a-half-minute dance with the water and rocks seems like a mere footnote in comparison to the darker days. Shaken and stirred but undeterred, this time Cotton avoided the hospital and crucially was declared fully fit to compete in the 2021–22 Tow Surfing Challenge.

17

THE FIRST TOW SURFING CHALLENGE

Big-wave surfing doesn't have a preordained calendar as such – it's impossible to set a clock or calendar to Mother Nature. But there are competitions, the most notable of which is the aforementioned Tow Surfing Challenge, held each year in Nazaré.

This season is different, though. Because of Covid and the lockdown that had scuppered much of the previous season, the competition was completely scrapped during the 2020–21 season. Because of this, there are instead, for the first time since the event's inception, two Tow Surfing Challenges this season. When they take place is hard to pinpoint, the date entirely open to the weather and when organisers see fit. The first is scheduled to take place in a window any time before the end of December 2021, the second from the start of 2022 until the end of the season at some point in March. The aim is to name the date when the waves are at their peak: when they are both the most eye-catching and the hardest to tame.

The World Surf League (WSL), the sport's global governing body, sets the date a few days in advance, after talks with the town hall and meteorologists, who pore over the swells and predicted weather patterns to try to ascertain the best possible day and time. Even with cutting-edge data, it is far from an exact science. First, an amber alert is put out to make it clear that the date for competition is imminent.

The clifftop becomes a bustle of activity. Booths are set up for the TV commentators, to house the attending media, and for the Covid tests that are still a requirement for the athletes taking part.

Two of those at the heart of Nazaré's surfing origin story are busy behind the scenes. While the event is run by the WSL, Pedro Pisco is the town hall's representative, helping with logistics on the ground, directing trucks and constantly either on the radio or his mobile phone. Another of the founding fathers of the big-wave movement here, Paulo "Pitbull" Salvador is ensuring the correct safety protocols are in place for when the green light is finally given. His domain is the surfers and their teams, while the local police are the ones in charge of the crowds that will inevitably swarm every bit of land overlooking the waves. Most surf and rescue crews are already in Nazaré for the season; others scramble from wherever they are in the world to make it to Portugal in time.

The date and time are finally decided upon: Sunday 12 December, with an 8am start. The surfers and their jet-ski compadres gather together in the harbour for a safety briefing from Salvador the night before, instructing them of the dos and don'ts, as well as the rescue operations planned for when things go awry, as they inevitably will.

For Steudtner, it is a rare moment of being an outsider in a contest, with his injury still leaving him consigned to the sidelines. But he nevertheless has a role to play, having been called upon by the WSL to add insights as a star pundit for their commentary team.

Andrew Cotton, quickly recovered from his near-death foray in the rocks in the lead-up to the event, pairs up with the American Will Skudin, better known as "Whitewater Willy" (a childhood nickname from his older brothers, which has stuck ever since), who flies in from the States on the eve of the competition.

An orange-bibbed Cosme, with the word "SAFETY" emblazoned across his chest, will not compete. Instead, he is one of the key jet-ski rescue drivers, deployed in case anything goes wrong. Von Rupp is with the Brazilian Pedro Scooby, a surfing rockstar who lives his life as quickly off the board as on it. Meanwhile, Maya Gabeira, devoid this season of what would have been a pairing with Sebastian Steudtner because of his injury, is trying her luck with Eric Rebiere for the very first time.

After a fitful night's sleep for many – as is often the case with the big waves imminent – the crews reassemble at the warehouses before sunrise the next morning, to wheel out the jet skis and make final checks on their surfboards and other equipment.

A nervous buzz emanates from them but, as daylight breaks, a heavy fog envelops the headland, making visibility virtually nil and competition an impossibility. The hope is that the sun burns off the fog in time, and thousands start to gather above the water for the best vantage point. But the fog hugs the coastline far longer than previously anticipated, and organisers reluctantly agree to postpone the competition by 24 hours. The crowds already gathered are left to pack up and return another day.

What a difference a day makes. After the false dawn of the previous morning, the second attempt at contest day begins with far better conditions. The skies are clear and the wind virtually non-existent – perfect conditions for big-wave surfing. However, the waves aren't of the magnitude anyone wished for or anticipated. Nazaré sometimes has a way of not living up to the hype, although these are still respectable, in the 40- to 50-foot range, good enough for the crowds who have covered the red clay clifftops for the second day in succession.

The contest is invitation only and surfers compete in nine teams of two, taking turns to surf and jet ski during the course of the heats, each of which last 50 minutes.

The aim is simple: to surf the best possible waves as an individual but also as a team. A panel of judges marks the surfers on the critical

145

line each one takes, while also looking for the biggest and steepest waves, with style also taken into consideration in the scoring. The calibre of waves a surfer or team gets (both in their heat and the order they surf within a heat) are largely the luck of the draw. How the surfers attack what the ocean offers up to them successfully is down to the competitors and their time-tested skills and instincts on the board and the jet ski. Each team competes in two separate heats, and the individual with the most points is crowned the winner. The team with the most combined points between its pair of surfers take home the team prize. There are also awards for the most committed surfer and the best female (of which there are three to choose from).

The preparations among the teams are varied. Some whoop and holler as they leave the harbour for the competition, while others pause in prayer and contemplation before exiting to the rougher seas. The world record holder Rodrigo Koxa and his partner Keali'i Mamala stuff Hawaiian Ti leaves down their wetsuits. A Ti leaf skirt is believed to ward off evil in Hawaii, from where Mamala hails, while a single leaf is considered good luck.

For some, the luck simply isn't there. Cotton, partnering with Will "Whitewater Willy" Skudin, a native of Long Beach, New York, has a big wipeout early on, landing square on his bottom; the force of the impact is enough to rip off the competition vest over the top of his wetsuit. In truth, while others flourish on the day, he and Skudin never get going. In contrast, the Ti leaves do the trick for Koxa, who, although taking arguably the biggest early pounding in his heat, recovers from it unscathed.

The clear favourites are Lucas "Chumbo" Chianca and Kai Lenny, who has just flown in from Hawaii. In effect, they are the Lionel Messi and Cristiano Ronaldo of the big waves. Usually a regular in Portugal for much of a season, the Hawaiian Lenny is a mere interloper this season, coming over solely for the first Tow Surfing Challenge because his then girlfriend (now wife) Molly is pregnant with twins, which are born the following month. At the time, Chianca is also an expectant parent, flitting in and out of Nazaré with his pregnant girlfriend Monise – the couple's daughter Maitê is born four months later. Both Red Bull athletes, Chianca and Lenny are known as the "Young Bulls", although Lenny conjectures that "daddies to be" might be a more appropriate tag this time around.

Their closest challenge is expected to come from Nic von Rupp and Pedro Scooby. Scooby is among those to have been brought back to life on Nazaré's north beach in a previous season, in his case thanks to resuscitation by Sebastian Steudtner. From the outset of this competition, Scooby is willing to risk it all by attempting to get a barrel. His first ride sees him swallowed up by the water. Picking the right wave is an instinctive art form executed in partnership with the spotters on the clifftop. Regrouping from the resulting rescue, both Scooby and Von Rupp admit they made a wrong choice, an easy thing to do with limited time, the clock ticking and pressure mounting. Von Rupp, at the controls of his jet ski, simply tells his partner to relax, despite Scooby losing his board to the jagged rocks and having to retrieve another just to continue competing.

But in the final wave of the heat, Scooby lands a barrel (effectively the air pocket of a wave as it breaks – the space between the wave's face and its lip as it curls above and round a surfer), and yelps of celebration reverberate from the clifftop. The Brazilian goofy – the term for those surfing in the less common stance of right foot forward and left foot back – moves to the top of the leader board.

Scooby and Von Rupp return to the harbour on cloud nine. Scooby says: "We had one minute left and I said, 'Let's go, Nic' – and he put me on a really good wave. He gave me a barrel – that wasn't me, that was my driver. The driver is the first part of the wave, he chooses the wave for you and you do the rest. He's my Portuguese brother. We fight sometimes, we laugh sometimes. Now, on to the second heat."

The lead is short-lived. In the end, Chianca and Lenny comfortably win the team award following a second round of heats, rewarded as much for their airborne tricks on the waves as for the waves surfed themselves. Other teams are left to dissect the whys and wherefores, some arguing Scooby's barrel warranted a bigger score, maybe even the individual win. The Brazilian instead comes up with the consolation prize of the most committed award. In celebration, he and Von Rupp spray each other with beer and Red Bull.

At an informal post-competition dinner afterwards, where they all dissect the day's events over food and drink, there is even an additional faux award for the biggest mishap. Consensus is that this belongs to Frenchman Pierre Rollet. Having looked like he'd rescued his jet ski from toppling over, he was sent tumbling by another wave in comedic fashion during the competition. He made it back to the beach with little more than damaged pride, and there's a pantomime element to it all. Amid the jeers and cheers, he laps up the sarcastic applause, arguably the biggest celebration of the day. Justine Dupont comes away with the other main award of the day – for the best female surfer, over Gabeira and Michelle des Bouillons. Crucially, everyone comes back to the harbour safely.

18

SAVING THE PLANET

Maya Gabeira

The women's award in the Tow Surfing Challenge is a new – and welcome – phenomenon. Introduced in 2019–20, there have been just two editions (with the 2020–21 contest scrapped because of Covid), and Gabeira's great rival Dupont has now won both. There's no malice between the pair – it is a healthy and respectful rivalry – but Gabeira would dearly love to add one of the bulky awards to the mantelpiece of her Nazaré home.

Though Gabeira lost out for the second time in December, another competition opportunity awaits her early in 2022. The date is currently unknown but she has a number of weeks to work out quite what her best partnership will be. Steudtner is still pounding the rehab work while she and Rebiere are in the infancy of a nascent partnership. The usual question marks hang over her.

At 34 years old this season, Gabeira is unsure if she has reached her peak as a surfer or if she will ever surf a bigger wave than the women's world record she achieved of 73.5 feet back in February 2020, at the last Tow Surfing Challenge before the Covid-19 pandemic struck. Another glass-ceiling moment – it was the biggest wave surfed by any surfer in any country that year, male or female. Plus, it broke the previous mark she had set of 68 feet. "To get the world record one time was a dream come true. To get it a second time was totally crazy."

The gaps between the big swells in the lead-up to the December 2021 Tow Surfing Challenge have given her time to repair and prepare any equipment, which brings her to Steudtner's warehouse – over which seagulls caw loudly, hoping for morsels of fish left behind by the neighbouring fishermen. A step inside each warehouse gives an insight into the surfer in question. In contrast to some others that are a little less meticulous and more maverick – with equipment often scattered around in makeshift fashion – there is German precision to this particular layout, in keeping with his approach. Two black Mercedes jet skis sit centrally, and similarly coloured surfboards line the walls. To the back is an additional room of discarded but still neatly lined-up surfboards that are no longer used. These are destined to be gifts to sponsors or else used for charitable auctions. This is the warehouse Gabeira and Steudtner used to share before she bought her house with its own garage, now essentially a surf warehouse.

It has already been a tough week and she has barely surfed. Her primary focus has had her glued to her laptop for lengthy online discussions in a relatively new role as a board member for Oceana, a non-profit ocean conservation organisation aiming to influence national and international policy over the world's seas amid the climate crisis. She finds it surreal she should be sharing a board with former presidents, Rockefellers, actors and billionaires. And yet while she might feel inferior intellectually, she is better placed that most to talk about the space she inhabits every day: the ocean.

In total, Oceana claims to have saved 4.5 million square miles of ocean. She is a relative newcomer to the organisation, having only joined the board of directors in January 2021. She is one of 30 members on the board – the others she describes as "brilliant minds". Within their number are the former president of Colombia César Gaviria, members of the Rockefeller dynasty and even the actor Ted Danson. For six hours over two consecutive days at her computer screen, she has listened and pushed her platform – but also been inspired, even amid the "brain fade" that follows the discussions.

There is still time for waves in the few hours either side, and after the second day, she sneaks off for a late foiling session. Standing on a surfboard with a hydrofoil (a sort of fin that acts as a lifting device) propels her above the water, giving the sense to anyone watching that she is improbably gliding over the water's surface. It is the perfect antidote to a more serious side of her working life.

Without Steudtner, with whom Gabeira set her world record, she had at one time feared she would have to turn her entry in the competition over to someone else. Instead, Rebiere travels from Galicia in northern Spain, where he runs a surf school, to team up for the contest. She jokes she has stolen him from his regular partner for the year, fellow world record holder Rodrigo Koxa, who had partnered up with Hawaiian Keali'i Mamala for the one-off competition.

The early indications with Rebiere are promising, despite the two having just three days to see if their partnership can click in the water, and she tries to see the positivity in her trial separation from Steudtner. "It's different not to have him," she suggests, "not only in the contest but generally to have him out. But maybe it's good too. It gives him and me a break. Maybe we needed a break and this season is less stressful. Maybe I needed it. He's so intense!" and she laughs heartily at the gentle ribbing of her close friend and perhaps closest ally in Nazaré.

There is a level of excitement leading up to the competition. In part, she likes the structure that a competition brings. But there is also excitement for the fact that, on competition days, Nazaré loses the usual Wild West energy of an increasingly hectic waterway by having a reduced number of jet skis in the water at any given moment. "More and more, it's become chaotic here. So it's nice to have one day where things are more structured and with more rules."

But her mind takes time to shift to the competition, in part preoccupied with climate change, the oceans and the challenges of the world, from talk of US President Joe Biden to senators, lawmakers and subsidies. She jokes: "I need to snap out of it and go, 'OK, let's get back to the really big stuff – like big waves!'" She knows her body and mind well enough after plenty of seasons in Portugal. Her back is sore, her physio kneading it back into shape as the training ramps up.

As she pulls out of the harbour with Rebiere come competition day, the clifftop is already pretty full, but she is not one to play to the crowd nor does she get any great buzz from the audience. Instead, knowing the clock is ticking gives her a razor-sharp focus. When surfing outside of a competition, it doesn't matter if a set of waves pass you by. In the competition, it is, as she puts it, "an all-or-nothing mindset" and an opportunity to take risks. Much of any big-wave competition is down to having an element of fortune in terms of the conditions and the wave that emerges in any given moment. "There is a degree of luck as there's priority and, if you don't have priority and the best waves come through … But I still feel I can pull off the best wave of the day."

But for whatever reason, the connection isn't quite there, they don't really bother the leader board, and again she misses out on the women's prize quite comfortably. Afterwards, she and Rebiere agree to go their separate ways. Despite their individual excellence, the partnership was out of rhythm and out of sync in the water.

As she had previously warned, there was no guarantee that two world-class surfers would necessarily click perfectly, and so it has proved. "It was OK, but I didn't enjoy my surfing; I didn't get the waves where I thought, *Ooh, nice.* I wasn't lucky. You need luck and our heats weren't the best timing for the waves. But you take the positives. That's just experience piling up, experience, experience, experience."

It leaves her back at square one, partnerless in the water and on the lookout for a new tow-in partner, scratching her head for who that might be – with weeks and months still left before the waves die down and the season reaches its conclusion.

19

CHRISTMAS TIME

Christmas is coming to Nazaré for this disparate group of individuals. The days are getting shorter – the darkness forces the surfers out of the water earlier each day – and the temperature is dropping, but the weather is still clement for the most part. There are indicators of the looming festive season dotted around the town in the lengthy lead-up. Some of the main drags are lit up with Christmas lights. On the roundabout that acts as the gateway to Sitio, the raised part of the town which overlooks the waves, stands a lit-up Father Christmas with a surfboard under his arm and a flashing message saying "Welcome to Nazaré" in Portuguese. This isn't the sort of lighting display that was around in the days before McNamara.

Increasingly, there are nods to the waves dotted all over the town. Sitio is surrounded by a wall to one side, built to fend off the sand storms during the seventeenth century. But the strength of the sand-storms was so great that, even with the wall, houses could sometimes be totally buried in sand. So a pine forest was planted north of Sitio to create a more natural and more successful defence. Part of the wall enjoys a modern nod with a giant mural – 300 metres squared – by the Brazilian artist Erick Wilson, himself a surfer. It is just one work from a wider project by Wilson to create 80 murals worldwide, this one highlighting the potency of Nazaré's waves.

As it edges ever closer to the 25th, some of the surfing fraternity and sorority return home to their families for Christmas, while others band together to become a makeshift family for the celebrations. For Gabeira, Christmas does not particularly resonate. There are plenty of occasions throughout the year when she misses her tight-knit family, but Christmas isn't a time she feels overly bereft of them. Her parents have long since separated as a couple – her mother still celebrates the holiday, but her father doesn't and hasn't since he was a young boy. Their daughter leans far more towards her father's approach.

Gabiera's father's dislike for Christmas dates back to his own somewhat defiant childhood, when he would fight against the shackles of family life. One festive period, he walked out of the house – as his daughter describes it, "He kind of bailed on the family, as he was very rebellious." When he returned some days later, his grandmother had died and his mum blamed him for the tragedy. "So he just hates Christmas, he's not into gathering [with] family. He just disappears or cruises at his house with his four cats. So Christmas is nothing, I don't care about Christmas, not at all. I just sleep." This penchant for sleeping – on Christmas or otherwise – saves her for the big days, the biggest of which are yet to come this season.

Even when she's awake, for much of the time, Gabeira, like her fellow surfers, seems to live her life in slow motion out of the water, almost like sleepwalking. It's like seeing a Formula One driver outside of their racing car; everything seems slowed down in normal life. It is an analogy she agrees with, the sense being that, given what she gets from her board, there is no need for thrill-seeking in the rest of her life. Life in and out of the water occupies both ends of the spectrum. She pushes the boundaries when she's in it, but when she's not, she's happy to be like a sloth, lounging at home in tracksuit bottoms and taking the necessary rest to prepare for the big days. "That's the most exciting thing I do – inside the wave, it's awesome, it's amazing," she says. "I keep all the excitement for that. I don't need anything else in life that's that exciting. I hope it's not something I need, after this is all over. I think I'll be tired by then of getting stressed!"

It is a far cry from the girl who stumbled into surfing as much via a curiosity as anything else. Her mother was a fashion designer, while her father Fernando Gabeira was a journalist who dabbled in politics and set up the Green Party in Brazil. He famously masterminded the kidnapping of the American ambassador to Brazil, Charles Elbrick, in 1969, as a member of the student guerrilla group known as 8th October Revolutionary Movement, demanding the release of 15 political prisoners within 48 hours. The aim had been to shine the light on the oppressive military regime running Brazil at the time.

Gabeira Sr told all in his book, which was turned into the 1997 film *Four Days in September*, starring the American actor and Oscar winner Alan Arkin. An advocate for gay marriage and legalising marijuana, Fernando Gabeira later stood unsuccessfully for mayor of Rio de Janiero before returning to journalism with his own TV show on Globo, a Brazilian television network.

None of the wider Gabeira family were interested in surfing, despite their prime location living just off Ipanema Beach. Instead, Maya Gabeira's interest was spiked on that very beach as an impressionable 13-year-old, when she touched a surfboard for the first time. A year later, she joined a local surf school which mixed children from affluent backgrounds like hers with other kids from the favelas – Rio's slums or shantytowns, of which there are about 600, housing an estimated 1.5 million people. One such favela was close to Ipanema. As she recalls, "The ocean was a bigger community, mixing a lot of different people together. In the ocean, it didn't matter where you were from."

So quickly had she embraced her new passion that within three years she had packed up and left home. As she put it, her parents "freaked out", but they came round to her life plan and understood the divergent path she was on, even though it was one they never would have chosen for her. However bad the accidents have been in the ensuing seasons, they've always continued to back her, which she credits as the number-one factor in her carrying on despite the hardship.

"We're very connected and there's a huge sense of trust from my parents to me. They really trust my craziness and back me up in it all the time. Every time that something happens, if I don't have a back-up in the industry or from my peers, it doesn't matter, as I have Dad, Mum, my sister." She can't think of times when they've questioned what she does, even amid the three surgeries. There is always that sense of unwavering support, despite her admission that it wasn't necessarily the career they wanted for their daughter. "My parents are very interesting, successful, hard-working people full of values and beliefs. I grew up in a political household, so being an intellectual was far more important than being good in sports. I failed on that one for them! It was nice to grow up in a completely different world and then find my own world out there."

Even two decades into her passion and career, she is still of the view that she could improve considerably, always judging herself and critiquing her own performance, as all the big-wave surfers appear to do. In the early part of the season, she conjectured: "With my knowledge and experience and [the] boards I have, I could surf the best waves of my life this season and be better than I was before. But I think for my first record in 2018, I was training a lot more than these days, and was maybe peaking performance-wise. But I don't know if I'll ever know 'Now I'm peaking' or 'I've peaked already.' It's a tough question to answer when you're in that moment."

And yet she is still driven to push herself – in her home gym early in the morning and in the water, whether surfing, foiling or driving a jet ski. But she is well aware of the limitations it puts on her life. In essence, in the season, it is: eat, sleep, train, repeat, a six-month mantra that rarely breaks its stride. Only after a big swell does Gabeira allow herself downtime to catch up on emails and the other side of her career: business. She talks herself down as a businesswoman, but is exactly that. These surfers have to be salesmen and women to keep afloat, both literally and financially.

Back in Nazaré, her build-up to Christmas is not without its blemishes. An innocuous visit to see *Spiderman* in the cinema causes an anxiety attack; she believes the combination of the loud volume and excess movement on screen triggered it. The attacks, when they come, sound terrifying. But she also has an affinity for talking them down at points, like getting rid of an unwanted set of hiccups. But then, she has known them since her teens, only getting a diagnosis of severe anxiety disorder at the age of 30.

For years, there was just bemusement. She believes it may have started from early childhood, during which she was asthmatic and prone to fainting or vomiting, often leading to a few days' hospitalisation at a time, with no real answers. In the hostile environment of Hawaii years later, the condition and the attacks worsened. She estimates she was hospitalised twice a year – but each time, it was explained away as one thing or another – before stumbling across her own initial self-diagnosis.

She believes that 2017 was probably the worst time imaginable. Back then, she couldn't attend social events or go to the supermarket for fear it would trigger an attack and a hospitalisation, which always ended with her having to have medication to black her out.

It's still there – it always will be – but she says: "Now, I'm pretty much free to do everything. I'm kind to myself. I take it seriously; if something's too much, it's too much. I tell people and there's triggers. Loud places – like a loud restaurant, even, is no good. And if I'm tired or something feels off, there are things I cannot do."

It's taken time, but she's now open about it. It was first shared with her family, then her Nazaré inner circle, and now she's even revealed its details on bigger stages, in giving talks about mental health. "I share because it's important. I have a severe disorder and I struggle with it. When it became extremely severe, my life stopped and I wanted to get better. I had to understand my triggers. And now, it's something I'm comfortable with, something I'm very open about. The only way to get past these things is to talk about them, [as] with all mental health."

December was her last time in hospital, and she hopes it stays that way. She was released in time for Christmas, which she estimates is her sixth in total in Nazaré. The highlight of the day is less turkey – and more water-based – it always is – as she solo foils through relatively flat seas without another soul in her stretch of the ocean. If there is any sense of loneliness, she doesn't let on.

20

ESCAPE FROM NAZARÉ

Andrew Cotton

There are times when some of those immersed in Nazaré can't wait to escape its clutches. So tight-knit is its big-wave surfing community that there are points when it can almost feel claustrophobic. Cotton falls into that bracket at various points during the course of a season, and yet, as soon as he goes away, there is still an inexplicable pull, the Portuguese waters like a magnet that always drags him back.

With no major swells predicted on the horizon, he and White use the Christmas break to pack up and head for the slopes of Les Arcs for a snowy Christmas week in the mountains of France before he returns to the UK in time for Boxing Day. As much as he enjoys clearing his head by snowboarding in the mountains, there is that perpetual fear of missing out on what Nazaré might be producing in his absence, a feeling almost verging on guilt.

"I do kind of feel guilty about leaving; I feel like I should be there," he says as passers-by drift past the café shacks at the gateway to the waves, unaware he is among the surfers they have come to witness. "It's an odd mix because, as much as I want to be there, I kind of don't want to be there either. This place just has that." It is a constant fear of not being around when the big sets of waves hit outweighed by the all-consuming nature of the place.

For the first week in France, he is constantly checking the swell charts, looking at the live footage of those in the water via the cameras set up on the lighthouse. Within a few days, he manages to wean himself off this drug of sorts, and it becomes a gradual separation from his mobile and the persistent need to check in on what he might be missing back in Portugal.

"It's tough, isn't it? But surfing's like that and Nazaré is even more like that. There's that thing I feel that there's maybe a great opportunity at the minute, so I feel like I'm underperforming or not doing enough. Maybe that's just me … I don't know."

Cotton says "I don't know" a lot, an offshoot of what seems an occasional lack for confidence, which, if true, is misplaced for one of the trailblazers of Nazaré. At times, he can seem to have a sense of not belonging, and yet ask around, and he remains a benchmark for many of his peers. Von Rupp is among those in awe at him still being at the forefront of the sport in his forties. The pair have partnered in the water in the past, the Portuguese star impressed that Cotton still scythes through the biggest of waves at an age where Von Rupp is not entirely sure he would still be doing the same.

Cotton's christmas festivities in France this year are different to the more familiar celebrations back in the UK. Cotton was brought up with Christmas Day being the centrepiece, and in Les Arcs, the major celebration peaks on Christmas Eve. With everyone having eaten and drunk themselves into oblivion, Christmas Day is a far more muted affair. Then he packs his bags once more to fly home on Boxing Day, followed by wholesale flight cancellations and a packed bus back to Bristol, where his dad picks him up and drives him back to Devon. It's like the old days, father and son heading down to the coast.

His dad Bob was a policeman – long since retired – who rose up the ranks to superintendent during a career that took him across the south-west: Falmouth, Plymouth and finally Bideford. Mum Christine was a part-time teaching assistant to fit around the two kids – Cotton and his sister Hayley, who is now a physiotherapist based in Bristol.

No one in the family had ever really surfed; his dad just decided, when Cotton was nine, that it would be a good time to introduce his son to it. It was Easter time, there was no teacher to guide him, and he was effectively just plonked in the water to fend for himself.

As he recalls: "My dad hired me a wetsuit, board, it was freezing cold, and surfing schools didn't even exist then. Mum and Dad stayed in the car, just left me to it. If you did that now, you'd probably be reported to social services! But it was the best thing they could have done, just to leave me to it. And although it was freezing cold, I just loved it straight away."

For years, it was always the same. Dad would hop in the car, drive him down to the beach and leave his son in the water to fend for himself. The younger Cotton relished the freedom of no teachers – he'd always struggled at school – and taught himself how to surf without a single lesson. And when he got out of the water, he would pore over waves in magazines in his bedroom – in his mind, the bigger and more spectacular, the better, even then.

For an asthmatic who was, by his own admission, rubbish at team sports like football and rugby at school, it was the perfect healthy outlet for him in those smaller waves back in the early days. He would often sit in class thinking about when the next session in the waves would come. More often than not, it would have to wait until the weekends, and very few of his mates surfed, so he entered an entirely different circle of friends.

Growing up close to Braunton, a gateway to North Devon's surfing hub, he was nearly perfectly placed – although the village of

Yelland was on the wrong side of the river meaning that a trip to the surf beaches involved a half-hour car trip.

At 14, he joined Croyde Surf Club. Initially, he would leave his board in Croyde or Braunton and catch the bus. As he got older, that turned to hitch-hiking before he bought a moped. As soon as he finished school, he left home and started renting a flat in Croyde.

Around this time, he started to earn a name for himself by winning local surf competitions, which brought about the first sponsorship deal: free wetsuits from Second Skin, a Braunton-based manufacturer, while another local brand, Gulfstream, provided him with a board. As an impressionable teen, he felt like he'd already hit the big time.

His parents were understandably apprehensive about a life in the waves – less in terms of safety back then, and more about a potential livelihood. There was no obvious pathway into being a pro surfer, no guidebook telling him what to do, or any talent scouts out on the North Devon coast checking out the prospective talent in the water.

But, despite all the uncertainty, for the last two years at school, being a pro surfer became the sole aspiration. The response was always the same: "I was told it was never going to happen, it's impossible, this isn't a realistic choice, you know?" Determined to prove people wrong, and adamant he wasn't going to college – "I didn't want to do that, as I fucking hated school" – he instead wrote to every surfing company he could think of, asking for a job.

Surfboard Factory were the ones that gave him his first big break. He started at the bottom, by sweeping the floor of the factory. Laughing, he says, "It was probably cheap child labour" – but, while the majority of his friends were at college, the sea was visible from the factory, and he could surf most days after work. In time, sweeping led to Cotty doing minor repairs around the place and then eventually building up to making surfboards. For 10 years, he worked there. The pay wasn't great but, as well as his monthly salary, he got free surf-boards and, when the factory shut down from Christmas to March with no business to speak of at that time of year, he would go travel-ling in search of waves elsewhere.

Now, in the passenger side of his father's car on the way home from Bristol, this time there is no trip to the water. Instead, he has ahead of him a solid 10 days of eating and playing Xbox and, occa-sionally, football with his son, Ace, all the while checking when the next swell might be making its way to Portugal.

This Christmas spent with the two parts of his life – his girlfriend and subsequently his children and parents – cannot have been more different than the previous year. On Christmas Day 2020, he woke up in Nazaré in the camper van which was his home for that full-blown Covid season, unable as he was to travel home. He was on his own, and later shared lunch with a few of the camera crew stranded in the town filming the HBO series *100 Foot Wave* to mark the occa-sion. He watched from his laptop as his kids opened their presents on FaceTime.

Reflecting on the decision to stay fully immersed in Nazaré last year because of the Covid travel restrictions, he admits Christmas Day was one of the tougher days he experienced: "It's a little bit strange and sad having to do the Christmas thing with the family on FaceTime, but you still get to see them. And anyway, I think there must have been so many people around the world that experienced Christmases like that that year. It's strange times and I don't see it as a hardship. That's just how it had to be. And the kids were fine. It was my folks I worried about more, as they were self-isolating."

Getting the balance between his passion, his job and his family life, and where to be and when, is difficult – a constant juggling act, and one he still hasn't mastered. It understandably put a strain on his marriage to his former wife, Katie, who bears the burden of his absence in parenting for much of October to March. And his parents are also very hands-on with his two children – he also has a teenage daughter, Honey.

The family know the stopover will not be indefinite; a swell will emerge and the lure of Nazaré will once again become too strong. For many, Christmas is also a time for reflection on seasons past and present. Cotton is his own harshest critic, to the extent that he cringes even at the prospect of watching clips back of himself in the water. At the same time, though, he argues that such a critique, married with doubt, is not uncommon among his peers. "You never really like your style," he says, dissecting his own. "I'm just so critical of it; it feels really good but it looks so shit. For me, looking at good surfers, it's about making things look effortless. They flow really nicely, that's the art of it."

Despite the discomfort of the exercise, he still pores over footage to assess, maybe address his positioning on the board, to correct an arm too low down in one moment and raised too high in the next in the battle for balance. "Sometimes you'll fall and you won't realise why you've fallen. It's important to watch back. The only reason to do that is just to get better."

It's all about improvement for the next big swell, which the forecasts suggest is hitting the Portuguese coast in early January. The time has come to pack up his one life on the Devon coast with his family and head back to his other life.

21

CAN'T GET NO SATISFACTION

Nic von Rupp

Satisfaction in the water is much sought-after, but rarely achieved. Now into the new year, Nic von Rupp is contemplating the Tow Surfing Challenge that took place a few weeks ago, and his part in it. Sitting outside his warehouse, his girlfriend Matilde Reymão Nogueira is feeding Maya the dog, who is expecting puppies, and trying to stop the pregnant dog from eating fish that was discarded by the fisherman and is slowly rotting in the winter sunshine. Maya aside, Reymão's attention is predominantly on reading over her lines for the next day of soap opera filming. Surfers, spotters and film-makers saunter by at various stages – the warehouses are perpetually a busy highway for foot traffic – and Von Rupp flits from Portuguese to English in the various conversations before turning his attention to the events of the Tow Surfing Challenge, and the subsequent swell a few weeks later, in which he excelled. He is in contemplative mood; he often is.

Twenty-four hours out of the water after this big January swell, of which he was arguably its star, Von Rupp is wondering about his place in the sport. He is partly smarting at a video from the day put out by the World Surf League entitled "Lucas Chianca Steals the Show at Epic Nazaré".

There is no animosity towards his friend and rival, just an annoyance in the portrayal of the day's events. He is not arrogant enough to think he was the standout performer, but is frustrated the accolades have not been fairly apportioned. "The guy is truly amazing – and it's true he steals the show most of the time, but that wasn't the case yesterday. I shouldn't complain, because the WSL [World Surf League] has been good to me, but things like that do suck when you've put in so much effort to be out there, plus people agree I was one of the main performers of the day and they write that. I caught maybe 20 waves in the morning and put in more time out there than anyone else. That's just how it is. You just navigate your way through it all."

By the time he talks about it publicly, his blood is no longer boiling and he is relatively sanguine about it, in part thanks to Reymão talking him down from his "fuck these guys" attitude at the start of the day. He has taken it on board and, as the sun prepares to set on Nazaré for another day, he has mellowed, knowing such gripes are pointless and only damaging to him. So he brushes it aside and packs up for another day, the car loaded with boards for the drive back home, his passenger reading out her lines along the way.

Even if the praise had come his way – in fact, any adulation – would it ever be enough? The short answer is no. "You're always looking for more. Not being content makes you push further, but you have to navigate your way through it. You can't let it affect you negatively, you have to take that frustration, or whatever you want to call it, and channel it in a positive way, to build on. 'This is what I did wrong' – and then build. And, fuck, my career's been good. I'm happy; I can't complain. And it can't always be rainbows and strawberries, can it?"

January marks a shift for the Portugal native. It is his last big outing of the season alongside Scooby, before the latter flies back to

Brazil to take part in the reality TV show *Celebrity Big Brother*. He will prove popular with the public as one of the mainstays of the house. Scooby transcends surfing. Von Rupp likes to call him "a rock star" but, as his partner, there must undoubtedly be an underlying wish Scooby would focus more on the surfing and less on his hedonistic lifestyle.

But despite the sometimes maverick nature of their partnership, it works. Both are at the top of their game as surfers and jet-ski drivers. But Von Rupp is his own harshest critic. Even having reached the pinnacle of his sport, he ponders the "what might have been" from many a surfing session. In any competition or even day out in the waves, there is an internal sense that he could always do better.

His assessment, in reflecting on the Tow Surfing Challenge, is that Scooby brought his A game, while he himself was a little below par and the high standards he sets for himself. "We were really close to winning that one. Scooby got an inside barrel, and there's so much risk doing that. People don't do that – it's inhuman." Most observers, Von Rupp included, felt Scooby's barrel ought to have scored more, but he wasn't about to go kicking and screaming to the judging panel. He believes his main rivals, Lucas Chianca and Kai Lenny, also warranted higher scores for their chop hops (jumping and spinning in the air on their boards, a concept similar to skateboarding tricks, while in the wave). "Kai and Lucas are insane with those flips. They're next level. Doing that on a 50-foot wave is high-risk. Did we deserve to win? I actually think those guys are pretty legit winners and I was happy for Scooby with what he did, but not so happy with me."

Watching Chianca, in particular, surf is like Lionel Messi with a football at his feet. The Brazilian has a natural ability to do things many can't – or don't dare – do. While the majority of the big-wave community are content simply to be riding the wave and then just getting out safely, Chianca performs jumps on the steepest of watery slopes, then turns, barrels and cuts back into the wave. It is a high-risk, fast-moving dance which he makes look remarkably easy. And the funny part is that he rarely falls because his control and balance in the choppy waters is without equal. And like Messi, there is a modesty amid all the achievements and accolades. Chianca laughs, almost embarrassed at the suggestion that he is the best out there.

Chianca is like the Duracell bunny without an off switch, with high levels of infectious energy. Day has turned into night, and all the lights are out across the harbour, except inside the garage of Chianca's sponsor Red Bull, its floor splashed in the paint of the company's colours. He is adding a snapped board from a recent session gone wrong to a makeshift wall of fame/shame celebrating the misdemeanours in the water. A photographer and cameraman follow his every move as he tinkers with jet skis and talks through plans for the morning – with the aim to be out on the water at 7 a.m. Most crews have decided against going out, but his – he calls them the "dangerous team" on more than one occasion – fully intend to surf the entire following day.

He is the absolute heartbeat of that team: a perpetual nervous gusto, both knees tapping as he sits talking in his car, his fingers constantly fiddling with his phone, the gear stick or anything else he can find in the car as an outlet. He's so high energy that those around him talk of intentionally giving him myriad tasks to perform before going out on the water, in order to burn off the excess. It never entirely works, and yet they persevere. Standing on the clifftop, if you listen closely enough over the noisy volume of water, you can hear him screaming, louder than most, on a surfboard or jet ski. "Sometimes I bark in the water. I love to bark to let out the pressure," he says, and off he goes, barking and howling into the night sky, head tilted back as if to high-light his bizarre approach, before dissolving into laughter again.

Chianca feels a natural tie to Nazaré. Always has, from the moment he stepped foot here. The religious cult of Nazaré is also in Sacramento, where he grew up in his native Brazil. Having the same church gives him comfort and almost a sense of protection in the water, as if he is untouchable, with what he calls "Mother Nazaré" on his side. Despite the ferocity of the water — far bigger than anything he encounters at home — he says it is here that he feels safer than anywhere else in the world.

"It's a crazy wave, but I just know I'm protected here. I know something is going to help me here. I don't know what, but it always helps me here." Every time he goes out, he prays — in his head and alone — the same Brazilian prayers: pleading for him, his team, in fact for everyone in the water to come back safe, feel strong, be good in the waves and be healthy.

There are times when things have gone wrong. In his career, he estimates he has rolled his jet ski some 10 times here, his surfboard infinitely more in the early days, and yet there is now an air of invincibility about the 26-year-old when he's in the water. It is he who is perhaps most regularly surfing the biggest waves, combined with running the riskiest lines, doing the aerials (jumping on and off the board in the midst of a wave), but also charging in to rescue his fellow surfers, whether they're on his team or not.

In an often selfish sporting world, he genuinely loves helping other people — whether towing or rescuing — although there are times he says it sometimes becomes too much. But mostly he gets as much pleasure from friends riding the big waves as he does doing it himself.

It's on the wave that he feels most free, the time he feels he is living his life to the fullest, shutting his eyes in conversation as if to transplant himself to that place and sensation. It is the adrenaline that is addictive, the connection between the wave and the board, which he admittedly makes look so easy. For him, it is a dance. "I think I'm just going to dance with the wave and dance like the wave wants. If she shows me something new, I'm just like, 'Let's go,' and I do it with love." He also loves to embrace the fear, saying it's his best friend out on the water. "Being afraid is good – it helps you get stronger. To be afraid is one of my limits – and I think when I pass it, I feel stronger."

When he first set eyes on the wave in Nazaré, his initial reaction – shared by a lot of his fellow surfers on their respective debuts – was how much bigger it was than he had anticipated, 10 times the size of the waves he had grown up surfing in Brazil. His father, who is an accomplished surfer but had not been a professional, came with him and made it clear he was not willing to financially support his son in such crazy conditions. His response was quite simply, "I don't want to want to pay for you to die."

So Chianca's father instead stuck to funding his son's smaller-wave ambitions, the money from which Lucas quietly saved and eventually used to launch a big-wave career, which sparked into life in 2017 – a year after his first victory here – when he won the paddle surfing competition, beating far more established names. It was then that he decided to work on being the best, to prepare his body physically and his mind mentally for the following season.

His philosophy is different to that of many others in his sport. His mindset is that the size of the wave doesn't matter, he still plans to surf it the same way, whether it's 10 or 100 feet. That involves a remarkable level of trust and self-belief in his own ability. "I always feel like I'm free and ready to rock. Everyone loves what I'm doing. I'm doing the best I can, as I want to do harder and better, and just progress and mature on this type of wave."

He has surfed all manner of big breaks around the world, but says Nazaré is the one that defines him. And it is one where he always insists on having fun – whatever the conditions, however perilous the situation. "They call us the dangerous team because we're always ready to rock anywhere in any conditions. It's our work and we know it's super dangerous but, if we don't have fun, it's not the same for us."

He is in Nazaré for the start of the season with his pregnant girlfriend Monise; the couple's daughter will be born beyond the season's end in May, when the couple are back in Brazil. There are other surfers that have warned him that being a parent can change the risks one is subsequently willing to take. Though he plans to be a doting dad, he does not believe that parenthood will change his approach to risk. "I don't feel that. Now is the time to make titles and get the big waves. I need to rebuild my mindset and keep solid and stronger and rebuild, because I am more than just me in the world but now seriously taking care of someone else. It's my baby, my girl's baby, so it's us. This is pressure. The big waves aren't pressure – this is pressure. And I think it will make us grow more and more."

Like Von Rupp, he has the headache of looking for another partner when the next monster day of waves comes. Scooby is incarcerated in the Brazilian *Celebrity Big Brother* house, while Chianca's partner Lenny is back in Hawaii and, as it transpires, not coming back for the rest of the season, as fatherhood is imminent. With both Von Rupp and Chianca partnerless, it is a natural fit for them to pair up. The two of them talk about the idea and neither take long in agreeing to the pairing. It has its consequences, though. With two teams effectively going into one – including rescue drivers, spotters and the like – it inevitably causes other relationships to break up within their own teams, albeit temporarily. It can ruffle some feathers, but that's the nature of the business.

Von Rupp dry coughs as he talks about the potential partnership – the final vestiges of having Covid two weeks earlier, the second time he has been stricken by the virus. As with people from most walks of life at this time, the pandemic is a feature of the big-wave surfing community, ripping through it at certain points during the course of the season, and certainly the early part. This time, his symptoms are relatively mild, and, crucially, his lung function is not diminished, and therefore will not delay the timing of his return to the water when a swell comes for him and his new partner.

22

THE HOSPITALISATIONS

Three surfers have been admitted to hospital in the course of just one January day in 2022. Justine Dupont, Pierre Rollet and C.J. Macias are all being treated with injuries varying in their degrees of severity.

Dupont is towed into a big wave but, as she goes to turn at the bottom of the wave, it is as though her board comes to an abrupt halt underneath her. She is catapulted off and finds herself dangerously close to the rocks. As she describes it in a later Instagram post, it's "the place where no one wants to end up". Her partner Fred David first tries unsuccessfully to get to her and then more waves pound on top of her, pushing her closer and closer to the rocks. In the end, Chianca finds the narrowest of entry points and, more critically, an exit for him and Dupont. He carries her on to the beach with the lifeguards, and she remains conscious throughout. Her succinct summary is simply: "This is completely part of the game when you do extreme sport," while Chianca is buzzing with the adrenaline rush of his audacious rescue.

Dupont is checked over in hospital before quickly being released, but hers is not the first hospitalisation of the day. That dubious honour belongs to Rollet, who wiped out on the very first wave surfed by any team the whole day. But neither is quite as horrific nor as played on repeat as that of Macias.

He is the brother of Nicole McNamara, wife of Garrett. And his association with Nazaré dates right back to the early days with the McNamaras and Cotton. A former high-level beach volleyball player, at 6 feet 5 inches, he stands far taller than any other surfer in that particular stretch of the Atlantic Ocean. At the season's start, he talked almost as though he was slightly tormented by the wave. A deep thinker, he claims to be at peace with it, although is still reluctant to tackle it on its biggest days.

On the day preceding the accident, things have finally clicked for him, at long last attaining the synergy he has aspired to. It is roughly a decade in the making. Always slightly overshadowed by what he calls "the legends of the surfing world" – notably, the force of nature that is his brother-in-law – at the end of the day, it feels like things have aligned, and demons from past poundings put out of his mind. In those moments, he has at last a sense of belonging. Riding one particular bomb, he comes out of it absolutely euphoric. Macias laughs at the recollection: he was so high in the moment, his first comments were "Is it the world record, is it the 100-foot wave?" He chuckles at the recollection. Others laughed too, at the time. It was barely half that.

If the wave of the preceding day was big, the one he tackles the following afternoon is comfortably the biggest he has ever ridden and, for a time, he looks to have it completely under control, with a confidence matched by the cheers that greet him in the water, on the fort and from those watching on the clifftops. Buoyed by his new-found confidence, he steadily gets himself into a more critical position on the wave. Just ever so slightly mistiming his exit, he quickly loses control and is thrust forward.

He is just a fraction away from escaping, his first reaction being, "Oh my God, I made it," before his arm crosses his midriff as he tries to steady himself at such high speed. Instead, it has the opposite effect and throws him totally off balance. "At that point, I knew I was done for." He tries to turn his way out of the danger, but it is too late and he is flung like a 6-foot skimming stone across the water's surface. The natural instinct is to put out his arm to break his fall – a move that, in hindsight, has pretty catastrophic consequences – hitting the water's surface rapidly and then being thrust deeper and deeper towards the bottom of the ocean by the ferocity of the wave.

In addition to his arm positioning, the other major error is his choice of vest over the top of his inflatable wetsuit – a white one. Despite his gargantuan size, in the similarly coloured white water, no one can spot him. The jet skis circle, the spotters go silent on the radios, straining their eyes through the binoculars to catch sight of the latest stricken surfer. For five minutes, he is gone. For his sister Nicole, standing by the small red lighthouse on top of the fort, it is particularly harrowing.

Reflecting on it a few days later, she says, "It felt like the end of the world – and that's the first time we've lost anyone like that." Nicole is the only one to spot him when Macias first emerges but that is it; he doesn't pop up where a surfer normally would for the next breath after the next wave passes, or at least not that she can see. "I spotted him when he popped up the first time. Then another wave came, he had two seconds to take a breath and then the next wave was on him. I knew where he should pop up again and I never saw him pop up again." Meanwhile, her husband tries to reassure himself Macias's life vest, incorporated in his wetsit, will inflate and, whatever the circumstances, the stricken surfer will eventually come to the surface. In the back of McNamara's mind is the thought, the doubt, that the life vest may have been ripped from his torso in the torrent of water.

All Cotton recalls hearing over the radio is shouts of "We can't see him! We can't see him!" mostly coming from a screaming Nicole. He remembers the feeling of helplessness as he bobbed up and down on his jet ski trying to spot Macias, waiting for the radio call to go to the inside of the wave to scoop him to safety. By this point, Macias is all too aware, despite the carnage he finds himself immersed in, that no one can see him. He's gone into survival mode, surrendering to the pounding, assessing his body, not yet feeling the pain that will shortly envelop him.

"I'm getting ripped all over the place and I'm going deep. It's been a while already, it's probably going to be a while longer." He thinks, momentarily, that he can wait out the storm. "And then, oh man, my arm. I could suddenly feel it really hurting." His life vest automatically inflates, allowing him up to the surface initially before his eardrum bursts, his ear pinging and then ringing. At points, he is unable to work out which way is up due to the sensory overload as he is repeatedly thrust under the surface.

By now, he is going into damage-limitation mode, holding the hurt arm to protect it from further harm. A keen yoga enthusiast, his great strength is his breathing, the one consolation for his helpless sister – "If there's one thing C.J. knows best, it's breathing." She reassures herself he'll be OK, but can never be sure. He grabs the morsels of breath whenever he can, two breaths here, another there, even a half breath at points amid the washing-machine effect of his pounding. By this point, the waves have settled down to 12, maybe 15, feet high – he gestures upwards to the ceiling in the large conservatory where he is reliving the experience, as a size comparison. It doesn't seem like that much respite, but then, he is grateful for any at all.

It's now been a solid five minutes – an agonisingly long time whether one is in the mêlée or helplessly watching it unfold. He is finally spotted. Alemão de Maresias, the Brazilian surfer and jet-ski driver, locates him on the third peak of waves, way out from where he initially comes off the board and just 30 metres out from the beach. De Maresias reaches out an arm to pull him up on to the sled at the back of the jet ski. Macias hands over the one functioning limb but can't find the strength to get himself up on the sled at the back of the jet ski, causing him to spill out into the water once again.

That's when De Maresias and Cotton first hear his screams of agony – as he is washed up on the shore moments later. The American remembers putting his feet on the ground, relieved to have survived the nastiest wipeout of his life, but then the pain surges through his body, making him feel physically sick. People are shouting at him to dig his feet into the sand to make sure he doesn't get sucked back out to sea. Instead, he collapses in the water and starts being dragged back in before Orlando, a neighbour in his temporary Nazaré home, comes in to pull him to proper safety this time, before he is placed on a spinal board as a precaution.

As Cotton also helps to drag him on to the beach, his first thought looking at the state of his arm is that Macias has snapped it. A trained lifeguard, he has never seen anything like it, the arm disfigured and bent in an impossibly wrong direction. Cotton says: "It was great to have him back on dry land, but his arm is really fucked. Fucking hell. I thought, *Fuck, that's such a gnarly break, how has he done that? I remember thinking, I'm over this shit. Is it really worth it?* And then you feel a bit responsible – he's out there because we're egging him on. But it was the first time he really wanted it. He wanted to be on the rope, he really enjoyed it right up until that point."

Macias readily admits some moments are almost comical in their recollection, despite the severity of his situation at the time, and he's laughing just 24 hours on. "I'm in this surreal moment looking up at the blue sky, uber aware of the whole moment. I'm grateful to be breathing, I know my spine's OK and I'm not paralysed. And I'm in immense pain – oh my God, I broke my arm, this is incredible. Then someone would slightly touch my arm and I'm like 'argh', I'm in so much agony. Then I start seeing loved ones, everyone's so happy to see me alive and I'm happy to be alive." He gets in the back of the ambulance that has pulled up on the beach and a whole other journey to recovery begins.

Throughout it all, he never thinks it is game over, telling himself again and again, "I'm not going down today," and afterwards, his attention turns to others, already aware as he is how traumatising it must be for friends and family. For his girlfriend Pavana, it is her first time properly watching him surf Nazaré. Standing next to his sister Nicole at the time, she recollects with some understatement that it was not the best experience of her life. Part of her brain would engage the worst-case scenario; the other part was hoping for the best. The moment she sees him staggering on to the beach, she runs down with Barrel, the McNamaras' son.

Twenty-four hours is a long time in Nazaré. Not long after Macias's release from hospital, he is back recuperating at the house in which he is staying with Pavana and his parents, next to that of his sister and brother-in-law. The first indication of things having gone wrong is there on the doorstep – his brand-new green surfboard was snapped completely in half by the force of his wipeout. As he pulls up in one of the golf buggies the surfers often use to get around in Nazaré, he unloads his giant frame from the passenger seat gingerly, his arm in a sling, sporting a cast which runs from his fingertips to right over his elbow.

The whole episode brings back myriad emotions and continues to do so for weeks and months afterwards, although a future in which

Macias and his partner might not return to Nazaré seems unlikely. They already have plans to eventually open a café-restaurant there. There's something about Nazaré that brings back people even after the very worst moments there.

And there is a sense of guilt, too, amid it all. "I felt bad putting people through that moment and putting my body through that traumatic experience," he says before he arcs his back and laughs in over-the-top fashion, tilting back his head and looking up as he does so. "In a strange way, I was loving it, inviting loved ones into deeper levels for their feeling for life. I didn't want to torture them, but I was curious about what that experience was like ... surviving a beating on a giant, full-on day. I was curious about that and this pain, being the one we think is dead and wanting to pull him out of the water. In a sick subconscious way, I was curious of it all – but one time's enough. I'm good. I'm like, 'Thank you!' I think I got away with it."

In the days afterwards, while he is upbeat and still has plans to return when fit again, others are still haunted: his sister, brother-in-law, Andrew Cotton, all those caught in the race for life to find his battered body. For days afterwards, it remains the main talking point, the accidents of Dupont and Rollet relative footnotes in comparison. But the Nazaré fraternity and sorority never dwell on the bad, the "what if"s, the "what might have been"s for too long. There's always another swell looming.

23

NEW PARTNER, NEW PROBLEMS

Maya Gabeira

Gabeira is lying prostrate on an outside sofa on the grounds of her home, her eyes closed with her arm across her face to block the glare of the winter sun, directly above her. A friend of hers, who is preparing a spot of lunch in the kitchen, jokes it looks more like a session between a psychiatrist and a traumatised patient than a dissection of a series of back-to-back days in Nazaré's choppy waters. Apologies are proffered for her inability to summon even the strength to get up and greet anyone.

The exhaustion is understandable. For her, the early January swell has been an unmitigated disaster. Before the sun was even properly up on its biggest day, she and her newly formed team were already bobbing around eagerly in the water, this time she'd switched allegiance from Eric Rebiere to another Frenchman in Pierre Rollet. On that first wave of the day, and before most other teams are even out in the water, Rollet's season is over. In turn, Gabeira's own session is nearly ruined with Rollet out of action and two flipped jet skis washed on to the shore.

It's barely sunrise and Rollet is sitting in an ambulance after taking a pounding from the waves. The medical consensus is that he briefly lost consciousness. Doctors will later diagnose broken ribs, while his knees badly swell up the following day and require further investigation. Visually, it pales into insignificance compared to Macias's tumble, which some conjecture is the most violent impact the town has witnessed, and yet Rollet faces a lengthy spell on the sidelines recuperating.

With the emergency services on hand to treat him, Gabeira's priority switches – there is not much time for sympathy here – to getting back in the water immediately. But the tractor in place to help the skis back into water is not in position, just a motorised dune buggy. So she has to drive that to and from the harbour. On a normal day, it is barely a five-minute trip, but in order to return both jet skis and start again from the harbour, she has to find her way through the traffic of day trippers flocking into Nazaré to catch a glimpse of Gabeira and her peers.

When back in the water and with Rollet hospitalised, she teams up with Pierre Caley to tow her into the waves, with David Langer stepping in as her second rescue. The chance of catching any big waves – or "bombs", as she likes to call them – seems somewhat farfetched.

"I'd never surfed with David before and he had never really driven Nazaré when the waves are big, so it was just a challenging, challenging day. I got one bomb which, fuck, was a miracle with what we had." She found herself on another big wave come the afternoon, but she was forced to adjust her line on the board, ending up near the rocks – and her would-be rescuer was flipped off the jet ski. By 4.30 p.m., she was left stranded on the beach once more, a day to forget finally at an end.

She is quick to shrug off the falls. On her first of the day, she edged a little too close to the rocks, but was quickly rescued while her life vest inflated. She came out unscathed. In the afternoon, she was forced to pull her inflatable vest once more when given a pounding, but again came away uninjured. Some days just don't work in Nazaré for whatever reason, something she accepted long ago.

The frustration is that her aspirations had been good for this swell. In preparation in the days leading up to the bigger walls of water, she and Rollet had caught some good waves; the Franco-Brazilian combination clicked as a pairing immediately – only to be undone by misfortune on the following day, at the point when the waves were at their biggest. By her estimation, it was the most marathon of days in Nazaré, starting at six in the morning in the gym and ending back in the harbour by 5 p.m. As she calls it, "the longest day of my career". "Now I'm tired just because I haven't stopped for days." The days either side of the Rollet hospitalisation and her double wipeout, she says, have been a lot of fun.

The last four days of this particular swell started with a slight gripe about her scapula, or shoulder blade. She was hampered by a deep knot there, she decided to treat it with more surfing rather than the usual, more typical visit to the physio. It does the trick.

Whatever the injuries, they are always shrugged off. Two weeks previously, she broke her nose when she was ridden into by a jet ski in a botched rescue attempt. She mentions it nonchalantly for the first time, in passing, like it was a small cut which needed the tiniest of plasters. Having had infinitely rougher days in Portugal and infinitely worse injuries, it's understandable. The mishaps that are not life-threatening barely get a raised eyebrow.

And while she is relatively unscathed in the grand scheme of things, this swell has not ended well for Rollet, Macias and Dupont. And not to be heartless but, of those, Rollet was her only concern. There's too much else going on to widen the net of concern further. "I don't get fazed unless someone gets unconscious. If people are injured but they're conscious, fuck, it's part of the game. You're going to get injured at some point."

And then she immediately flicks once more from one side of life to the next: from the waves to business. As well as the documentary being made over the past decade, she has diversified to become a children's author with a first book, aptly called *Maya and the Beast*. Loosely based on her own life, it tells the tale of a young Maya, scared of life because of asthma. The only place that fear dissipates is in the water, even when coming face to face with "the Beast" – a giant wave. Her trick is to tame the wave and show the rest of the town not to be so fearful.

Plus, she has come up with her own sunscreen brand, Blue Aya, which launches the following summer. She has entirely funded it, started it from scratch, and got a laboratory to create it using natural ingredients. There are different varieties for specific skin types, but the ingredients are largely the same: coconut water, kelp, zinc and green coffee extract, among other things.

Despite all that – and other ventures in which she is involved, which make her one of the highest-earning surfers on the circuit – she downplays any suggestion she is awash with business acumen. But with a film, book, sunscreen range and no shortage of other sponsors, she clearly has her head screwed on and surrounds herself with the right people. "I'm not a businesswoman, but I have those around me," she explains. Using the example of the sunscreen, she notes that she has the expertise from a life spent outdoors of knowing what feels good on her skin, and her fellow surfers do too. The other pieces of the jigsaw, she has slotted in over time: the scientist that develops the formula in the laboratory, her mother (whom she likens to her CEO), and a marketer to help push the brand. That leaves her to "do what I know how to do".

But amid all the business ventures, everything always comes back to the water, as it has done for the past 20 years. She calls it her "everything place".

"It can be scary, it can be happy, it can be draining, it can be energising, it can be everything – all the emotions you have out there. It does me good for sure – OK, maybe not at this extreme. Everyone says sports is great, everyone should do sports. And then you talk to the biggest athletes in the world and many are all fucked in their body, as there's a limit when you go over the edge, and it's not that great for you." She says this still prostrate on her back garden sofa, and questions whether the moments of intense adrenaline are a drug that's actually good for her. At this point, she concludes, "I don't think it's healthy. It's a drug, but I don't think it's healthy."

But after lunch and one of her "nanna naps", as she calls them, the questioning quickly evaporates. Her location quickly erodes any of the bad. For all the physical hardships, it's hard to tire of the view on the drive from her mountaintop home, the lighthouse in the distance. On the bright, blue-sky days, the sun almost points round the far corner to north beach, luring her back into the water even when she's reluctant. Every time on that drive, she still feels its hypnotic pull.

All those involved with the surf of Nazaré talk of its magic. For each person, that magic is different in its identification. For Maya, it is simply in the waves and the stunning backdrop. "Anywhere you get waves back there – and a cliff that beautiful, and the sunrise and the sunset, and the mist and the fog and the sun. That I think is the rawness of the place and the potential and the crazy waves. And the people are kind; they're all very welcoming." These past days, it's the waters that haven't always been so welcoming.

24

THE LIVERPOOL EFFECT

Sebastian Steudtner

When Liverpool won the Champions League back in 2019, their manager Jürgen Klopp was left trying to uncover new ways to inspire his players and reinvigorate them after they'd already achieved the pinnacle of European football. In his quest to give them an additional psychological edge against their domestic rivals and to avoid his star-studded squad turning stale after their continental triumph, he reached out to Sebastian Steudtner, of all people.

On the final day of the team's pre-season training camp in Evian, in south-eastern France, and just days out from the start of the 2019–20 season, he asked his countryman to both give a team talk and also teach the footballers the sort of breathing techniques Steudtner himself uses in his pool training sessions and out in the big waves to stay alive. As well as teaching them aerobic exercises and breath control for when you're in a state of panic, he also spoke about the whole mantra of staying calm under pressure.

Klopp and captain Jordan Henderson have since paid tribute to the German surfer for the impact the exchange had on the players. Steudtner, for his part, brushes it all aside, in particular some articles that pushed the parameters of the story's retelling to suggest the surfer was the mastermind of the Premier League title win that would subsequently follow.

In the opening session in the pool that day, the breath-holding ranged from just 10 to 90 seconds at best. By the end of it, there was a straight duel for underwater supremacy between defender Dejan Lovren, who has since moved away from Anfield, and striker Mo Salah, with the pair nearing the four-minute mark by the end of it; Lovren was the last to surface.

It was a session that clearly resonated with those there. For another defender, Virgil van Dijk, Steudtner's messaging of dealing with pressure particularly had meaning. Comparing Steudtner's experience of big-wave surfing to the relative triviality of his own big-game pressure, the Dutchman said, "He was like 'one slight mistake and life could be over'."

Much like Klopp and Liverpool, in his own quest for self-improvement, Steudtner is always looking at avenues outside surfing, often casting his eye to methods from other sports and athletes in order to achieve even the most marginal of gains. Being injured and out of the water has given him even more time to do so.

Boxing is probably the sport he turns to most, continually drawn back to it because of the parallels he sees between that sport and his own – and not just the poundings he takes. "It's the same thing – you have to be prepared to die. That's the first thing, at a certain level, and that's not because boxers or surfers die left and right, but it's the mentality you have to bring into the ring that has to be 'I am going to kill you or you'll kill me' – full stop." But the analogy goes beyond that. "It's a dance, a strategy. It's the most beautiful sport, nothing is more technical than boxing, nothing. I love boxing. If I didn't get into surfing, for sure it would have been boxing." At his height and weight, he would probably be in the lightweight division. You could comfortably envisage him being in the ring and, with his muscular frame, more than capable of holding his own, whomever the opponent.

Russian and Mexican boxers are the fighters he most admires – the manner in which they strip their lives down to the most basic terms, taking themselves to a forest hideaway or some other Spartan existence for the most simplistic of pre-fight training camps. But the businessman in him also looks up to the British boxer Anthony Joshua perhaps more for the commercial acumen, which has seen Joshua accrue a net worth in the region of £200 million and rising, than for what actually plays out between the ropes.

Steudtner's own business partnerships are partly financially driven, but they are also a symbiotic relationship aimed at improving the technical side of his surfing operation. No stone is left unturned during the course of the season; everything is aimed at him improving, even when not in the water.

At the Porsche Development Centre in Weissach, just outside Stuttgart, he briefly takes over a wind tunnel. In place of the usual sports car stands his surfboard, with him on top of it. The German manufacturer uses its cutting-edge science from decades in the car industry to refine the aerodynamics of his body position, board and wetsuit. As the company's scientists pore over the relevant data, they ascertain that even the slightest change of Steudtner's position on the board can greatly improve the aerodynamics. It is an approach to the sport that no other surfer is currently undertaking. "It's cool," he says of the experiment. "They treat me like a car. And it's an exciting process to test all these things and see what's possible."

By his own admission, he is driven to pushing the limits of what might be achievable, even if much of his testing and tinkering fails to reach fruition. He admits, "OK, maybe 80 or even 90 per cent of new things don't work – but that's just how it is, always trying and trying.

It's the same with surfing. You try all the time and most of the time
you fail." On top of the wind tunnel operation, he is also partnering
with Siemens as part of a research project on the biomechanics of
big-wave surfing. It is a study that is not expected to be completed
until some time in 2025.

Steudtner ponders whether his unusual drive to push boundaries
unlike his peers might be partly down to his own early influences and
his adventurous nature growing up. As a child, his favourite place
to go was his aunt and uncle's farm, recollections of which bring an
immediate smile to his face. There was fishing in the river – he and
his sister catching them with sticks, like a real-life Tom Sawyer and
Huckleberry Finn – and they would kill their own chickens for the
evening meal by chopping off the animals' heads. For a then impressionable youngster, it was the ultimate adventure playground.

The farming couple made a big impression on Steudtner too, and
it still resonates today. He recalls the time his uncle accidentally cut
his hand open, to the extent that blood was pouring out of a massive
gaping wound. He simply sat down and stitched himself up. And his
uncle's motto of "If it's my time, it's my time" could just as easily apply
to his nephew in his choice of profession. For Steudtner's uncle, that
day finally came at 64, when he dropped dead from a heart attack.
The surfer's aunt, meanwhile, lived on and was diagnosed with cancer
at age 70. After undergoing initial treatment, she essentially said "sod
it", defied regular medicine and pursued her own approach and has
continued to confound medical expectation to live a decade beyond
the doctors' expectations.

The family were originally very wealthy in the early twentieth
century, owning a large farm with hundreds of acres in a picturesque
valley. His great-grandfather fought in the First World War, and his
grandfather in the Second World War, posted to Italy; the job of his

battalion was to destroy any resources that remained in the area and ensure there was nothing left for the enemy to employ when they arrived. That largely involved him killing animals, a part of his life that perpetually haunted him for his remaining days and from which he never fully recovered, according to the family. As his grandson puts it, "He was never the same again." In addition, it became known in the locality that he was no fan of Adolf Hitler. Word got out and, as the family story goes, someone snitched, which left the family on a deportation list. They avoided that fate when the war finished shortly afterwards, he forgave his accuser and, like much of the rest of Germany, life simply moved on.

The sleek lines of Steudtner's glass-fronted new home in Nazaré, with its view overlooking the ocean, is in stark contrast to that old family farm. His roots, at least for much of the season, are here in Portugal, although it is only his seasonal home. His spell injured on the sidelines has given him plenty of moments of reflection on both his past and future – and yet he has no idea when that time will run out, when the drive to be in the big waves will diminish.

As much as he itches to get back in the water, he seems to thrive in the face of adversity – right now, it's the injury plight that drags on and on with still no end in sight. But in some ways, he likes it like that. Perpetually being at the top without a care in the world, he insists, would simply not suit him. He draws on another sporting parallel to highlight it. "It's a constant chase, right? At a certain point, you have to run out of performance. It's natural; it happens to everyone. Win, win, win or perform, perform, perform. Unless you're someone like Lewis Hamilton that's so obsessed, at a certain point, you're done. If I was Lewis Hamilton, I'd be as bored as hell. How boring is it to win and win and win? Now things might have just got a bit more interesting for me."

For all his comments, there are still likenesses between him and the seven-time Formula One world champion. Only a year separates them in age, they have similarly spent a lifetime in their respective high-octane endeavours and both have railed against their sports. In Hamilton's case, it is in terms of the lack of diversity in Formula One and wider motorsport. For Steudtner, safety remains his fight. But there is also the shared sense that whatever they achieve in their respective disciplines, it will never ever be enough.

Complete fulfilment is hard for him to attain. His familiar refrain is, "I'm not satisfied" – and not just because of the current injury, the broken foot which put an end to his seasonal partnership with Gabeira. He winds the clock back to his early days in Nazaré, only his second season, and one of the biggest days he can remember. The date is not important to him, just the recollection that both he and Tom Butler had surfed some of the best waves of his life, with the military doctor Axel Haber also in situ.

Butler was bouncing off the walls in ecstasy as they began to pack up at the end of the day, while Haber was equally pleased for his two friends. For Steudtner, the sensation was different. Instead of celebrating the rush of that day's water work, he was dissecting what he could have done better, lines he should have taken, how the session could have been improved, with half an eye on next time. Occasionally, it can gnaw away at him, but it is also the thing that has made him improve above all else. "It means you don't enjoy the thing so much, but that's why I improved a lot. I have friends in business and they say the same thing."

Butler's absence still leaves a void in his life. Close friends and long-time surf partners, Steudtner would dearly love to have him back at his side. Finding a partnership that inexplicably clicks – as his with Butler did from the very outset – is hard to attain, but the

Cornishman's reappearance does not seem imminent at any point. While they are opposites – what Steudtner calls fire and ice – which equated to fighting like crazy at points, it somehow still clicked. Some relationships in Nazaré that shouldn't work just do. "Tom is and will always be my brother. He's genuine, he's honest," a facet he thinks there is not enough of in the town. Theirs is and always has been an unwavering loyalty to one another.

And yet loyalty is not always a buzzword here in Nazaré. Steudtner is quick to point out that some "would stab each other in the back in a second" if it served their purposes, and he laughs at the nonsense of it all. It is not necessarily a criticism, just a reality of the sport and the waves that they all pursue in a perpetual quest for one-upmanship.

He says of his profession: "It's not like a basketball court, where it's your turn. If there's more surfers, that means less waves – and it's a greedy sport. If I want to catch waves, I don't think about you because you're in my way; so you're naturally competitive. There are all these vibes that happen in surfing, a localism like, 'I was here first.' You have to be a hunter and be competitive naturally. It's a myth that surfers are all chilled, smoke weed and help push each other into the waves. If you catch the biggest wave, you'll get famous quickly. You've examples of Garrett, Maya, me. It's whatever you need to do or feel you need to do."

25

THE BIG MOMMA

Sérgio Cosme

Sérgio Cosme's left shoulder is dangling out of its joint, hanging limply at his side after a surfing session on a relatively innocuous January day. He is living proof of the proverb that bad things happen in threes: first, the knocked-out teeth, then the ACL, now the shoulder.

He looks down at it in slight disbelief, this result of falling on a rare foray out on his surfboard this season. Coaxed and cajoled into making a surfing return by his peers, Cosme was reassured by his physiotherapist that the reconstructed knee could withstand the rigours of swapping the saddle of his jet ski for the surfboard. He falls on one particular wave, and the knee holds firm – but out pops the shoulder joint. He suspects it is more as a result of wear and tear than the individual wipeout, a knock-on effect of breaking his collarbone years ago. Acting as though it is little more than a mere inconvenience, a fellow surfer pops the dislocated shoulder back into place for him, and off Cosme goes into the waves again. The pain is limited but, unbeknown to him at the time, it will mark the beginning of the end for his surfing for another season.

In all, he will make a total of just four visits on his board into the bigger waves all season. Each time he tries to surf, out pops the shoulder at some point. Going forward, the bigger problem is that it is also the arm he reaches out with from the controls of his jet ski when scooping a stricken surfer to safety, the arm he will stick out from the water when looking to be rescued himself. Another of his peers, the Portuguese surfer João Macedo, teaches him a simple technique for popping it back every time it comes out of place. He opens his arms slowly from the bottom to the top like he's praying with outstretched arms. As he puts his arms together at the top, the dislocated shoulder slots back into place with a click and no grimace of pain. Well aware this method is no more than a stopgap to keep his season going, he eventually concedes to a doctor's appointment for the shoulder to be examined. Further surgery is among the options but, having spent too long on the sidelines with his other injuries, he is reluctant to be operated on just yet.

The unlikely analogy he turns to in order to explain his predicament is that of a plane crash. "With a plane, when it crashes, it's often not one problem but several small problems altogether. It's more or less the same with me and my body." While not a medical expert, he conjectures the Covid lockdown is partly at fault. In many ways, he believes his body had not been put sufficiently through the rigours of the waves, given the various lockdowns in the preceding 18 months. But he also admits it is a wake-up call for him to slow down as he edges ever closer to his forty-third birthday in September.

Despite the ongoing problem with his shoulder limiting his capabilities, his prowess as a rescue driver is so revered that he is still regularly sought out for employment by his team, other Nazaré regulars and one-off visitors. And in that quest, Cosme sets out to limit the dangers and injuries to the surfers around him. But when he is within the surf team, alongside Von Rupp, he is not directly paid. His money instead comes from sponsorship deals – among them Tudor watches – or else prize money in particular competitions. And yet it has never been the money that acts as his driving force in the water. "There's no money to pay me if someone dies in my arms," he says somewhat bluntly. "Sometimes I prefer to not earn money in terms of safety. I need to earn money on the jet ski but, in the big days with my partner, I prefer not to think about money."

Like the surfers he has towed in and out of peril, he has fallen foul of these waters on his surfboard with the effect of damaging more than simply his brittle shoulder. Back in 2017 was the one time he thought a lifetime spent in the water might be over, not to mention his own life.

Taken out by a wave, he was dragged across one peak after another, the result being that when he was finally spat out, he was hundreds of metres away from where he had taken to his board. He was lost. He remembers it as 20 minutes, perhaps longer – although the dangerous moments often feel more prolonged in these choppy waters – that he waited in the vain hope that someone would eventually come to his rescue.

Casting his mind back to those 20 minutes, he can vividly recount his thinking pattern at the time. Exhausted, he pondered how long he had been bobbing helplessly out in the water, not spotted by his would-be rescuers. Further still, he questioned how much longer he might be stranded there.

There was also the consideration of what might come next, a moment that has helped shape his daily approach to Nazaré's waters ever since. "I try never to think about death. When you think you are dying, your percentage to die is starting to increase. It's better that you don't think about death. Normally, I say in Nazaré – or this sport – you should be prepared in a situation that you are almost dying or ready to do so, so you must be calm. Why? Because if you stay calm, you are more focused about what you can do to not die here. If you stay stable, you won't be nervous – you increase the probability to live, so that's the only choice and thing to do. So when something happens to me, I try not to think about anything bad. I try to see an exit going out. When you see the exit, you need to think about your death. You distract your mind. You can say, 'No worries, it's a short life but good life.' But I remember that time thinking, *I don't know what will happen*." He eventually made his own way back to shore, scrambling on to the sand, breathless from his beating but crucially alive. It is a moment that he regularly remembers this season, to remind him how to act when things go horribly wrong.

His first time surfing in these waters had been back in 2015, with Rodrigo Koxa – a partnership now disbanded but a friendship consolidated for life by the day Cosme towed Koxa into an 80-foot wave to break Garrett McNamara's previous world record. For a number of reasons, it was an event that very nearly didn't materialise. Back in their first season together in 2015, a nasty wipeout saw Koxa churned around under the surface, each time getting barely a half breath before being battered again. The experience left the Brazilian with PTSD and questioning his own place within the big-wave community.

For Koxa, who wears his heart on his sleeve perhaps more than any of this band of surfers, it is an emotional retelling of that moment seven years ago. We are inside a Nazaré surf warehouse following one of Koxa's recent wipeouts this season, from which he has come out relatively unscathed. His latest mishap makes the bearded surfer, the son of a psychotherapist, reflect on the past. The incident at the end of 2015 he still describes as "the worst time of my life", as he not only nearly lost his life but also his livelihood. In the ensuing weeks and months, he lost all his sponsors and was facing a lengthy rehabilitation from the psychological trauma of it all. The spill had sent him close to the rocks and his team couldn't get to him to rescue him.

As he plotted his rehabilitation, it was Cosme with whom he partnered and trained, and whom he credits for his place in Nazaré's annals. "We have a great connection," says Koxa. "He's a great friend. We trusted each other and we came together."

It was almost baby steps for Cosme, who was part guide, part psychologist, part confidant and finally part training partner, as he gradually lured Koxa back in. Cosme recalls how his friend was nervous and didn't want to be in the water. "It took a lot of work to get back, and I'd done that work with him," he remembers. "He almost died there, and I told him to get past the bad time he had. I tried to help him and said, 'Koxa, let's go to the water.' I told him, 'Don't worry, I will guarantee your rescue for you' although you can never guarantee a rescue! He first said, 'You will not be there.'" But every time Cosme did catch him and hauled him on to the float at the back of the jet ski. And so the trust and confidence, both in his partner but also simply in being in the water, grew. At that point, recalls Cosme, "I started to see the old him come back."

The moment the comeback was complete, that things finally clicked and the mental demons were eventually put to bed was on his record-breaking day in November 2017, a record that still stands as the 2021–22 season counts down – but could see itself erased from the record books by Steudtner in time. For now, in this moment, it remains Koxa's.

As if to prove his confidence in the water now, he recalls the end of his latest big Nazaré swell, in which he got hurled to the bottom of the ocean floor – the first time he can remember that happening – and had to wrestle with the power of the water to not have his wetsuit ripped clean off. By the time he was eventually rescued, he had lost his boots, the wetsuit was filled with sand and his foot was twisted in the straps of his surfboard, which effectively ended his big-wave season. His board finally washed up on the shore an hour and a half later, where it was retrieved and sent back to the harbour for him. Having previously come back from the brink, the Brazilian is sanguine about it.

Just outside the warehouse stands a brand-new Mercedes branded with "Koxa Bomb!" on it and a silhouette of him surfing. When the sponsors left in droves, Koxa Bomb! was his self-funded rebrand – paid for by the jet-ski and surfing lessons he gave. It is a mantra that he likes to repeat over and over again.

"All my life, I train for that moment," he says of the 80-foot 2017 record in his slightly broken English, "and then my life makes sense. I focus every day to surf big waves and one day, I get that one. I'm always looking for the bombs. I tell myself, 'I'm the bomb, the Koxa bomb!' I have the message 'go bigger', that everybody can go bigger – bigger in your life whatever you do and think. Always you can do more. That's my philosophy and, for me, it worked. For me, the world record means that my life makes sense."

Despite being the man to have surfed the biggest wave of all time in the record books, he does not boast riches. He was so short of funds in the aftermath of a moment that went viral that he struggled to make it back to Nazaré, among those he conjured up a deal with were a series of restaurants to feed him on a given day to help keep him out there. Big-wave surfing has made very few of the surfers wealthy.

Sérgio Cosme likes to refer to the Nazaré waves as a single entity – in his words, "big momma". Amid Koxa's PTSD, the rehabilitation, the doubts, the nerves, the battle with confidence in the water, the term was coined in the moment when it finally slotted into place for Koxa. When he jumped on the rope, Cosme asked him what he wanted; the Brazilian's reply was that he wanted "the big momma". Cosme explains: "It's a mythical wave, but he saw me and said, 'I want big momma.' I said, 'You realise you need to wait for that wave?' and he was like, 'No worries, I'll wait.'"

For one and a half hours, the pair bobbed in and out of the water waiting for the right swell, not catching a single wave in that time. When the "big momma" eventually came, they screamed over the roar of the waves and the jet-ski engine to work out which of three potential waves to go for. They opted for the second. Cosme towed him in to perfection, and looked over his shoulder as he rode the jet ski up and over the monster wave. The rest was now down to Koxa. With each rewatching, the wave looks bigger, Koxa cutting from top to bottom diagonally in a race to ensure he is not enveloped by the giant swathes of water behind him. These are the fine margins between a record-breaking wave and potential ignominy or hospitalisation.

When Cosme came to his rescue, Koxa was delirious in the water, screaming to his partner about the wave of his life as Cosme repeatedly shouted back "rescue, rescue!", all too aware of the volume of water and the size of waves still pounding down on them both.

"This is because we were in the worst place possible to take time to commemorate the biggest wave of his life," Cosme recalls. "Suddenly, I'm thinking this is going to fuck the jet ski and everything. He's on a big high, saying again this is the biggest wave of his life as he gets on my back and I'm like, 'Not now, let's get to the other side.' I was still concerned about our safety. I'd never seen something so big and never expected such a big wave."

Every big wave, every new record further cements Nazaré's status in the surfing world. The pair's double act brought them to New York City's Times Square on a trip with McNamara and Nazaré's mayor Walter Chicharro, where video of the feat was played out on the enormous electronic billboards, a picture of which still hangs on the wall in Chicharro's office. Despite Cosme's part in it, the record books don't credit him. Instead, the record solely states the name of Koxa, who graciously says, "It is both [of] ours. Without Sérgio, I'm not on the wave." Of course, the rest of his peers know his vital role in it, but wider recognition escapes him, all the various viral clips of the epic venture on the internet only referring to Koxa. Much like Cosme's plethora of rescues, it isn't always about the recognition – instead, he is safe in the knowledge of how crucial his role is.

26

PUTTING NAZARÉ ON THE MAP

The mayor

Surf spots have a propensity to go in and out of fashion. Some remain constants, such as Mavericks in northern California or Bells Beach in Victoria, Australia. But depite being a relative upstart within that world, Nazaré is the "it" destination for big-wave surfing in Europe and, those in the town would argue, in the world.

The sheer volume of all comers hailing from Braunton to Brazil attests to that. The ultimate marketer of its future is the wave itself. There is no other wall of water that's yet been uncovered that is as consistently big.

But central to keeping Nazaré on the map as the season ticks to an end and the focus moves to the one to come is Walter Chicharro. As the town's mayor, he effectively calls the shots in Nazaré. He is sitting behind his desk at the town hall. The wall in front of him is taken up entirely by a photograph, with the lighthouse in the foreground, of Nuno "Stru" Figueiredo breaking the kitesurfing world record back in 2017. On the desk behind, neatly dotted over the wall, are photographs of him standing with Andrew Cotton at the Big Wave Surf Awards, the Times Square snap celebrating Koxa's world-record big wave surfed in 2017, and one with Pope Francis in Rome, just two days before the town's 2018 Tow Surfing Challenge. In it, the Pope is blessing a small statue – one of three similar pieces – central to the religious sect of Nazaré; one remains with the Pope, another with a local priest in Nazaré and the third in the mayor's office.

Religion is at the very heartbeat of Nazaré, from the chapels dotted around the town to the street names – even to the ships used by the fishermen. Legend has it that the name Nazaré comes from a statue of the Virgin Mary that was brought from Nazareth to Merida, Spain, by a Greek monk in the fourth century. Supposedly, four centuries later, King Rodrigo, the Visigoth ruler who had been defeated by Christian forces, and Friar Romano fled with the statue. Before his death, Romano hid the statue inside a grotto in the promontory of Sitio, where it lay undiscovered until shepherds stumbled across it in the twelfth century.

The story gets rather fanciful with the introduction of the commander of the castle of Porto de Mos, some 20 miles away, who was hunting one day in 1182. While he was chasing a deer at pace on horseback, the deer fell over the edge of the clifftop. The commander, Dom Fuas Roupinho, called for the Virgin of Nazaré in prayer, and his horse stopped in an instant. He built a memory chapel in the spot as a tribute, and it still stands in the top left-hand point of Sitio, with the main beach of the town just behind it. On the other side of Sitio is the Sanctuary of Our Lady of Nazareth, built in 1377 under the orders of King Ferdinand to meet the increasing demand of pilgrims to the town.

Chicharro is apologetic for being late – a meeting to decide next year's budget ran over. As always, surfing is central to any budgetary discussions, the most important facet to have put Nazaré centre stage above all other draws to the area. He understandably talks up the town and its wave as Portugal's biggest attraction, putting it on a par with the footballer Cristiano Ronaldo and ahead of port wine.

He proudly talks of how Facebook owner Mark Zuckerberg used the term "Project Nazaré" as the name for the company's augmented reality glasses. He's made contact with him on Facebook … and is still waiting to hear back.

This season coincides with the start of another four-year term as mayor, but the big-wave season began as Chicharro only just returned to full health, having been recently hospitalised with pneumonia. The mayoral elections took place while he was in his hospital bed, and yet he still won another term (which he says will be his last), despite being unable to deliver any final moments of campaigning. He is adamant the illness never got to a point where it was life-threatening, but that the episode was scary enough after the realisation that he was struggling to breathe.

He is the quintessential Mr Nazaré, born and brought up in the town. And although it was his predecessor who was the mayor when Garrett McNamara was first brought to this place, Chicharro has been central to both keeping the spotlight on his town and pushing forward the big-wave movement.

Like everyone in Nazaré, his life is indelibly linked to the water. He says his surname literally translates as "big horse mackerel" (a culinary favourite in the town) and, while his own working life originated in hospital sales, it is marine life that made him – he hails from a long line of Nazaré fishermen.

He never met his grandfather, who died on a ship while in Canada fishing for cod and had an earlier brush with death during the Second World War. While his grandfather was on board the boat *Terranova*, it was bombarded by German forces. He was presumed dead and his company sent a telegram to his wife, Chicharro's grandmother, letting her know that he was missing. Understandably, assuming her husband had passed, she adorned the traditional Nazaré mourning

NAZARÉ

dress of black from head to toe, and never heard any further word in the intervening weeks and then months.

Eight months later, she was hanging up the laundry one sunny morning when she spotted a man looking like her husband start coming down the street in front of her. Thinking she had seen a ghost, she promptly fainted. "And nine months after that, my mother was born," says Chicvharo, laughing at the plot twist of a much-told family story. "And I have to say that I exist because the Germans bombarded a Portuguese vessel where my grandfather was." That his grandfather's life would eventually be ended by another marine tragedy while fishing for cod is sadly not a new phenomenon to Nazaré. "All of us from Nazaré have some tragedy from the sea in our families' history," says its mayor of the familiar tale for those living in and around the town.

Growing up, Chicharro's mother ran a lodging for summer tourists, which he says is the reason for his good English, which is delivered with a Portuguese lilt. He remembers the town bustling with people throughout the summer months and then being virtually deserted of any outsiders as soon as the colder, wetter, darker autumn days crept in. The only other notable exceptions were perhaps Easter and New Year's Eve, both standout events on the Nazaré calendar.

Now he says proudly there are tourists 12 months of the year. The economic boost to the town has not gone unnoticed. More restaurants are popping up, new roads and car parks are being laid to meet the demand of visitors, and an industrial park has been built from scratch, with an increasing number of big businesses coming on board. He proudly points to the number of people using the funicular from town up to Sitio and the gateway to the wave.

In 2013, visitor numbers were at 600,000 per year. Within six years, that number had doubled, he claims, higher than a similar

208

attraction in the capital, Lisbon. With an increasing number of nationalities visiting the town – as attested to by the visitors' book at the lighthouse library – as he says, "Nazaré is now a global brand."

It is his abiding mission to keep it that way. While Nazaré was gaining popularity before his initial election in October 2013, his constant aim is to expand its reach. His philosophy is, "We have to show the world we're a very powerful product." The increasing numbers to the town suggest his approach is working. As well as his constant push to communicate the message of Nazaré, another achievement reached on his watch was to bring the World Surf League to the town in the shape of the Tow Surfing Challenge. And the clock is ticking for the second edition of the contest in the 2021–22 season. The event has simply helped add further credence to what the big-wave surfers are doing, beyond the death-defying clips they put up on their own social media feeds.

There is no denying that the "discovery" of the Nazaré wave has totally altered the shape of the town. "The structure of the local economy has changed," says its mayor. "Some companies have been attracted here because of the global awareness made by the wave. Tourism is still the main industry here, but we needed to change from three months in the summer to have a year-round capacity to host and entertain and show the world what Nazaré has to offer. Now we've gone from quite a renowned Portuguese and European brand to a global brand."

So where would Nazaré be without the uncovering of the big waves by McNamara and the town hall team? Its main politician argues it would still be a big summer tourist spot rich in history and its ongoing connection to the sea. But he admits the area would not have what he calls "the kind of power and success" the wave has given it. One of the main things that's changed, in his view, is the way that brands look at Nazaré. Initially, there was a struggle to get many, if any, sponsors to sign up to events there. Now it seems to him like they are queuing up. In the harbour, Mercedes has its own lounge dedicated to entertaining clients and hosting big events. Red Bull and Yuki Brand have their own notable headquarters in the harbour too. On competition days, such as those organised in conjunction with the World Surf League, a slew of other sponsor names emerge. For Chicharro, the breakthrough was the 2018 visit to Times Square when Koxa's record-breaking wave was emblazoned on the big screens. It was essentially global proof and acceptance to the mayor that his strategy was the right one.

During his tenure, the lighthouse has been transformed into a makeshift museum. Inside is a room explaining how the canyon works to create the monstrous waves. In two other rooms stand a variety of beaten-up surfboards belonging to the surfers in Nazaré's waters, each briefly telling their own tale. Inside the last room of the lighthouse is housed a display showing video footage of the big waves in action, filmed as a part of a project. Up some heavily worn-down steps – unsurprising for a building dating back to 1577 – is the roof of the lighthouse, from which people can watch the waves. Entry inside is just a euro. But when the first teams entered it to use as their base for big-wave surfing a decade or so ago, the smell was putrid, the space filled throughout with fishing nets that had been discarded there for years on end; their removal was eye-watering, back-breaking work.

On the rooftop, a faded yellow line with the request for people not to cross it is the only safety barrier. A crumbling black outer wall of just two feet is the gateway to a deep and dangerous drop below. In fact, there are more signs advising against smoking at this spot than the potential perils of getting too close to the edge. But on the big days, when the crowds truly gather, the roof is shut to the public, kept clear for spotters, teams, officials and the media. Chicharro is an occasional visitor on such days, if work commitments allow.

The lighthouse and the clifftop as a whole are in desperate need of restoration and modernisation – Nazaré has not quite moved with the times as yet. Part of that is because strict rules from the Portuguese environmental agency effectively block any plans – for the time being, at least – for a viewing platform. Lengthy discussions have also been held about a total renovation for the lighthouse, which will have to come at some stage. The road is also in need of restoration, although agreement is in place of a 50–50 deal between the Portuguese government and the locality to resurface it. In Nazaré, as the mayor puts it, "things take a lot of time". Nothing moves particularly quickly, often to the chagrin of its surfing winter inhabitants.

Despite that, Chicharro says he has good relations with all the town's surfers and, having never surfed the waves himself, he is part in awe of them and part bemused by their antics, like much of the rest of the town.

"I would say we look upon the surfers as crazy," he says. "We know they haven't got all the screws in their head! Until the harbour was built here in the eighties, there were a lot of people dying in the seas. The mix of fishermen and surfers is quite interesting because, at the end of the day, they face the same dangers and problems. They both depend on the seas: one needs to catch the fish, the others need to catch the waves. At the start, I think there was some sort of surprise: 'What the hell are these guys doing?' Nowadays, the population knows them. They're popular and recognised by the people, and we see them as one of us. We see them as our brothers, our citizens. They live in the midst of us all and they move from being strangers to our common and fellow citizens."

In addition to pushing the Nazaré name, his other main goal is keeping the surfers safe. Tragedy, which would undoubtedly have a negative impact on the global brand, never seems that far away when he ponders the surfers' daily activities, and it is something that plays on his mind as the town's mayor. He points out how the town hall now employs lifeguards on north beach, tractors and others to pull stricken jet skis to safety. They liaise with the fire department, police and the sea captain to control the public. He is trying to get national government backing to build a small hospital container on the beach, to be used for the big days. Away from the beach, the surfers have access to the gym at CAR Surf (the high-performance hub), and also the town's swimming pool, with diving courses offered to aid the surfers. "Our main worry is that they come back to the harbour safe and sound while trying to get the rides of their life." Up until now, they always have – despite some hideously close calls.

27

MR FIX-IT

Lino Bogalho

It's universally agreed that, if you have a problem in the town – however big or small – Lino Bogalho is the man to call. He's the surfing community's – and the town's – Mr Fix-it, often referred to as "El Patron" by the surfers.

He can seemingly hire out any equipment, track down the smallest screw required to fix a jet ski, or erect a custom-built warehouse from scratch. And if not, he knows someone who can. No job is too small to bother him nor too large to solve. As he sips on a cold Sagres beer on Nazaré's main waterfront, he claims it isn't uncommon for him to receive a call from a troubled surfer at three or four in the morning and, at times, it feels like he has a hand in everything that plays out in the water.

His main business is Nazaré Water Fun, which has a shop on the town's main beach waterfront but also runs dolphin tours and rents out jet skis and land buggies. Spend any time in Nazaré, and you will regularly see him darting around on his scooter, liaising with surfers at the harbour one minute, directing operations with as many as five radios from the roof of the fort the next. He likes to think that no one has spent more hours on top of the lighthouse pacing around as the spectacle unfolds beneath him. Ross Clarke-Jones, an Australian and one of the early big-wave surfers in Nazaré, likes to say there are plenty of ocean legends in the town but that Bogalho is the only "land legend". And it's hard to avoid Nazaré Water Fun. Business is clearly booming – the brand is omnipresent, with advertising hoardings dotted all over the town.

Squat and barrel-chested, sporting a beard with plenty of flecks of grey, he is rarely if ever out of shorts – be that in the depths of winter or height of summer, and often head to toe in Red Bull Racing gear, which is among the items he sells from his shop.

He never intended to get involved in the waves. To this day, he is adamant he has not once set foot on a surfboard. His friend Garrett McNamara regularly tries to lure him out on one, and the answer is always the same: a definitive no. But he is passionate about the water and has been from day one, although he stumbled into it by default. He only meant to help out for a week when McNamara and the town hall team first assembled. Well over a decade on, he is still involved – and far more extensively than when it all began.

It all started with a jet ski. More precisely, his own – a Sea-Doo 250 horsepower, which was one of the few in town at that time powerful enough to deal with the big water. He lent the machine to the town hall for its mission to crack the big waves with McNamara and thereby make Nazaré famous.

The then mayor had given permission for the big-wave project, but not the finances to buy a jet ski. The first watercraft, which Cotton was driving at the time, flipped and got lost in the white water despite their best endeavours to relocate it. The police found it at four in the morning when it emerged, completely demolished, on the other side of the lighthouse. So Bogalho provided his.

This time, McNamara, knocked down by a wave, was unspotted by those on the lighthouse and in the water and was spat out a mile down north beach. It meant an exhausting and lengthy walk back up the beach. So, to save time and energy in future, Bogalho brought the first of his buggies to the beach for the next day to transport surfers and boards alike as and when required. He wasn't paid for the additional help or equipment; McNamara's then girlfriend, now wife Nicole took him aside to ask him why on Earth he was doing it.

The truth was that he'd already been bitten by the big-wave bug, just like those in the water. He knew it was a risk to be ploughing his time and money into this, but he also believed in the project from the outset and had a passion for it. Back then, it was, he says, like a small, tight-knit family.

Year on year from 2010, things slowly built up. Each year, beginning in October and packing up at the end of March, he served this small big-wave community. Then, at the end of the third winter season, he decided *not* to pack up and instead looked into expanding into the summer market.

So he first bought a 6-metre rib boat for tourists he named *Guilhim* after the rock in front of the lighthouse – the one the surfers do their utmost to avoid, and where Cotton found himself caught up earlier in the 2021–22 season. That then spawned more jet skis, and then he was on to building warehouses for the likes of Mercedes and Red Bull, the ones that now adorn the harbour alongside the fishing vessels. So much has the business bloomed that he now employs seven permanent members of staff year-round and 35 in the summer. It is not uncommon in the summer for the dolphin-watching boat to go out on four fully booked trips daily. Sometimes his daughter works with him, but mostly she is studying marine biology at Portsmouth University in the UK. At times, business is so full on – too full on – that he dreams of packing up and retiring to Africa. But friends and family tell him he is so attached to being a Mr Fix-it and problem-solving that, within two weeks, he would get bored, want to pack up and get back to the madness of it all. He is inclined to agree.

Amid the current chaos of this season, he likes to don rose-tinted spectacles and hark back to the old days, when it was just a few of them. Obviously, the increased tourism has been good for business. But at the same time, it brings more fractiousness between the various surf rivals. It also equates to more people in the water, many of them not sufficiently adept to deal with the big waves. Those deemed too inexperienced, he simply turns down if they are looking to hire jet skis or other equipment for the day. His overriding concern is safety.

"From the first day, I said, 'One day, something really hard is going to happen, someone is going to die'," he says. "We always have to stay prepared and have a set-up to make the risk lower. I worry all the time about death."

He is always looking to improve – whether that is around safety or the Nazaré experience. He is working on a safety helmet for surfers in conjunction with those behind the Volvo Ocean Race – a round-the-world sailing challenge nearly half a century old – with a communication device built in. And for the entertainment side, he wants to drag big-wave surfing kicking and screaming into the twenty-first century, with more of a show for an ever-growing audience. He looks to the transformative example of another event, the America's Cup, often referred to as the "Formula One of sailing", to make it all a more televisual experience, with people able to watch live from any number of cameras, and with graphics to boot.

For now, if they're not watching on the clifftop, the only way to view Nazaré's surfers is by logging on to the webpage praiadonortenazare.pt/live-cams/ that 24/7 has three cameras filming from the fort – one of the main beach, the other two the big waves on north beach – or else watching the online clips once the surfers eventually upload them.

28

SAFETY FIRST

Sebastian Steudtner

It is Nazaré's answer to Groundhog Day: Steudtner caught in the repetitive nature of the day-to-day, all aimed at getting back out on the water. Rather than acting as though he is trapped on some sort of non-stop treadmill, he seems to relish the challenge of his rehabilitation.

On a typical day, the alarm sounds at seven o'clock and he drinks warm lemon water and takes a little carnitine in order to kick-start his metabolism. By eight, he is in the local swimming pool, after which he eats a breakfast consisting of oats, almond milk, banana, chia seeds and two scoops of protein powder. A gym session follows between 11 a.m. and 2 p.m. – he's usually sharing the space with the local bodybuilders, against whom he is dwarfed – then a late lunch, rest, some work calls and emails followed by a cardio session, typically an assault bike or else a ski trainer, before an early dinner.

The daily plans are all laid out for him every week by his Serbian trainer. If it is repetitive, he doesn't complain. Instead, he is buoyed by a hopefully moveable, improvable target date, and all his work is aimed at speeding up his recovery to enable him to surf big waves before the season is out. Even if that doesn't prove possible, there is hope he can etch his name in the record books even without picking up a board. There is genuine excitement, even belief, that the monster wave he surfed in the preceding 2020–21 season has broken Koxa's 80-foot world record.

Even without the record and out of the water, his mark is indelibly felt in the community each day. There are those in it who owe their lives to Steudtner, not that he would ever name names. He does at least let slip that the first person he saved from possible death in Nazaré didn't even thank him afterwards. He has perhaps done more than anybody to improve safety and diminish the perilousness of such a pastime for him and others out in the ocean. At times, the battle to get safe in such an extreme sport can be a frustration – change does not come as quickly as it should or as he would like.

"We're so, so lucky no one has died until now," he says, the exasperation apparent in his strained voice. "I've had the most bizarre conversations with people about it. They all agree someone will die and more needs to be done safety-wise. But when the time comes to do something more, people are like, 'It's not my responsibility.' It does frustrate, and I see it as a responsibility. I have to do it. A death could happen so easily with the amount of jet skis in the water. If a jet ski hits you in the head, that's you done." He can reel off the close shaves, one of the more vivid memories being seeing a jet ski fully out of control and leaping from left to right at high speed. Had its trajectory been just a little straighter, it would have hit a surfer bobbing up and down in the water square on the head "Watching just that moment," he says, "it's amazing no one has died."

The prospect of death perpetually overhangs those in Nazaré, even on innocuous days. It began first with the sense of unknown in the early days, and now the dangers are amplified because of the added volume of people in the water – the plethora of jet skis and visiting surfers who are not as adept as they should be for such enormous waves.

When Steudtner first arrived, he was similarly ill-prepared, like most Nazaré newcomers, but he has changed that, season upon season, in an attempt to bring safety standards up to the twenty-first century.

Central to that has been Nuno Oliveira, Nazaré born and bred and a trained ship captain, who spent five months at sea in his career, then said to himself, "Fuck this!" and realised it wasn't the job for him. Instead, for a decade he served as a lifeguard on the town's main beach when the summer holidaymaking hordes invaded the town.

Some lifeguards can have a lifetime of work without tragedy and trauma troubling their watch. For some reason, his shifts were known in local lifeguarding circles for regularly attracting the drama, though that was not of his own making. Different moments still stick in his brain – trying to resuscitate a man in front of his family and being unable to bring him back to life is the sort of thing that is forever etched on his mind. It is the often mild-looking incidents on that main beach – rather than round the coast on north beach, with the big-wave surfers – that are what he calls the ugliest of his lifeguarding experience.

And yet he has still been on watch for many of what could have been the dark days of the big-wave community, the surfers' near-death moments: for Alex Botelho and Maya Gabeira in their respective hours of need. He still shakes his head in disbelief that Botelho survived, going five minutes without breathing. "Most people would have died three times over already – the guy's just a beast to survive that when all the signs are that he's already finding a room up there," he says as he looks up to the skies.

Fittingly, he says this sitting and talking outside the church atop Sitio as day turns to night. Despite not being religious himself, Oliveira notes how locals and surfers alike talk of a celestial being watching out over them. "We always say that the Holy Mother of Nazaré has been doing such an amazing job keeping them safe. Take Andrew Cotton this season, floating around in the rocks – and during that time, not one set of waves came and hit him. So she does a good job to protect them. There are so many things that can happen. You can be hit by a board, jet ski, the blast of a wave can break you. At least until now, no one has died, and I hope that continues for a long time. It's such a risk. Most don't want to think about the risks because they think it will compromise performance; you need to be a bit crazy to do what they do."

Much like Steudtner's efforts, Oliveira's contributions mean that tragedies that might have already struck within the surfing community have been kept at bay. As well as playing a part in Botelho's rescue, he was also central to Gabeira staying alive all those years ago. There was a point he recalls even arguing with her surf and jet-ski partner Carlos Burle over whether mouth-to-mouth resuscitation was necessary on top of the compressions he was doing on her heart to revive her on the beach following her accident. Holding firm to his lifeguard experience, he ignored any doubters questioning his approach, steadfastly stuck to what he was doing and, as he summarises some years on, "The bottom line is: she's here."

Oliveira was lured into the big-wave surfing fold by Steudtner, in his early days with original surf partner Tom Butler. Unprepared, the German had asked what was needed safety-wise. They were the first to take on board the advice of having something as simple as a bottle of oxygen to hand on the beach. The change since then has been night and day. Now, on the big days, the beach has lifeguards (plural), a nurse, a doctor, an ambulance, and a tractor, the latter to help drag the stricken jet skis to safety.

For the 2020–21 season, Steudtner even set up a safety association with the town hall, much of it paid for out of his pocket, effectively employing Oliveira and another lifeguard, but it was disbanded the following season much to Steudtner's frustration. Now, Oliveira has walked away from the waves to focus on renovating a house and raising his young daughter. On the big days, he still feels a pull, missing the adrenaline rush in his life. There may come a time when the lure proves too much and he returns.

For Steudtner, safety remains a driving force. "It's so important. We're in a sport that has a lot of attention but sometimes no foundation. I have an eye for safety, but the bureaucracy around it I hate, because it's like being back in school." Much like with the technological advances he pursues, Steudtner likes to think outside the box with the company he keeps and how that can make him better equipped and, critically, safer. He is probably the truest out-and-out athlete of those at Nazaré, pushing both his physical and mental capabilities. In every situation, he looks to get better. Among those around him on the biggest days, when he's fit to surf, is former military doctor Axel Haber.

An ENT (ear, nose, throat) specialist in the German medical system, Haber crossed paths with Steudtner when Haber was also a German kitesurfer away from his day job. They got talking and Steudtner invited him to Portugal, where his fellow countryman slept on his couch during a stay back in October 2013. A keen surfer himself (although Haber will only surf north beach on its much smaller days), his medical background meant that he was interested to know what safety protocols were in place. "What's your plan when something goes wrong and the shit hits the fan?" was Haber's key question. A shrug of the shoulders and an uncertain glance were the first answers. The doctor's advice was that, at the very least, a neck brace, oxygen tank and IV drip were required on the beach. The pair surfed together, got along well and have worked with each other ever since – although Haber makes the point that he is a friend who just so happens to have medical skills and watches Steudtner surf, rather than being the on-call doctor to save those in danger.

While progress can be slow, safety is constantly evolving and improving. Steudtner's team was the first to carry a defibrillator on the beach, while the town hall has worked on improving things too. But in Haber's eyes, there has always been the inevitability that a death would one day come to Nazaré's waters.

"The only reason it hasn't happened is that the place has only been surfed for a few years until now. It's not a question of if, but when." Haber did an ENT course on sinus surgery and the surgeon in charge put up a picture of a forest, with the warning there was a tiger somewhere within the trees. "He said, 'If you go to the mountain often enough, you'll see the tiger.' Even if you do it 30 to 40 times safely, it does not mean the tiger is not there. If you walk it often enough, you will see the same for Nazaré."

Steudtner feels strongly that things are still not safe enough and that improvements still need to accelerate. The key to any major event in the water is to get the surfer in question to hospital as quickly as possible for the necessary treatment. And from past experience, Portugal's medical system does not fill him with confidence.

On one occasion, an elderly man had a heart attack while on the clifftop above the waves. Steudtner tried to do heart massage on him, but there was no defibrillator to hand and, by the time the ambulance arrived, the man was dead. Drawing parallels to the surfing, he said of another event: "Imagine if someone drowned. Guess how long it would take for an ambulance to get there? I helped save a guy on the motorway who was stabbed – road rage. His son was trying to calm him down while he had a knife stuck in his heart. Thankfully, it didn't go through but we had to look after the guy for 40 minutes until the ambulance came." Haber was on hand to speak him through it all over his phone.

Steudtner estimates he has spent close to a six-figure sum on trying to improve safety at Nazaré, but he is bemused rather than embittered by it. He makes the point he is one of the lucky few to have made good money from big-wave surfing. While others have to count their pennies, he has accrued more wealth than most. As a result, he says: "When I started to make money, I started to look ahead at what I could contribute to make the sport better. I realised quickly that if anything life-threatening happens, we did at least contribute to making things safer."

29

THE RISKS OF THE BIG WAVES

Most big-wave surfers have to be relatively blinkered to the dangers of their passion and profession for much of the time. It's like being a Formula One driver, fighter pilot, BASE jumper or any extreme sports athlete, for that matter. But bubbling under the surface, there is the memory of the waves gone wrong, and the devastating outcome.

With the poundings taken at Nazaré, there are the obvious hospitalisations and broken bones, this season merely adding to the list of walking wounded. But there are inevitably concussive impacts too, the effects of which are only being uncovered bit by bit in football, rugby and American football in recent years. Quite what the impact of the big waves might have in the mid- to long-term on those who surf them, no one entirely knows.

There are some in Nazaré who wear helmets of sorts in the water in a bid to add a layer of protection and hopefully negate the threat, and various innovations are being researched, aimed at improving headwear for the big-wave surfers of both the present and the future. Steudtner is among those who struggle with wearing a headguard of any kind – the sensation puts him off balance. Cotton occasionally wears one and is increasingly opening his eyes to the effect of repeated waves pounding on his head. He is among those to have read and recommended Derek Dunfee's excellent 2021 autobiography *Waking*

Up in the Sea, which shares the physical and mental effects that big waves have had on the American.

In December 2012, Dunfee suffered a monstrous wipeout at Cortes Bank in the North Pacific Ocean. He was found 10 minutes later, barely conscious, miles out to sea. Somehow, he survived. But while it was clearly the most traumatic and dramatic moment of his career, the concussions had already begun the year before. Those first severe concussions made him sensitive to any slight bang on his head. It was similar to vertigo – a foggy nausea which he would slip in and out of for weeks, sometimes months, on end. Even now, after the publication of his book, it is a challenging subject for him discuss, and we wait until he's having one of his good days to talk about his experiences in big waves.

"I committed my life to big-wave surfing and had a really amazing big-wave career," he says of the good. "I accomplished more than I dreamed of and I was fortunate to have the success I did, which made it easier to stop."

But the impact of the repeated head injuries means that he has to think hard on the simplest decisions in his daily life. If he's in a car, he can only be the driver, meaning even a taxi ride is a no go. The impact of being a passenger can cause him to get sick, and it impacts his mood and balance for hours afterwards. His right eye has a hard time focusing and only functions at about 30 per cent of its original capacity. He does daily online exercises to help improve his vision and spends time in a hyperbaric chamber at home every day in a bid to address the damage to the brain. These tube-like chambers provide 100 per cent oxygen, giving the body more oxygen than it could normally inhale thereby helping to fight bacteria, reduce inflammation and support the blood–brain barrier. The dark days have been incredibly dark. At points in the past, he would drink to the point that he no longer cared about his survival, or even surf big waves recklessly, thinking that might be the simplest way to end his life.

But things are looking brighter, and simply writing the book has helped, serving as a cathartic process for him. The hope is also that Dunfee may aid others having to go through what he did and facing some of the things he still does on a daily basis. Others he has crossed paths with during his 20 years as a big-wave surfer have increasingly reached out to him, sharing similar stories. But there is still almost an omertà, or silence, among many big-wave surfers over concussive effects, thanks to the bravado that goes with such an inherently dangerous pastime.

"I can understand why lots of big-wave surfers don't want to talk about it, because it's so difficult to let go of that ego. I've learned a lot about what's normal and what can be really bad. And I went through a lot of shit. There's not much talk about protocol and the amount of time to take [someone] out from the water after a big wipeout. Now, I don't ever tell people what to do or to wear helmets. If anything, I just explain what happened to me and certain things I did to get better. The biggest thing with that is time. If people have a bad concussion, it might take as long as a year or two to get better, rather than thinking of it being a month or two."

He knows he will never truly be OK, and the reality is he does not know what health issues there might be lying in wait for him. For now, his aspiration is simply to live a normal life, or at least a semblance of one. But he is not alone in dealing with the negative impact of the ocean.

Shawn Dollar's story is no less traumatic, its impact no less devastating. At his peak, he paddled into some of the biggest waves in history. His first world record was a 55-footer at Mavericks in 2010, his second a 61-footer at Cortes Bank, where Dunfee came so viciously unstuck a decade ago.

Surfing off the Californian coast one day back in 2015, Dollar made the near-fatal decision that day to go out by himself. Having taken a fall, he cracked his head at speed on a boulder the size of a car. He heard his neck breaking on impact, felt it and thinks he went in and out of consciousness in the immediate aftermath.

Amid the dazed and confused sensation, he knew he needed to remain conscious in order to have any chance of staying alive. "I knew if I'd gone unconscious, I would have drowned for sure." His other survival instinct was to move his body into a position to protect his spinal cord from further damage. "I broke a lot of other bones to fight the force but I protected the spinal cord. In any survival story, you either choose to fight or give up – and I didn't let myself give up." In excruciating pain, he was swept off his board at least a dozen times, and had to paddle through rocks and climb over further rocks on the beach to get back to where he had left his stuff, and from where he might be able to get help.

Slumped in a heap at the bottom of a beachside cliff, he dragged himself up. He then had to hitch a lift with a fellow surfer to hospital three hours away. He rang the hospital to pre-warn them that his neck was broken; their response was relatively nonchalant and disbelieving, bearing in mind the fact that he was able to pick up a phone and make the call.

From the moment doctors saw his first CT scan and evidence he had broken his neck in four places, the mood changed. "I remember the whole room went dead silent and no one would talk to me. I think the chances of surviving something like that intact were like a million to one."

Of all the injuries, the one to his head has perhaps been the hardest to overcome. He is well aware he may already have chronic traumatic encephalopathy (CTE), a disease linked to repeated blows to the head and one only diagnosed by an autopsy. "Right now, I feel like I've recovered and I'll live a long and healthy life, but I don't know – and every day I take supplements and make good choices for my body and brain. But sure, I worry about Alzheimer's and dementia, which are precursors to this [CTE]. I just have to hope."

Having gone through what he did, he wants people in Nazaré and other big-wave spots to wake up to the dangers of concussions in the monster breaks. He believes that is happening, with some using hyperbaric chambers for treatment after the event, and he is also pushing for more helmet use at the various big-wave spots around the planet. He has tested out all the latest models but has yet to find one that is properly comfortable. Still, the worry is there both for himself and others heading into the future.

"A lot of people don't learn about the issue until they're forced to. I hope no one else learns my hard messages. If I'd had that 10 years earlier, I reckon I would have been shit out of luck. But I worry about all of them now, a lot, in the big waves. It's very dangerous and there seem to be a lot of surfers not aware of the concussions. No one wants to hear the message; I wouldn't have heard it. But the main message is there are ways to recover if you're hurting. Be safer and more preventative. I don't want to stop these athletes. At the end of the day, people should be able to take risks."

The injuries that are seen are easy to quantify, like C.J. Macias's snapped arm and Cotton's broken back. Those that live under the surface, less so – as Dunfee and Dollar can now attest.

30

A TIGHTROPE WITH TRAGEDY

Sérgio Cosme

For those responsible for trying to keep death at bay, like Sérgio Cosme and Alemão de Maresias, the prospect overhangs and plagues them. They all agree – some won't say it, but it lingers in the mind – that tragedy can come at any point.

Cosme is in a small group of what are seen as constant lifesavers: elite jet-ski drivers, known more for their driving than their surfing. Another very capable surfer heralded more for his audacious jet-ski rescues is De Maresias, whose surname literally means "man of the sea". He had helped in the search for C.J. Macias earlier in the season.

At 52, his face is weather-beaten by a lifetime in the ocean, but it rarely comes without a warm smile. Having just gotten in from a morning helping his fellow Brazilian, the skimboarder Lucas Fink, he has his red wetsuit round his waist, is sipping on a small bottle of Sagres beer and eating a quickly rustled-up baguette filled with ham and a Spanish omelette before going out again this afternoon. The names of his children are tattooed on his left arm: Clara, 18, his daughter from his first marriage; Rene, 12; and eight-year-old Samuel. His greeting is always the *shaka*, a Hawaiian surfer tradition of a salute with his thumb and small finger extended on his right hand.

Before this season's start, he was invited to team up with Maya Gabeira and a then-fit Sebastian Steudtner, but turned it down, deciding against a season in Nazaré. Then Garrett McNamara called with a similar request and, despite his initial reluctance, he was persuaded into a change of heart by both McNamara and his own wife Renata to make the trip over to Portugal.

He has flown back and forth from his native Brazil all season. For him, the pleasure derived from towing someone into a big wave matches that of actually surfing it. In essence, he's content to play the sidekick role. "I'm pretty happy to be part of a team and make them happy. I say, 'Your happiness is my happiness.' You do have the same feeling towing a big wave or surfing it. When you find a good wave, it's pretty much like surfing it. You find the wave, put the guy or girl in the proper position, get the barrel, come off and make good. This is an amazing thing. You see the guy riding the wave, connecting and making it out perfectly. He's happy and I'm happy."

Like Cosme, he is slightly haunted – and it shows in his face as much as his words – about any potential black day on the horizon. There have been too many close calls to mention this season alone – from Cotty's dance with the rocks to Macias's season-ending, limb-twisting fall. But even before Marcio Freire's untimely, tragic death in the subsequent 2022–23 season, there have been darker days in seasons past. For De Maresias, the worst prior to that was as recent as 2020 with Alex Botelho, who still has issues with his lungs and the psychological effects of his darkest day in the water.

As De Maresias retells the story, tears well up in his eyes. He is still spooked by his struggle to rescue Botelho, only managing to do so on the fourth attempt, and dragging his limp body up on to the beach, where he had to be resuscitated.

Two or three times, he tried to scoop him out of the water but simply couldn't amid the ferocity of the white water. In the end, he ditched his jet ski and leapt into the water to try to get Botelho's face above the surface and enable him to breathe or at least not take on more water. As he remembers it, "I'm a specialist in towing and rescue but, in that moment, I was a surfer swimming with a friend. That was one of the heaviest moments of my life."

In the days afterwards, it ate away at his core. He recalls a perpetual feeling of sadness as well as a sense of discomfort reliving it and of entering the water again. Remembering the vivid sensation, he says, "My heart was so broken." But a day before flying back to Brazil and his return to the bosom of his family two weeks after the incident, he got word from Botelho. A close friend visiting him in hospital sent De Maresias a video message from the surfer. At the core was a message of thanks for saving his life. Botelho has struggled since, so too have those who witnessed the incident. As for De Maresias, he can talk about it now, but is still bothered by the unfairness of it happening to a surfer who is universally liked. "There are so many assholes in the water, but Alex is such a kind guy, an angel."

There are plenty, Sérgio Cosme included, who think the Botelho incident could have been avoided. Ahead of the competition and on the eve of Botelho's accident, Cosme had pushed unsuccessfully to have a grabber – effectively a second rescuer – on the back of his rescue jet ski. The thinking was that Cosme would have had additional safety back-up to assist should things go awry – as they did. Tellingly, at his insistence, he has had a grabber behind him for both of the Tow Surfing Challenges this season. While he is meticulous in his safety precautions, he argues that not all others are, and he is increasingly concerned about the lack of preparation by a lot of people entering the water, be that on paddle days or tow days.

"Sometimes people don't care about their lives," Cosme says. "If I don't care about my life, it means I will put your life in danger as well. You suddenly get some pumped-up guy who just wants to go in the water to get more likes or activity on social media. Normally, people say we're crazy guys for going to Nazaré on the big days. I may be crazy, but I do the sport I love; I train for this and every day focus for this. We're crazy – but good crazy."

He instead takes umbrage with the ones he calls the "stupid crazies", the ones who go out in the water unprepared and seemingly without a care in the world. It increasingly gets under Cosme's skin, both in terms of the risk to themselves and those around them, but also in the madness of such an undertaking.

Occurrences of this nature are becoming more frequent. Sometimes he shrugs his shoulders at such an approach, and other times he finds himself forced into at least having a quiet, polite word. Out of the water and back in the harbour, he may offer up: "Guys, I like your attitude to come here to challenge yourself, but where is your safety team? If you don't have one, then please don't be here." The reality is that if big-wave surfers don't bring safety teams, the onus falls on Cosme and De Maresias, and in so doing, limits the protection for *their* team and possibly the prospect of towing them into the wave of the day.

Cosme has gone into harm's way countless times in order to save others not on his team. On one occasion, he flipped his jet ski in an attempted rescue, costing him €1,500 in repairs. And there are times he's done rescues, similar to those of Steudtner, for which he is not even thanked, the assumption being he'll be on hand whatever the situation to scoop people out of the water and back to safety. But he is safe in the knowledge that lives have been saved in Nazaré because of him. Asked if he has saved any lives, he admits: "In my opinion, I think yes. In God's opinion, almost for sure yes. I want to believe that for many people I was there to take them out. But it's not just me. The other guys on the jet skis are no different … just the same as me."

His own skill sets are both a blessing and a curse. When he undertook a course to become a lifeguard, his instructor said to him he would be a lifeguard his entire life. At the time, he didn't quite understand the message. This winter, the true realisation of that message only just properly sank in. Watching one guy go out in the water on his own near a rip current, Cosme decided to stay at the water's edge for 20 minutes until he was assured the guy in question was out of the water and back in a safe position. At that point, it dawned on him what the instructor had meant, and today safety is his biggest priority in Nazaré. As he puts it, "I'm concerned about safety every second, every hour."

That concern starts the moment he sees a big swell on the forecast. His own internal questions and nerves kick in. Once out in the water, his own team are the number-one priority for him, although not ever to the detriment of another life, his eyes always darting over the water to see others who are potentially in danger, in particular those with less experience in the Nazaré wave.

On the jet ski, he has to have a 360-degree view of the waters around him. If things aren't quite to his liking, it begins to make him feel uneasy in his seat. "If I don't feel everyone is safe, then I start to feel concerned for everyone. This is me and probably why they call me the guardian angel. You cannot forget someone's life just because they're not in your team."

It is why, at the end of the day on the return to the harbour, the first feeling for him is always one of relief rather than elation at a good day, a mission accomplished with no life lost or, for the most part, no one seriously injured. "Even if we come back with a broken arm, it's relief because we're alive and at home, and we just need to be grateful at the end of the day."

31

THE SECOND TOW SURFING CHALLENGE

Andrew Cotton

The negative impact of the Tow Surfing Challenge in December 2021, on the eve of which Andrew Cotton ended up by the rocks, is still there, albeit in the back of his mind, the irritation of how it played out and what he might have done differently still marinating in his thoughts. So quickly does the focus shift in Nazaré that there are always new opportunities and potentially even bigger waves. In seasons past, Cotton might have had a year to dwell on the rights and wrongs of his approach to the contest. But the knock-on effect of the Covid-impacted previous season means he has another stab at success with the second Tow Surfing Challenge in early February.

He has had weeks to ponder how he might approach the same stretch of water differently. Cosme is on board as a rescue driver, with his human grabber on the back in case things go markedly wrong, while also ensuring his shoulder, with its propensity to pop out of joint, stays in place on this occasion. And Steudtner is once again consigned to giving his insights from the commentary booth rather than dipping his toe in the water. For him and his ailing foot, the contest is still too soon to risk it. He's close to fully fit, but not close enough to push the boundaries just yet.

For Cotton, it is the chance to properly make amends. Still bothered by his own perceived failings in the previous Challenge in December, he ponders how best to make his mark two months on, coming to the conclusion as he stares at the waves on the morning of the competition that instead of surfing to his left and out to relatively safety as he had done last time around, he will turn right, towards the lighthouse and the rocks, where a few weeks earlier he had danced with death. It is a calculated risk for the reward of higher points from the judges. But it also one mitigated by the fact that the waters are less chaotic come competition time, with a more cohesive rescue operation for all those in the water. With Cosme and his grabber roaming the waters, Cotton finally concludes it's a risk worth taking.

Others tinker with their boards, jet skis and remaining equipment in the days leading up to the contest – as much to burn off the nervous anticipation as any methodical, practical preparation. In contrast, Cotton is only just flying into Lisbon Airport from a stint surfing in Mullaghmore. It is the sort of timeout from the hype of the contest build-up that he craves, one he describes as helping him get out of the bubble.

In Ireland, there are none of the egos, no surfers clambering for fame – it's just the purity of him and his mates battling with Mother Nature. In Nazaré, it can feel crowded, claustrophobic at points. Some lap up the crowds cheering from 100 to 200 feet above. At times, they can be treated like celebrities or superheroes, undertaking what is unthinkable for most normal folks. "I definitely don't feel like a superhero," he says of how he's perceived. "There are people that like the crowds, but I was kind of doing my thing before that, no? On Garrett's world record day, there was no one here."

Leaving his arrival so late from the stint in Ireland, he is not on site in time for the usual safety briefing by Paulo "Pitbull" Salvador, which is a prerequisite for any competition. But, as a veteran of Nazaré, Cotton is arguably the most well versed in the line-up in terms of what awaits the following morning.

It is not until 7 a.m. on the day of the competition that he and Will Skudin, his partner in the previous contest and back again from the States for a reunion, come face to face. But their time partnering each other in the last Tow Surfing Challenge compared to this one is like night and day. Whereas in December, they struggled to find any modicum of rhythm – Cotton in particular – this time, they immediately gel and click as a pairing, alternating equally between towing and surfing in the opening heat.

Turning right towards the rocks at high speed takes immeasurable bravery and, despite a heavy wipeout in his opening heat which requires him to take time out to recover his breath and his senses, Cotton keeps going for the same high-risk approach, wave after wave. Explaining his thinking, he says: "With the contests, they've been scoring the surfers that surf to the right higher, so I decided to focus on the rights. It's a bit of a sketchy move – you're going right towards the cliff and, if you lose a board, it's hard to get rescued. So, you're rolling the dice a bit, but it's a good time to do that in a competition when there's lots of safety. I suppose it's about wanting it. It's a commitment. If you're hesitant or worrying about injury, you're going to hurt yourself, kill someone or kill yourself. Everything else is just shut out."

This place is perpetually about rolling the dice. He does that by edging his board towards the waves that smash against the rocky cliffs on which the lighthouse stands, despite it going against his natural instincts for survival. Each time he turns right, he questions internally whether each wave is makeable, the same question resonating in his head: "What am I doing?" It is a constant internal battle. Everything in his mind is telling him to stop, but somehow, he just keeps going.

Some days, he can strike out with this approach; on this occasion, it is the opposite outcome. He ends the day with a podium finish in third overall in the individual standings, with just Lucas "Chumbo" Chianca and the Australian Jamie Mitchell ahead of him, who has flown in from Hawaii where he lives with his family.

Cotton's goal may have started with victory in mind, yet he is still stoked by the outcome in the aftermath. The disappointment following the December competition has finally been erased from his mind. "The last time I was like, 'Fuck, this is embarrassing.' I felt like I'd let myself down massively, like an imposter and a fraud. So it was nice to have some good waves. You still want to win it but I was behind Chumbo and Jamie Mitchell. Chumbo's the best guy in the world and Jamie's a big-wave champion, so that's a respectable third. Of course, you want to beat those guys and, in a heat, anything's possible."

While others celebrate late into the night, high on the euphoria of another notable Nazaré day, Cotton spends the evening packing up once more to fly back home to Devon. Now into mid-February, there is not yet the sense that he can finally rest on his laurels at another season done, another season survived. He knows he can't truly declare this campaign finally over, and gear up for a spring and summer of preparation. "Four days later, a massive swell can come in, so it's not like it's job done. It's going to be a busy few weeks. There are always more swells. I think if you were like any other sort of other job or athlete, you'd have a proper schedule: 'On these dates, I can't work.' But I can't say that to the Atlantic, can I?"

There is relief not to have joined the walking wounded for another busy day at the Lisbon hospitals, roughly one and a half hours from Nazaré, that treat the surfers. On the opening wave of the entire competition, Justine Dupont's season is over – she breaks her ankle. Changing her direction on a wave to dodge the wakes from two jet skis, the Frenchwoman can't ride out the wave and gets enveloped in white water. Underwater, her foot somehow gets stuck in the straps that hold her on to the board in competition. She feels and hears a crack and a pop, and knows immediately something is majorly wrong. Returning to the harbour, she just sits on the wooden walkway, being consoled by her team – a lost soul stunned more seemingly by the season's end than the actual injury.

Dupont's first instinct is to bemoan missing out on competing with a new partner –one of the sport's rising stars, Tony Laureano – and to apologise for the subsequent impact on him in the contest. That is quickly followed by the realisation that the season is well and truly over.

The day is bookended by hospitalisations. For Jamie Mitchell, from the highs of vying with Chianca for the win, it ends disastrously on the very last wave of his second heat. Pushing himself to the limit and beyond, he decides to risk it all to win outright. After he turns into a wave, it goes horribly wrong and he gets utterly pounded. The first hope is he is simply winded – he's certainly left breathless – by the impact, but as he is carried back to the harbour face down on a jet ski, he's almost lifeless. One of three people hospitalised that day – Portuguese surfer Antonio Silva also suffers a heavy concussion (along with Dupont's break) – the scans later show Mitchell has a compression to the back, an L3 injury to Cotton's L2. But it is, the Briton says, "a very similar sort of injury".

For Cotton, Mitchell and all those in the field, there is a pay day of $3,000 each for taking part. The winners of the team award and most committed surfer award pocket another $10,000 – not necessarily the biggest payday given the high stakes involved – and there is $9,000 for both the best male and female performance. With Mitchell left learning to walk again, stranded in Nazaré and unable to go back to his family in the United States – albeit temporarily – Cotton is among those left pondering what exactly the point of it all is, despite his own good showing. His personal delight at a successful competition is partly countered by a frustration at the risk-reward imbalance.

"There were three people hospitalised out of the field – that's a pretty high percentage [from 18 entrants]. It just shows how dangerous it is, and that's not reflected in the money or sponsorship. It's a bit of a joke. If you come third or you come last or you end up in hospital, you get $3,000. You're using your own equipment and fuel. I've written off my ski before in a contest and none of it really makes financial sense. Jamie risked it all and broke his fucking back. That's a year out, that's a fucking nightmare. If he'd won, he'd have got nearly $10,000, but I know that's not why we do it. But you can't help wonder: is it worth it?"

He has asked himself that question countless times, and yet the answer he always comes back to is still the same – yes. He suspects a day will eventually come when the answer is no longer in the affirmative. But that isn't now. On this occasion, he is not left to count the cost – financially or physically – but others are.

32

A WOMAN'S WORLD

Maya Gabeira

A season that had promised continuity at the outset has provided anything but. Gabeira has found herself bouncing from one surf partner to another. At the start of the season, it was Sebastian Steudtner, whose campaign was ended on his opening wave. The surfing marriage with Eric Rebiere was short-lived before an amicable parting in the waves. And then Pierre Rollet found himself in the back of an ambulance at the start of the year.

Gabeira could be forgiven – her various partners too – for thinking her season is cursed. But always the optimist, she believes she has finally stumbled upon a winning partnership with another partner in crime. This time it is the Frenchman Pierre Caley, who describes himself as "half lazy, half crazy", the latter half a prerequisite for Nazaré. Just simply being in the line-up for the second Tow Surfing Challenge he will later list as the highlight of his entire year. He had previously teamed up with Gabeira on the day Rollet was hospitalised.

On the first wave of the day, Gabeira's main rival, Justine Dupont, is already out of contention, the competition and the rest of the season with that broken foot. But Gabeira still has the French-Brazilian Michelle des Bouillons to beat in a straight head-to-head for the women's award. Placed in separate heats, they vie with each other for the top gong.

In an inauspicious start to her own opening heat, Gabeira's jet ski is almost immediately knocked out of action, while she is thrown off her surfboard and hurled around in the washing-machine effect of the water, her limbs flung asunder. Things could hardly have gotten off to a worse possible start, but importantly, her body remains intact to try again. It has echoes of the woeful start in the water for her and Rollet just a few weeks back. Even before she is rescued, her thoughts turn to her own competition hopes and the sense, in her mind, "I've fucked my chance." She allows herself a quick cry out the back of the waves, away from prying eyes. But after deflating her vest, which had automatically puffed up in the pounding, and realising there are no new injuries, she composes herself and gets ready to go again.

Before the heat is over, she finds a good wave and sets up a solid marker to put her at the top of the female competition. A first Tow Surfing Challenge win looks hers, as Des Bouillons endures struggles of her own with partner Ian Cosenza in her two heats. But adding a twist to the competition on her last wave of her second heat, Des Bouillons catches her best wave of the day, one that catapults her up and ahead of Gabeira – a successful final throw of the dice – and ensures the Brazilian needs a strong performance in her final heat.

The pressure, nerves and expectation are getting to her, despite all her experience and her status as a world record holder. In some ways, that pressure is further amplified with Dupont out of the competition and Gabeira now the expected favourite. In the aftermath, she will talk about hating that pressure with a vengeance, but, in a warped way, she loves it too.

She makes no secret of the fact that she has never liked to feel rushed at Nazaré – that's when accidents happen – but this time she is, and she has no choice but to respond with immediate effect. As it stands, with the clock ticking dangerously close to the competition's denouement, she does not have the sufficient points total to beat Des Bouillons. It looks like another chance has gone begging. "You start getting scared of failing, that creeps in and the whole mind games kick in," she says, looking back on the topsy-turvy nature of the competition.

But the girl from Ipanema produces the wave when she needs it most. The Nazaré magic finally materialises when she is at her lowest ebb and, with it, she is catapulted past Des Bouillons to come away with the award. It is remarkably, she says, the first competition award of note of her career, and one that leaves her with the rare sensation of being lost for words. The aftermath will prove nothing more than a blur of memories.

She knows there is a slight asterisk to the win, with the absence of the injured two-time winner in Dupont, and, afterwards, she says she would have loved to have been able to compete against her for the win. Such a head-to-head will have to wait for another season and, in any case, it is a mere footnote to one of the best days of her entire career. "That was the first time I'd won a pro competition in the World Surf League, and I don't know if I'll ever win again." And the tears flow for a second time that day. The first time, tears of stress aboard the jet ski and her thinking her chance had vanished; this time, they are tears of pure, unadulterated joy. "I cried when I was told the score and I will always cherish that moment. It was an incredible experience and living all those emotions with Pierre that day." It ranks her tenth overall of all the competitors in the field – male or female. The smiling celebrations and euphoria of the moment turn to exhaustion as the exertions – physically and mentally – take their toll. "I'm so old for my first win," she says. "I didn't think it would happen. I never thought this would happen – it was a long path to get to this point."

Her victory comes with a $9,000 prize. As for the trophy, it initially takes pride of place at her home, a daily reminder of her success. But in time she will move it elsewhere, to the office of a new business she has long been plotting. Be Aya, set up in one of the unused warehouses at the harbour, will offer people the chance to experience Nazaré with her and her wider team during the course of the subsequent 2022–23 season. It will be the latest addition to her business empire, on top of her new sunscreen range, and yet she laughs at the premise of a widening operation. She shrugs her shoulders at any praise of her business acumen. To her, she is first and foremost a surfer, a contest win only cementing that.

33

FLARE-UPS

Nic von Rupp

Surfing is notoriously territorial. Localism features from Hawaii's famous surf break Jaws to California's Mavericks. Those with home advantage take precedence over visitors when it comes to the waves. Nazaré, in contrast, does not suffer from the same fate. In part, it is down to the fact that outsider Garrett McNamara was the first to surf the big days here, rather than any of the locals. It's also due to Nazaré's history in big-wave circles being barely a decade long – not enough time for tribalism to take hold. It is very much an international hub, with all comers from all destinations across the planet welcome.

Despite being the most local of the big-wave surfers, Von Rupp likes the lack of ownership – the theory being that it should make for a more harmonious existence. "Surfing being territorial – that's just the code, and the code isn't really implemented here. If you're in Hawaii and the best wave of the day comes, 100 per cent a Hawaiian will take it. It's the same in Tahiti. Culture-wise, it's deeper in places like Hawaii – Brazil too. That's how it is, that's the code. In Nazaré, I won't pull my local card. I'm pretty respectful. I believe in harmony; I'm not that greedy that I need to fuck someone over. I'll wait my turn."

Equally, he wants the respect back – both as a surfer and as a native of Portugal. People from all around the world come to the local waters he and his fellow Portuguese surfers and jet-ski riders, like Sérgio Cosme, call home. "I can't deal with people talking shit to me. I do feel like I at least deserve some respect," says Von Rupp.

Respect can sometimes be hard to attain at Nazaré. There are big egos pushing for their moment in the spotlight – whether that's about getting the biggest wave or claiming you already have. And there's always this sense of "my wave's bigger than yours" bubbling below the surface. It creates friction and fights both in the water and out. Slanging matches are not uncommon out on the surfboards and jet skis, in the quest for the best wave, and can blow up into physical dust-ups.

The battle of the egos has possibly been exacerbated in some quarters by the spotlight being on Nazaré more than ever. With HBO filming the excellent documentary series *100 Foot Wave*, everyone wants his or her moment in the spotlight. Von Rupp has been part of filming series three throughout the season.

"There's a lot of tension, as everyone wants to be famous, make money and be successful," he says. "People want a piece of it and, if they don't get it, they're pissed. It's a shitshow at times. You have to try to focus on yourself and not bother about anything else, because there's so much bullshit. I try to get on with everyone, and life's hard enough without the fights, but I won't take shit."

It's hard to imagine Von Rupp in a fight. He seems too affable for it. But he had a deeply rooted system of right and wrong instilled in him from a young age by his parents. If someone oversteps the mark, he's not afraid to raise an objection to it. It leads to the occasional run-in. There was a notable one this season, with a rival he prefers not to name.

He and his team had been vying for waves and performing the usual dance between jet ski and surfer, both in their own set-up and that of their rival teams. In one particular moment, his jet ski and that of a rival came precariously close to a high-speed run-in, the consequences of which could have been hugely damaging physically and financially. The guy in question angrily confronted Von Rupp in the immediate aftermath, as though the Portuguese surfer and his team were solely responsible for the near miss. Von Rupp tried to pacify the situation in the heat of the moment by suggesting they talk later that evening at the warehouses, when the dust had settled.

The surfer with which he had effectively butted heads in the water never showed. When their paths finally crossed, Von Rupp asked for the reason behind the no-show, wanting to get to the bottom of the spat and clear the air. Instead, the guy lost his temper in a flash, directing a barrage of invective Von Rupp's way.

The vitriol continued unabated, testing Von Rupp's patience. So to his non-Portuguese abuser he mentioned localism for the first time, querying what would have happened if Von Rupp had showed that level of disrespect in his rival's country and waters. The confrontation intensified before coming to a head in a physical altercation.

There was no shortage of onlookers, and no great surprise at the clash. In such a high-octane world, there are moments when things just explode. But they are quickly forgotten. Each season has its moments, each character has their blow-out – some, it has to be said, find themselves in the midst of the mêlées infinitely more regularly than others.

All scraps aside, the second Tow Surfing Challenge has come at a price for Von Rupp. He packs up after the contest, nursing damaged ribs from one particularly violent fall, the pain of which was initially anaesthetised by the adrenaline rush of victory for the team award with Chianca. The following day, he can't even lift his arm for a simple task like reaching for crockery from the kitchen cupboard or even cough without wincing in pain. His doctor diagnoses heavily bruised ribs and tells him under no circumstances should he return to the water for at least a month. With the ribs already weakened, he is warned another accident could mean a broken ribcage and/or a punctured lung.

Essentially, he has been told his season is over – time to focus on rehabilitation and rest before beginning the long build-up to the next season. But he is at least going out on a high, his final chapter a team victory in the Tow Surfing Challenge to go with the runners-up spot from the one in December.

There has been something freeing for both Von Rupp and Chianca with a temporarily new partner, a new outlook and even approach to the water. They have surfed the same waters from Nazaré to Hawaii, and partied together in those same locations in their younger days. Since the two are normally tied to Pedro Scooby and Kai Lenny, respectively, getting a rare chance to work as a team, says Von Rupp, has been "a guilty pleasure". But their collaboration came with the expectation of being the favourites to win.

"I wanted him to keep that title from last time so there was pressure to not let him down or let myself down. It was amazing to go with Chumbo. He's such an amazing surfer and we've kind of pushed each other for a long time. We're similar surfers, with the same drive and same vision of what we want to achieve. It's cool, as he's a beast and it releases my inner beast as well."

Following the competition, Von Rupp has a celebration meal for 20 people into the evening, and then the next day, a small dinner arranged back at his home. Bruised and battered, gone are the nights of wild celebrations into the early hours of the morning that he and Chianca might have had in the past.

34

AGAINST DOCTORS' ORDERS

Nic von Rupp

Nazaré never really leaves you, even when you're away. The lure of it has this inexplicable stranglehold over those that surf it, even those on the periphery. Nic von Rupp has come to accept that his season is over, so packs his bags and heads over to Barcelona for his girlfriend Matilde Reymão Nogueira's birthday, a rare opportunity for the pair of them to get away. These four days are Reymão's only free time between the start of the year and the end of June, amid all her filming commitments. It doubles as a holiday and, in theory, a point to mark the end of his latest big-wave chapter.

But while they're in Barcelona wining and dining with friends and seeing the city's sights, the charts show another gargantuan swell edging its way to the west coast of Europe. The early forecasting is once again that it could be the biggest of all time, although, as ever, with no guarantee it will live up to that expectation. The swell looks near perfect this time, coming from the north-west – creator of the biggest waves – and, while things can change between now and its arrival in Portugal, the sense of excitement begins to build for Von Rupp and others at the prospect of a monster day, possibly the last big one of the season. It means his mind starts to shift back to Nazaré, the thought of potentially defying his doctor's advice and thinking about one last go at the big waves despite the state of his ravaged body.

Eating away at him is the idea this could be that 100-foot day that's long been talked about and he won't be there to see it and surf it. But balanced with that is the impact it has on his relationship and everyday life. It reminds him of the fact that he'd hate to date a surfer, perpetually packing up as they do at the whim of the latest swell. So, conversation between boyfriend and girlfriend shifts to his need to get back home. There is no great objection from Reymão. "She gets it and we still had our full time in Barcelona. We're supportive of each other – with our busy schedules, if we weren't, it would be very complicated."

His planned return to Portugal coincides with two days before the swell hits, the timing such that the couple's Spanish holiday has not had to be curtailed, as others have in the past – even though his mind has occasionally been elsewhere for the latter part of the vacation. But on arrival back home, the advice a week and a half after the doctor signed him off for the season remains the same: still do not go back in the water. He plans to do it anyway, and tells himself if he straps himself up, he can still make the magic happen. The lure of the water when big waves are afoot can be that powerful, going against every sensibility, medical or otherwise.

"I can recover when I'm in my grave," he says, deadpan. "If I was walking and breathing, I had to be there. It could be one of the best days ever. It was no choice; it's the nature of my job. When the big swell comes, you've got to be ready."

The primary trick, says his doctor, is to not suffer another big fall. This is Von Rupp's aim, but it is hardly assured in such volatile water. Partly conscious of it, partly oblivious to it, his first wave of the day fails to totally live up to expectations and he cuts it short, nonchalantly tailing off to the side only to be scooped up by Chianca, once more his partner in the water.

Take two – his second wave of the day – is far less forgiving, giving him perhaps his biggest wipeout of the season and damaging his shoulder badly in the process. The speed is immense – taking him by surprise on the top of the board, the water not smooth enough, his fins underneath the surfboard struggling for grip and not giving him the necessary security as he skids over the surface. He wobbles, the balance begins to go, he recovers but his regaining of control is too short-lived before the wave closes on him and he has no choice but to effectively jump ship. But as he does so, it sucks him back in and he is completely annihilated by the force of the water. Chianca again swoops in quickly enough to rescue him from further danger, but the damage is done. Von Rupp is shaken up and needing to take time out.

After a moment catching his breath, with already bruised ribs and now one shoulder not functioning, he can only hold the rope behind the jet ski with one arm because of the pain from the new injury. Surely this is finally the end for his 2021–22 campaign? But on he goes and surfs wave after wave – grimacing in pain – from dawn till dusk. Taking stock of his new injury, the potential rehabilitation and repair can wait.

"I hurt my shoulder really badly, but I just kind of set my beast mode on," he says when back on shore. Even with the injured pair of ribs and the shoulder, he simply couldn't stop. It is an eye-catching sight, Von Rupp being towed holding the rope with just one hand, an impressive balancing act between glory and oblivion. Sometimes the strength of the tow is too much, the rope wrenched out of his hand. As dusk approaches, he is not afraid to admit he was counting down to the session and the season being over, the body battered, his now frail frame exhausted.

As it transpires, it isn't necessarily the biggest swell of the record books. The direction of the wind isn't quite perfect, denying the key first peak waves – but he argues it was still worth it for the rush, and some gargantuan waves were caught even with his body being in rack and ruin. It's not quite the day of days, but the waves have still topped out in the 70-foot range. It is possibly the biggest swell of the season, and that night, the surfers disappear to the town's various restaurants to mull over whether records might have been broken, to dissect who surfed what, the lines, the barrels, the wipeouts, the missed opportunities. For Von Rupp, the pain is immense, but worth every minute for the bombs he got. As for the records – not today.

On reflection, the overall feel of the day is different. The egos of which he and others have spoken dissipate, in part because of the sheer volume of huge waves – enough for everyone – and everyone comes out of the water happy and without any immediate hospitalisations. All in all, a good day in the water. They don't always end this way.

This time Von Rupp is officially done, whatever swells might still come, even the mythical ones in that 100-foot range. For him, there is no event to mark it, not even a clink of glasses in celebration. He is mentally and physically tired, the season having taken its toll once more. Initial hopes and plans to celebrate the day with his camera crew fall by the wayside. As day turns to night, and the warehouses at the harbour are shut up and people disperse, a little after 10 p.m. he finally shuts the boot on his car. It's time to drive down the coast, get back home and contemplate another season surfed and survived, as well as a lengthy rehabilitation programme. In the rest of the week, doctor appointments and physio sessions await, a late spring mending his body before the work begins over the winter to prepare for the next summer. It later transpires he has broken a small bone in his shoulder which will need three-and-a-half months of rehab.

For him, there is a sense of satisfaction at one of his best ever seasons – but still, there is also that endless gnawing sensation that he could have done better, not just in that particular session but in the season as a whole. It is the same ending felt along the length and breadth of Nazaré's surfing community. But he knows he will be back next season and many beyond that. Nazaré is ingrained in him more than any place he has ever surfed.

In this Mount Everest surfing, it is a climb with no finite ending. At school, it was always the dream. In the classroom, he would draw waves on his book and pine to become a professional surfer. His parents were supportive, but always reminded him that school had to come first. It's prepared Von Rupp for the day when it does end. There is that constant voice in the back of his head saying that his surfing career will one day be over, and there needs to be something more. His business skills mean he already has his own surf accessories company, and he is always looking on the horizon for new ventures.

But he argues his peak as a surfer has not yet come. Some are still at the top of their sport in their forties, even their fifties, while Von Rupp is in his early thirties. Whether he will be one of the old timers still mixing it in the big breaks, he has no idea. There is nothing he wants more than a day in the ocean. The pull is twofold: one, to ride the biggest wave of his life, and two, to stay alive. It's a constant balance between one and the other.

"There's stuff that people don't do because they're afraid of dying. Fuck, if I want to make history right now and be the most famous guy in Nazaré and perform like no one has, I'll pull into a giant barrel. You pull that off, it's the peak of your career." He pauses to reflect the machinations of such an undertaking. "You need the balls to do it and the skill and the knowledge. People would expect Chumbo, Scooby, Sebastian, me to maybe do it – but the risk, man. Fuck, the risk. Fuck! I want to live. Maybe I'll feel it one day and the right wave comes along. But it's a thin line. It's looking death straight in the eye. If you're under for two waves, it's life or death – that's a solid minute and a half." That might not seem like a lot, but it's a hell of a lot when you take into consideration you've had all the breath knocked out of you before that, and you're being flipped around in the currents not knowing which way is up or down. It is a relentless tightrope walk; the goal to ride big waves and come out in one piece. For another season, he has done just that.

35

THE COMEBACK KING

Sebastian Steudtner

No one season is the same, but with 2021 having long since turned into 2022 and this campaign meandering towards its final throes, Steudtner has come to accept that the single, bone-breaking wave that injured him might summarise his entire campaign.

His work rate has been non-stop in his quest to get back, following all the guidelines for his rehabilitation, from weights to pool work to dietary requirements, and well beyond. He's buried his body in training alongside the local Portuguese bodybuilders, and he's stuck to the stringent dietary plan laid out for him by his personal trainer to the letter of the law, cutting out the carbs, leaving his body as lean as possible for an impending point of return, whenever that might be. But as the days of the season tick on and January becomes February, the big swells appear to be diminishing and, with them, his chances of a return.

For a standard 20- to 30-foot day, which are in abundance in Nazaré throughout the winter months, it isn't really worth the risk when his foot is not fully repaired. And even as he thinks and says out loud that the season is likely over before it has even got going, and his focus should shift to the next one, in the back of his mind there is one potential caveat … if a truly big swell comes, it may just be worth taking a chance.

As a consequence, he is perpetually checking things over, scrolling across the forecasts to see what might lie on the horizon in a week or two rather than pack up and leave Nazaré for home. And then signs of the swell come in the third weekend in February, the one where Von Rupp hotfoots it back from Barcelona only to injure himself yet again, ending his season.

With all his experience, Steudtner knows better than most not to get carried away in the potential excitement of the prospect ahead. And yet this one seems different. Initial reports weighing up its size and wind direction suggest this could be a moment to risk making a return for. Steudtner increasingly begins to ponder whether it may be possible to get back out in the water. He knows it is a risky decision with regards to his foot, having worked so hard to get it nearly right. But one could argue the greater risk in such conditions is instead to his life. Having not surfed a single wave of any size since October, it is bold to throw himself into waves of that magnitude. Plus, much of his equipment, which has sat idle with him injured – the surfboards, the jet skis, the radios – is not even ready and needs dusting off.

Like any decision he makes, it is methodical, every step of it clearly thought through and talked through. The first point of contact is a call to his surgeon. There is only one proper question, and that is whether he risks damaging the foot further if he takes to the waves. The surgeon reassures him that structure-wise, there is no risk; it is simply a matter of whether he can cope with the pain it will inflict. So, he is left to ponder what the pain will be, whether he can handle it and if it will hold him back at the business end of a wave. As he puts it, "You have to be 100 per cent confident and can't have any doubts going into a wave like that."

The advice on a Monday morning from his physiotherapist is much the same as that of the surgeon, so he takes to the waves – albeit smaller ones topping out at about 15 feet – for the first time in four months. It is a homecoming of sorts, with Steudtner back in the place where he feels most comfortable. But for all the usual bravado, there is a tentativeness as he plants his feet, understandable after so long off the board and out of waves of any size.

When he returns to the physio the following day, the foot is badly swollen, reacting to having been pushed in a way to which it has grown unaccustomed. His initial fear is he has fallen at the first hurdle. Undeterred, his physio reduces the swelling with treatment, tapes it up and gives him a series of exercises to do in order to build up the foot until Thursday night – the eve of the day the waves are expected to be at their peak.

"It's stressful," says Steudtner, understating the enormous mental and physical undertaking, not to mention the hustle of getting a team together in time for such a swell. "I don't have anyone or anything ready at all. I've no team because I had no season. So I am getting my equipment from scratch, really. I have to get the surfboards ready, the jet skis and figure out the entire thing." And throughout it all, everything is filmed, cameras following his every move. That might heighten the stress for most, but filming is a necessity in Nazaré, to get the short clips to put out on Instagram feeds and YouTube. For Steudtner, there is a wider documentary about him being plotted for release at some point in 2023. And as the clock ticks into the early hours of Friday morning – the dawn of the supposed big day – it only gets more stressful. While others within the big-wave community become full of excitement and nervous anticipation about the incoming swell, he is left to ponder the magnitude of the undertaking ahead of him.

His decision to return brings with it a reunion with Maya Gabeira, his planned partner for the season who had to look elsewhere for stand-ins. But with all other surfing teams finalised for the season, he needs further back-up, so he goes back to his roots and picks up the phone to bring over Daniel Goldberg, his original tow partner from their earlier days in Hawaii. He also calls in a doctor from Germany to act as medical support in case things go awry, perfectly possible in light of the injury he is carrying, not to mention the fact his body is not as match-fit as usual for the gargantuan waves.

In the dark before first light strikes on Friday morning, they gather at the warehouses to fine-tune their equipment and get ready for the water. Having collected themselves, they head out of the harbour with a sense of nervousness and anticipation. In his first waves of the day, nothing feels right; this is partly down to the foot, and partly down to his own rustiness.

So much of surfing is about balance and feel. The injury means he is out of position on the board while on his tiptoes, which, in turn, pitches him forward into the water and, more often than not, off the board. "I couldn't really put pressure on my back foot on the tow rope, so I ended up being very light-footed," he complains. As he is towed in, he can't take his usual lines, he can't quite get the rhythm in the heart of the wave as he normally would. At times, he comes out of waves before they have begun to reach any great size. At others, he has tumbles that would never normally happen to him.

Amid the barrage of uncertainty, never, though, does he question his being out in the water – despite the uphill struggle. Giving up isn't really in his vocabulary. But is it worth the fight? At first, no. But eventually, yes. First one big wave, then another, then others follow as both the confidence and rhythm seep back. And with it, the foot holds together, and the pain is manageable with Steudtner's performance nearly back to normal. Unlike in the early days of his recovery, it isn't that jolt of pain, like a knife cut deep into his foot. Instead, that has been replaced by a constant ache – although the adrenaline acts as a sort of anaesthetic to the still-damaged foot.

He returns to the harbour partially elated at his big-wave surfing return and the rush, partially disappointed he hasn't managed more (as is always his wont). In addition, he is completely and utterly exhausted. For all the gym work, his body is not fully in tune to the endurance required for the rigours of a big-wave battering. That the hoped-for 100-footers have been replaced by mere 70-footers – although the truer calculations will ensue in the coming months through the official measuring process – was preferable for a body out of the swells for so long. "I think that was a good thing for me," he says of the day's waves, which were big enough to warrant a comeback, but not so big as to force him to surf, while injured, the 100-footer he'd sought for years. "Luckily, it didn't translate into reality, but it was still one of the biggest days of the season. And I'm glad I did it – and not just for me, but for the team experience."

Big-wave surfing can be a lonely existence, pushing ahead on your own as an athlete, businessman and financier of a solo operation. In this instance, when the entire focus of the team was on Steudtner, he cannot be prouder of the team effort, Gabeira among those essentially sacrificing much of her own day in the waves to enable her friend to ride the big waves. She is elated for him. He repays the favour a few days later by towing her into a few more big waves, after deciding his particular one-off day was sufficient to feed his need for the 2022 season, which was in danger of becoming an entirely damp squib.

His comeback riding deep into the heart of the waves should be the ultimate high, but he argues it is the opposite. "It's funny, but having seen how much my team put in, that was the best part, realising how great my team is. The entire team did everything to enable me to come back." As he takes stock, he sees that is way more special than any wave ridden, any crash evaded. He knows he will get the sole credit for the comeback from those watching on the clifftop or online, and it makes him feel like a bit of a fraud. "It might only be one person on the wave and just that person getting the credit, but you have to look at the rest of the team. It's the same thing with Formula One. You don't necessarily know the guy who's the mechanic or who's changing the tyres on the car because you just know Lewis Hamilton. In our sport, that might be the guy changing the propellers on the jet ski who does it for the passion or for their own motivation."

And psychologically to have had a successful comeback before 2021–22 ends is also crucial. The last time he had gone into proper waves, his foot had ended up damaged in three places, leaving mental scars, despite his insistence to the contrary, as well as the more obvious physical ones. Now, the mental demons over the capabilities of that previously damaged foot are resolved; and instead of having to wait for a remedy to that before the start of another season, he knows the foot can hold up whatever the conditions. "It was good motivation to push me in training but, as the last big swell of the season, it means a big physical and mental difference going into next season, as I know already when I'm not quite 100 per cent that I can do it. You have to fall off the horse and get back on, don't you?"

With all the hard work in his locker, next season can't come soon enough. There may not be new record waves to measure or awards heading his way off the back of the day's waves, but the German perfectionist briefly – very briefly – allows himself to bask in a moment of success. In five days, he has gone from nothing to riding the crest of the wave at a time when he'd given up on the season. His one-off comeback is marked with a barbecue back at Gabeira's house with all the team, from surfers to drivers to doctors to camera crew, in attendance. The goal has been achieved.

For Gabeira, it proves one of those days that don't quite click. For what are bumpier waves than anticipated, she brings with her too light a board for the occasion. But there are still positives to take away from the experience, primarily the performance of Steudtner. For once, she is happy simply to play second fiddle. His return to action might be just the one day for 2022, but the indicators are good for a possible reunion between the pair for the 2022–23 campaign, should they opt to do that in due course. "It was nice to see Seb back and so strong," she says. "I expected him to do it, but we had to make sure that it worked smoothly for him. He really pushed it to get there. I'm proud of him."

Already, she's talking with Steudtner, now that he's back, about next season and who to surf with. Such talks continue right until the swells return in October. Either way, she'll be back in the water for another season in Nazaré – no matter the partner.

36

RETURN TO NAZARÉ

Andrew Cotton

In the aftermath of the second Tow Surfing Challenge, Cotton's body is sore, its older frame not recovering as rapidly as it once did. He describes himself as "ruined", having put so much energy into the contest, with his thinking being there was no need to keep anything in reserve. While still ready to return, part of him wondered if that might simply be it for the season.

Amid the wipeouts and waves, the event had been a good day for Cotton and, more widely, Nazaré, showcasing the town, the contestants and big-wave surfing in a favourable light (bar Mitchell's hospitalisation). Cotton still wonders if it is all worth it, but then he thinks of where he might be without it. In his mind, he thinks he'd probably still be on a building site.

Even now, in articles about him, Cotton is often referred to as the "surfing plumber", a throwback to his early twenties, when he underwent a plumbing apprenticeship at the behest of his father, after leaving his surf factory job. Rick, the guy with whom he did his apprenticeship, likes to take credit for turning him into a professional surfer by putting him off the job full-time! His one-time protégé agrees. Cotton has never been one to shy away from hard work. He didn't mind the hours, the early starts, learning a new trade or working on a building site come rain or shine. For these jobs, he used to think of lifting heavy objects as some sort of cross training for his time in the waves. And in the evenings, he would be back in the classroom studying at college. He qualified for an NVQ (National Vocational Qualification), but he would constantly try to fit the work around escaping to travel and surf, his limited income spent almost entirely on those pursuits.

His skill set was so good that he even built his own family home with his then wife Katie. But such employment was only ever a means to an end. As the big-wave surfing took off, he shut off the valve on the plumbing business. Now the only plumbing or building-related jobs he does are to help his parents. To this day, he says he does not really know if they're proud of what he's achieved in the water in the years since they first parked up the family car and plonked him in the Devon waters with nothing more than a surfboard for company or guidance. There is a clip in the first series of *100 Foot Wave* where they watch, avidly but nervously, from the clifftop as their son performs in a contest, later hugging him warmly, every bit the proud parents. They may have wanted a more stable, safer career for their son, but that's never been vocalised.

Discussion turns, as it often does both externally and internally, to whether he is earning a sensible living this season. His riposte is that, if he'd wanted a sensible living, he would have remained a plumber. The earning is a constant battle for many in Nazaré, him included, and yet he is better off than many. There are some key sponsors that have long been at his side – the energy drink Red Bull, the Devon clothing brand Saltrock and another company from his home county, the surf line Tiki. "I'm super lucky. I'm sponsored by Red Bull, I work with great brands that help me out, but everything's on a year-to-year basis. The scary thing is it's a year contract and, if they say, 'You're not sponsored anymore,' I'm actually fucked."

The finances are a perpetual struggle. Some of the surfers simply scratch around from one meal to the next and from one swell to another to stay afloat. Cotton's finances are not quite that precarious, but it remains a perpetual stress. A season comfortably costs £20,000. A full day's worth of petrol for the jet skis can be as much as £150, and the cost is on the rise globally. He sees some making much more than him, while others are financially clinging on just to be there. Sponsors aside, another revenue stream comes from various talks both in and out of the big-wave season. He has looked at widening the net to other options, and jokes as a surfing plumber that becoming the face of the hardware store company Screwfix might be the answer.

Of his financial situation, he says, "I'm not moaning about it. But it goes back to me thinking that I'll get that one wave and it'll all be alright. If you look into the running costs of everything, you're not even breaking even. But I suppose it's about what you want to do, and I just want to surf. I've thought about trying to do a TV show, and I do wonder if any surfers have exit strategies."

In the immediate days after that second Tow Surfing Challenge, he rests up and heads home to spend the February half-term school holidays with his children. His son Ace has yet to be properly bitten by the surfing bug – his father suspects he never will be. Instead, his passions are playing football and the Xbox with his mates. But Cotton knows seeing the big injuries Dad has sustained – laid up in a back brace or on crutches with his leg in plaster – have impacted Ace mentally. His son still regularly comes to Portugal to visit him during the season, the pair heading from a French ski trip to Nazaré when another big swell hits barely 10 days later (the one that ends with Von Rupp nursing two injuries rather than one for the off season, and the one that marks Steudtner's comeback). Like his peers, Cotton had been ready to say goodbye to Nazaré for another season, but talk of this swell, predicted by many to be the day of days, proved too enticing.

So the pair fly into Lisbon and arrive in Portugal's capital the night before for the potential 100-foot day that came up some 30 feet short. Cotton gets what he calls a couple of waves but has something holding him back: his son. Despite doing what he does, he is acutely aware of the risks of big-wave surfing – his son is, after all, named after Ace Cool, a big-wave legend who lost his life in Waimea Bay after he didn't return from a surf one November day back in 2015. Like many others, Cool, whose real name was Alec Cooke, wanted to be known as the Evil Knievel of big-wave surfing, and had had his share of close shaves in the preceding years. This time, he lost the fight. His body was never found.

Going back for this late February swell, Cotton sees his atten-dance as essential in case it ended up being a record-breaker of a day. When it dawned on him it wasn't, he took his foot off the throttle. "I didn't want to push it, and I had Ace with me. So I didn't really want to go all out. I almost felt a bit guilty to do that with Ace there. Our trip was the first time just me and him, and, if something happened …" he trails off as his thoughts turn to the unthinkable. After this, his mentality shifted to his responsibilities and playing it a little safer.

Ace makes no secret of the fact he doesn't like his dad tackling the big waves; Cotton says his son gets anxious being present. Ace won't ever watch from the clifftop, nor will he even watch any clips of his dad in the water in the aftermath of a competition or a day's surfing. His grandparents tried to sit him down to watch the first season of *100 Foot Wave*, in which Dad played a starring role a while back, and he wouldn't do it. "I feel bad about it. In lots of his younger years, I've been injured – a broken back, knee surgery three or four times. For three or four years of his life, I've been laid up at home unable to do anything. So I think he associates surfing with that. But he still understands that this is work, this is Dad's work. Unfortunately for him, my office is a 70-foot wave."

The ex-Formula One world champion Jenson Button once said that it was unthinkable for him to still be competing in Formula One as a parent, his argument being that he wouldn't be able push himself and the car to the absolute limit with someone else relying on his survival back at home. So he postponed fatherhood until after those Formula One days. In contrast, for Cotton, being a dad has almost been a catalyst for his career. If anything, it was the start of parenthood that acted as a trigger to take the big waves in an even more focused fashion, a sense of "now or never", to tackle the whole process more professionally.

That last big February swell in many ways marks the beginning of the end of the season for Cotton. He has surfed some of his biggest waves in March in the past – a notable one in Ireland back in 2012. There will be some more fleeting moments to come in the following weeks – some big-ish waves, some foiling, some filming with sponsors and even a programme with the BBC. Taking stock of the season, he isn't happy with it – he never is. The same feelings gnaw away at him: that he could have done more, the waves caught could have been bigger, the style of surfing could have been better. It is ever thus, and it's the thing that motivates him to work harder again over the winter and come back with the same renewed enthusiasm for the season. All the while, the same thought sticks in the back of his mind: "Maybe I'll get *that* wave."

But what is this wave? Is it the 100-footer? Will any wave ever be big enough to quench his thirst? "You're thinking this could be the one, but we're living in a dream world because what is 'the one'? We're not racing around or winning the FA Cup. Really, there isn't anything at the end of it. It's in your mind: *once I get that wave, then that'll be it*, but this is an addiction. Surfing is an addiction. You're in that position where you think, *One more and this'll be the last one, the biggest swell ever; I'll ride that wave and then that'll be it, and I can retire because I'll be able to retire off that wave.* In reality, it's never going to happen. But I think that's what you tell yourself."

Despite the questioning, the man who first saw those big waves in magazines in his boyhood Devon bedroom and dreamed of being in them, will always keep coming back to Nazaré as long as his body allows it. For him, it is the "place to be" in big-wave surfing, for all the talk of other spots, from Hawaii to the west coast of Ireland. Hawaii is more picture-perfect, Tahiti, too, with crystal-clear waters and bright blue skies. In contrast, Nazaré can often look ugly – down to the fact that some of the biggest swells often lend themselves to storms sweeping in from the Atlantic. But what it might lack in terms of picture-post-card beauty, it makes up for in the sheer volume of big waves.

While he's lost count of the number of days this year the waves here have been over 20 feet, in contrast, he says, such days are harder to come by in Hawaii, for example. A convert to Nazaré in its early days, Cotton argues he and other trailblazers have been able to prove the doubters wrong. "At first, it was taken here was a bit of a joke in the surfing world; but then the mainstream media caught up with those giant walls of water with surfers in front of the lighthouse. You want to be where the biggest waves are – and that's here, no question. If you want to be a big-wave professional and be good, you need to be here. This is where you need to train. It's dangerous, but it's the place to be."

Despite being firmly cemented here, there are times when he still suffers from imposter syndrome, where he compares himself to other surfers, and negatively so. It's that doubt that motivates him to work harder and keeps him coming back. And what else would he do? "For me, my attitude is: how long can I blag this? It's like I'm completely making it up – but I think everyone's like that."

As for when the end comes, he is unsure. At some point, his body will tell him it can no longer take the battering, that the size of waves into which he is towed must reduce. By his reckoning, that's not on the immediate horizon. Whether he can finally feel satisfied, at that point, with walking away, he has no idea. However, one thing he is sure of is that surfing will always be a part of him, even when he's old and grey – and no doubt back in Devon by then.

"Surfing is just with you until you die. It's one of those sports. I don't think you'll be doing 80-footers until you're 60, but you'll still be doing small waves when you're 80, with everything braced and taped together. Maybe, by then, the surfing doesn't matter, it's just about time in the ocean. There might be some days you don't surf, but you're in the water and you're loving it more than ever."

37

FROM RUSSIA TO RECORDS

Sebastian Steudtner

Surfing is an inherently selfish pastime: just you and the wave – everything else is essentially immaterial and a blockade to your goal. Steudtner makes no secret of the fact that he can be selfish in his quest, be that catching an individual wave or missing a family gathering for the call of a big swell. But at the same time, he is a surfer with a conscience. Was he always that way? He wonders if, when he was a younger, emerging surfer, it was the "me, me, me" that drove him on a daily basis to fight for relevance amid the bigger names he aspired to emulate. But at the same time, he remembers his parents always instilling in him the essence of right and wrong, of being respectful, and helping others less fortunate than themselves.

The day before the pinnacle of a troubled season – Steudtner's late February surfing comeback – Russian President Vladimir Putin orders the invasion of Ukraine. Like many, Steudtner watches the news reports on television, stupefied by what is unfolding in mainland Europe. He has ties to Ukraine. His link is twofold. First is his close friendship with the former boxer Wladimir Klitschko, whose brother and fellow ex-boxer Vitaly is the mayor of a heavily shelled Kyiv. His second Ukrainian sporting link is a lesser-known light in Vasiliy Kordysh. Before the war, Kordysh was a regular surfer and was president of the Ukrainian Surfing Federation – still is, although there are understandably far greater priorities now.

When Steudtner and Klitschko talk in the days and months after war breaks out, the German tries to steer the conversation away from discussing the war, his thinking being his friend has gone well beyond saturation point on that subject as the invasion drags on and on, creating unrelenting devastation. "He doesn't want to talk about what's happening, he wants to get his mind off the things on him. So we talk about boxing or surfing or other things."

With Kordysh, the conversation is different. Steudtner lends his Instagram feed to enable the Ukrainian surfer to give an impassioned appeal to a wider audience about the horrors facing the Ukrainian people. He also posts pictures of the beach in Odesa where Kordysh would regularly surf, and where the annual national championships would traditionally take place. Instead, the beach has been closed, its golden sands and the seas surrounding it scattered with land mines and barbed-wire defences in a bid to halt the Russian invasion on that coastline.

"I spoke with Vasiliy and then felt really appreciative going to the beach in Nazaré and surfing in the smaller waves with no worries at all. Vasiliy told me at the time a good swell was on the way to the Ukraine, but that no one could go surf as it's too dangerous." The mines have been placed by the Ukraine military to hamper Russian attacks on the port, and the public have been informed to stay away from the beach, though not told of the exact locations of the mines. A few days after Steudtner and Kordysh first exchange messages about the impact of the war, a local man taking his girlfriend to the beach drives over one of the land mines in a tragic accident. His girlfriend dies, their vehicle is a write-off, and the man is left in hospital with life-changing injuries.

Such stories are plentiful – detailing one utter horror to the next. In his bid to help, the German uses his wider circle of contacts to fill a large truck with vital supplies in Nazaré and get it driven all the way to Ukraine. It's pulled off in a matter of days. The idea that he might be sprinkling just a little bit of good in the world is lost on him, a sense of guilt the overriding sensation that he is left with, unable to do much more as the fully laden truck pulls away. "I get disgusted by how quiet people are. People are being slaughtered not far away from here in Europe. How can you not do something, how can you not help? That's a basic human condition. I wish I could do more."

And the plan is to do more, in time. He already has a project in Germany where children from disadvantaged backgrounds are taught how to surf over a 10-month programme, as well as given lessons in how to swim. At the heart of it is giving them a better understanding of being in the ocean. A similar proposal for Ukrainian children is put in motion, the finer points of whether it takes place in Ukraine in the future or with refugees coming to take part in a place like Germany yet to be decided.

"It's unfair how little support some people get. It's crazy to see how little responsibility people take in general, especially in the sports world." He's getting angry now – at the unfairness of the situation and the unwillingness of some to help. "Everyone is preaching about values, but no one's living those values. As soon as it touches their bank account, everyone's scared to do something. All I've done is just a few social media posts but, really, I haven't done shit. People with a platform and money need to act in moments like this. Without preaching, what is greater than helping others? There's nothing greater, is there?"

While utterly incomparable to his own plight, Steudtner is partly driven to help those impacted amid the Russian invasion by his own past struggles. His previous troubles pale into insignificance in comparison. But he remembers those that were willing to help him – and those that weren't – at a time when he had to return to life as a bouncer back in Germany, eventually arriving in Nazaré with very little money to his name, just big aspirations. He also sees the challenges faced by the new arrivals and those short of surf sponsorship in the town, who are now trying to find their feet and make a name for themselves. Where he can, he steps in to help.

Nazaré's surfing community is filled with people who are struggling, in a sport which occasionally is itself. The surfers all want to improve as athletes but, at the same time, don't have the capacity to take care of much apart from their jet skis and simply surfing the wave.

As Steudtner talks about their situation, he could easily be reflecting on his early days here. "It's tough. As well as surfing, they have to market themselves – and no one is going to do that for them. The young ones expect that to come to them; I did too, but it's a long time in coming. I do like to help. I don't want to do anything to get to the very top if it's not with good values. What's the point if you don't share? I'm as happy for getting a world record for Maya as getting a world record myself, and Maya's the same." He harks back to her reaction to his recent return to stress the point, and the end of his own difficult season.

Some struggle earlier in their careers, some later, and Steudtner likes to have half an eye looking out for them. "I hope I always have values of taking care of people around me and being respectful and honest. Being fair is more important than money." But, alas, this is not the outlook of everyone in Nazaré.

On a more selfish note, as the 2021–22 season ends, he is still pushing to have his October 2020 wave officially measured and ratified, bored of asking himself how long it takes to measure a wave. Two full seasons have now passed since he surfed the wave Steudtner believes should have etched him in the record books. Nineteen months on, and having broken a foot, fully rehabilitated, and returned to the waves in the interim, he is still on tenterhooks, no clearer to understanding if he has surfed the biggest wave of all time. "The sport's in an unprofessional state and that's why that measuring is unprofessional," he says more in a manner of acceptance than frustration.

The thinking among others is that, after the event, if you hype it up enough when it comes to a particular wave, people will believe it. There is always conjecture about who has ridden the biggest waves. Some argue the case for one particular surfer and his or her wave, while others will give their backing to another. Some simply shrug their shoulders at the nonsense of it all. Steudtner has always been fairly confident he has the world record, and yet he is none the wiser whether that is a reality. It has been universally agreed, Steudtner included, that he is not the first man to have cracked the 100-footer. That remains unachieved ... for now. And yet despite the silence from the measurers, he is still confident Rodrigo Koxa's mark has been bettered.

To find answers, he jokes he has been forced to turn himself into an investigative journalist – or, at the very least, a pushy athlete manager – to get to the bottom of it all. For months on end, he is simply met by silence from anyone who might provide answers to his questioning. Then silence turns to murmurings, and whispers begin to emerge that the record is looming.

Finally, on 24 May 2022, the news comes: his wave has been measured at 86.5 feet, a new world record. By just 6.5 feet, he has surpassed Koxa in the record books, the Brazilian's five-year reign ended. The moment is marked with a ceremony with the Guinness Book of Records, fittingly set up on the roof of the Nazaré lighthouse. He is all smiles on the day, despite the fact is it is now more than a year and a half after it all happened in the water below him.

There is happiness, and a sense of relief too, and he puts out all the right jubilant statements in the moment. Speaking to Guinness, he talks of his amazement at a lifelong goal achieved, the crazy journey to get to that point, the physical training, the behind-the-scenes work on his equipment and the management of building the right team around him. With the record, he now declares he has "achieved everything there is in my sport". On social media, he speaks of the childhood dream achieved and the hope that he has inspired others to chase their dreams as well, as he once did from Nuremberg to Nazaré.

And yet, at the same time, attaining the record all seems too little, too late. Amid all the celebration, this supposed moment of euphoria is laced with a retrospective frustration at the painstaking nature of it all. The fight not to just get this wave properly measured and ratified, but also what he perceives as a fight for much of his career for the necessary recognition. There is footage of a wave of his in Nazaré in 2018 which, at first glance, looks every bit as big as his one two years later, which has made it into the record books. The former was a wave that never gained any great traction with the same measurers.

Of finally having the record, he says: "It's great that it's confirmed and it's good to have it, but it's not like I'm jumping up and down with joy." In truth, he is not so much embittered as a little tired by the whole saga. "It's been such a long process. This is the longest it has taken in the history of the sport. It's the first time in the history of the sport that number wasn't given out on the day of the awards ceremony or 10 days later. There has been no explanation for it. I don't even know where to start."

And yet the record is his – at least, until next season when he and his peers will collectively try to better it. As for whether it is genuinely the biggest wave ever surfed, there will be those that say otherwise, even those that suggest Steudtner's is no bigger than Koxa's previous mark. It's the way of the big-wave world. As for the German himself, he believes there may well have been other waves surfed that may have been bigger but that were never measured, most notably the one two years beforehand.

"I've been surfing really big waves for 10 years – there's just no transparency. Go back to 2020 for me, and before that to 2018, and you will find evidence of bigger waves or the same size waves I've surfed. For me, it's nothing new because we haven't got a measuring system that's transparent. I don't know if this is my biggest, as I'm not a wave-measuring scientist. A giant wave is a giant wave in the way it feels. How fast I went on this record one was right up there. The vision I had up there when I changed my line was the big difference. It was very special."

The odd thing is that while the record is his, and it cannot be taken away from him until the circus converges on Nazaré for the 2022–23 season, it doesn't really change how he will approach the off season and the build-up to his next onslaught in the same waves. As the world record holder, the spotlight might now be on him now more than ever; with more sponsors potentially likely to come sniffing. But his aim for the coming year is still to tackle the waves in the best way possible, be they 15, 50 or 100 feet.

38

UNDER THE SURGEON'S KNIFE

Sérgio Cosme

Sérgio Cosme jokes that his shoulder is spending more time out of place than in its socket. Behind the smiles, he is coping with the physical ailment, but psychologically, the injury begins to eat away at him. His concern is less about him, and more about those that the guardian angel of Nazaré perpetually seeks to protect.

It gets to the point where he is no longer functioning at full capacity when it comes to jet-ski rescues, and he is plagued by the idea someone in the water might befall a worse fate on his watch because of his impaired physical state. He often likes to say you can never guarantee a rescue in Nazaré – he has seen enough close calls to know that – and yet he is still ill at ease in the water since his shoulder injury. "The thing that I need to guarantee is that I'm 100 per cent able to do my best," he says. "I don't know that I can right now. Maybe I've taken that risk before, but I don't want to do that again."

So surgery goes from a plan of avoidance to a possibility and, finally, to an inevitability. By the moment of the operation, he knows that its timing also means he will not be fully fit once the first big swells of late autumn come around again – be that on his board or straddling a jet ski. It means new plans will have to be made, his established team with Von Rupp rejigged at least until Christmas,

281

Cosme estimates. He jokes to his teammate: although Von Rupp has lost a driver, he's gained a spotter; his plan is to join the other spotters on the clifftop and keep a hand in with the team.

> "While I'm not able to get in the water, at least I can be a spotter and maybe teach someone to be a spotter for us for the rest of the season. These setbacks happen in life sometimes, but I believe there is a reason for everything. I'd prefer to have two years' worth of surgeries if it means I'm OK for the rest of the decade."

There is a "here we go again" element to surgery, following the operations on his knocked-out teeth and then knee. He is in the unwanted position of hospital staff being on first-name terms with him. But surgery is a success, the joint repaired. Now the question is how long he will be forced to stay out of the water.

While conversations turn to next season, his primary focus is on his own rehabilitation and getting back in the water as quickly as possible. He has not yet allowed himself to ponder how he will feel when the big days hit at the start of next season and he is consigned to dry land. But he knows it'll be a dagger to the heart – he has spent enough time on the sidelines to understand how hard it'll be, come October. "Put a Formula One or MotoGP driver on a track without being able to drive, and you'll see his face and his mood," he says. "It's the same. But I have to be grateful that I'm still part of the team. I could be in a coma in hospital or forced out of the sport. This is the team I created back in 2015, first with Koxa and then Nic."

It was as a spotter that he began in Nazaré, helping some of the first crews to surf it in its infancy, before he himself surfed it or pulled off his jet-ski rescues. Life has come full circle: he will once more mix, at least for a few months, with the spotters on the section of cliff that they make their base for every session. Ever the optimist, he believes it will make him better at his job once the time comes to return to the ocean, whenever that is. "I've done everything in the team: surfer, rescue, main driver, second rescue, driver of a camera-man, spotter. And it's important to do this. I think everyone should do this – because when you're out of the water, you understand some things better. You can understand some of your mistakes better; you learn to communicate better in the team."

Quite who is on the other end of the radio is another matter. Von Rupp will again be ever-present, but the make-up of the rest of the team is being considered during the summer months. Scooby has been a regular with them in recent times, but he missed the latter part of the season to film the Brazilian *Celebrity Big Brother*. Despite that, he will rejoin forces with Von Rupp, and there is talk of teaming up with another of the local crews to make a star-studded, all-Portuguese crew for 2022–23; but such decisions are likely to go down to the wire. These are the sort of decisions that can decide whether the subsequent season is a flyer or falls flat.

A trip to France for a sponsor event allows for Cosme and Von Rupp to both step away from Nazaré and have some time together to speak candidly about their hopes and expectations for when the action resumes in October. With regards to the idea that there is any bad blood between them from Von Rupp's decision to join forces with Chianca for the big swells for the remainder of the previous season, Cosme is dismissive. Reflecting on that time, he says simply, "I was more sad than mad … but in any case, I don't stay mad with him." It is the disparity of Nazaré surfing, both a team sport and a selfish, individual one where each surfer has to pursue his or her best pathway. "I've told Nic I don't want to change. This is a dangerous sport, it's extreme. Every small detail we can do combines to help save lives. If you're changing your driver or surfer every swell, you are dealing with a different approach every time. I know exactly where Nic will end up if he falls. I know he prefers left to right. You need to be connected with your teammate. Nic is my partner and I'd like to be the same with him."

The other perpetual discussion point is the finances. Both Cosme and Von Rupp bring with them sponsorship deals, ranging from Tudor Watches to Yamaha and Monster Energy. And yet a big-wave season has the ability to devour money, however seemingly sizeable the pot at the season's start. With rising fuel prices, next season is likely to be the most expensive yet. Cosme likes to joke that "towing is a sport of millionaires", and yet very few of them have actually attained that status. "Big-wave surfing really is like Formula One, and not just because it's the best or the most expensive – it's also a team sport. We need our jet skis, our teams, our warehouse, our spotters. In Formula One, the guys on the pit wall tell their drivers to go faster; it's their mechanics, their team directors. More or less, it's like that – but on the water."

How Cosme would dearly love a Formula One budget. Such riches are but a pipe dream. Rehab aside, it will be the usual battle to keep his and his team's head above water for the season. For what is his eighth season, it is the same, ever-present, and yet he wouldn't want it any other way. Part of the joy appears to come from the struggle to get there.

39

THE BEGINNING OF THE END

There is no grand crescendo to this big-wave season, no final monstrous wave capping it all off. Instead, given the grandiose nature of the past months in the water, it doesn't exactly turn to a trickle, but it does slowly fizzle out.

Unlike other sports, there isn't a cup final, a last race, a finale of any kind or a trophy to be handed over to mark the end. There is never a date that seals the season's conclusion nor a point where the wave – Cosme's "big momma" – packs up, only to return in October for another winter's season. It is less like the flick of a switch, and more a fading of the light.

Heading into spring, the swells gradually begin to diminish and, one by one, day by day, week by week, Nazaré's band of nomads steadily pack up for another season. None of the final days or weeks of the big-wave window come close to the really big swell that landed at the end of February, although big enough waves still pop up here and there in the aftermath and lure some back for a final dance. Injuries, family commitments or else an admission that it's time to leave lead the surfers away. Some – with their claws so entrenched in the big-wave surfing community and the hedonistic life it brings – hang on longer than others, refusing to let go of their passion, their livelihood, their drug.

When the season does finally end, life is quieter in the surfing corner of the town – in the Nazaré warehouses and in the harbour, where the jet skis would ordinarily take out the surfers each day. And the surfers' lives quieten too, for the most part. There is relief at having survived the season and at the chance to give the body a rest – the mind, too, from the stressors. But season's end can also be tantamount to a grieving process.

No thrill-seeking quite matches an immersion in the big waves, the life-and-death tightrope walk of the biggest days. Returning home to normal life, wherever and whatever that might be, can almost seem ordinary. The town itself is no less quiet, its year-round appeal keeps the tourists coming as spring approaches and then edges into summer, when it welcomes an influx of visitors chasing sea, sun and sand – rather than a glimpse of Nazaré's band of surfers.

In different ways, the disparate group of watermen and women try to chase a fix of sorts in the interlude before the next season.

Andrew Cotton toys with a surfing trip to Indonesia but, when it comes down to it, he has neither the time nor money for it. Instead, he packs up for the drive back to Devon to spend the summer with his family, girlfriend, friends and surfers in the smaller waves, where aspirations for the bigger ones began.

He darts to the States to give talks, to France for some cycling in the Alps and to a stint in Salzburg at Red Bull's headquarters, for the gathering of their British-based extreme sports stars, including the cyclist Danny MacAskill and the rugby player Jack Nowell. Most of the athletes talk to him about plans to retire in their early thirties. At 42, there is no thought of retirement for Cotton – and no doubt in his mind that he will be back to Nazaré next season. "It's not like rugby or another game, surfing's something you do forever," he says. "It can be love-hate, but I need it." Even in the off season, it is all about the big waves and the preparation for them, both technical and physical.

Much of the summer is spent thinking about the winter ahead. Long bike rides and working closely with his personal trainer are aimed at enabling him to be fit enough for another year in Nazaré's waters. But there are the technical preparations too: sorting out a new trailer and jet ski, as well as tinkering with some radios he's adding. Then there are the finances. Some years, it feels like a case of wondering how he can beg, steal or borrow what he needs. Often, the success of his financial ventures is reflected in where he ends up staying. Plans are to lodge in the same prime-location holiday house rather than cramped in the back of a camper van. That is partly financed by a pre-season talk in Venice, the sort of high-paid job that keeps him afloat for another season.

In contrast to Cotton, Nic von Rupp makes his way to Indonesia with Reymão. Images posted on Instagram of a picture-perfect idyll show a rare getaway for the couple. There is horse riding in the ocean, stunning, deserted beaches, and drinks with friends to celebrate a birthday – his thirty-second, a moment which allows time for reflection. Come autumn, a national campaign starring him is launched with Visit Portugal, to attract tourists to Nazaré and the rest of the country. And amid all that, there is the constant rehabilitation for both the ribs and shoulder, to enable him to be back to full fitness for the season's start.

In person, Maya Gabeira can act like she's laid-back to the point of horizontal, but hers is an off season jam-packed and seemingly mapped out from start to finish. There is a US road trip with friends, Oceana board meetings, a talk to the United Nations in New York and the world premiere of the documentary about her life. She acquiesces and agrees to watch it, having previously refused to do so.

Viewing the past 10 years of her life is a cathartic process which makes her reflective of the past. Sitting in her seat for the hour-and-a-half viewing, she feels a wave of emotions: vulnerability, fear and, finally, with the standing ovation and overall response, simply contentment. The suffering she underwent, particularly in her earlier days in the big waves, is an overarching aspect of the film.

On her return to Nazaré at the summer's end, she goes training with Sebastian Steudtner and tells him how she doesn't feel ready for the next season, that she has low expectations and that she is no longer sure about pushing it to the limit on the big days. Steudtner's response is, "Every fucking year, you say the same thing," and she bursts out laughing, knowing it is the truth.

In her heart of hearts, she still has a commitment to the wave and her sport; there is an overriding feeling that "I'm not near being done yet". And yet, at the same time, there is the beginning of a gradual shift. "I want to surf big waves, but I want to do other things and put my brain to work, and contribute to society". With the Oceana board, such a quest continues, while at the UN she opened up about her own mental health struggles.

It is surreal for her that the waves and her place in them should have brought her to this point. Having had a propensity to change partners last season – through injury, rather than any fault of her own – she and Pierre Rollet, rather than Steudtner, have agreed to renew a partnership which had previously ended with the Frenchman in hospital with damaged ribs and knees.

Steudtner's scientific approach to the off season sees him dart from leaning on the technology of Porsche to having his patience tested by the Portuguese builders of his dream home, which should have been finished long ago. With his season over and his one-off comeback complete, he starts plotting with his team how to tackle the next season, now that the foot is back to 100 per cent functionality. In the interim, he has the occasional foray into smaller waves to either surf or foil.

He wants some quiet time, although his quest for perfection in sport and in the house build means that he doesn't really do quiet for long. He gets bored too easily, the mind always racing, the next project on the horizon being planned. With his body now repaired, it is all with a view to being the best prepared he can be when the large Atlantic swells once again hit Portugal's coast in October. Does it bring with it expectations, as a world record holder? "I have no expectations. I just want to surf." Finally, the body, as well as the mind, is ready to do so.

Sérgio Cosme faces an off season of repair and rehabilitation. The shoulder is getting better week by week, as he undergoes another period of reconditioning much like the previous two endured for his teeth and ACL, albeit with a different part of the body to repair. While others know they plan to be ready to hit the first big swell when it comes in October, for the Portugal native, there is the frustration of no set date when he might be back marshalling the waters from the seat of his jet ski as Nazaré's guardian angel. The safety of Von Rupp, and the many others he has saved or could save, is poorer for his absence.

Come September 2022, the messages between surfers, spotters and camera crews begin to ramp up. There is conjecture about when the first big waves might come, and conversations begin to lay bare the desire to catch Nazaré's next set of bombs. Most reckon the collective itch to return usually kicks in around September.

Whether one is surfing waves in Indonesia, working in a Porsche tunnel, toiling in injury rehabilitation, brushing shoulders with the great and good of New York, or surfing the small waves of Devon, such activities can only garner one's interest for so long. These are quickly forgotten, as rose-tinted spectacles look ahead to what awaits. Soon, they begin to count the days to when they can relocate to their various winter homes – a false countdown that doesn't know when Mother Nature might bring back the monster waves in which they thrive.

Cotton is among the earliest to return, but he knows it must come with a balance. He has too often made the mistake in seasons past – his peers also – of hitting the early part of a campaign too hard. They all have their stories of a season cut too short too soon. As Cotton puts it, "[If] you come out too hard and too hungry and pick up a big injury in October, it can be a very long winter. I've been there." As the months, weeks and days click ever closer to the start of the season, he can have all the aspirations he wants about competition wins, record waves and new lines. But his plan is less complicated than that: to go out and enjoy himself. "Keep it fun. Otherwise, what's the point?"

Even having spent months watching them surf the big waves, I still find it hard to fully comprehend why they do it. It is too simplistic to say it is just the thrill-seeking, the chase for that one wave, whatever that might be: 100 feet tall or a perfect barrel. It is about a shared experience for the individual teams on the water and the wider community out of it, from surfers to jet-ski drivers and camera crews.

But it is also about a quest for survival in the sport and staying alive. Having come closer than perhaps anyone to losing their life, for Gabeira, the lure is quite simple: it is the desire to come back. "Surfing one wave is something special, but to survive it is something else. I can only be a great big-wave surfer if I stay alive."

All have survived this season. The quest for survival will begin in earnest again soon.

ACKNOWLEDGEMENTS

Nazaré's big-wave surfing community could not have been more welcoming on this journey. My five main characters – Sérgio Cosme, Andrew Cotton, Maya Gabeira, Sebastian Steudtner and Nic von Rupp – must get the biggest thanks for letting me into their lives and for all their patience amid the perpetual questioning.

There are endless others in the town to thank – Adrian 'Strodgy' Cordeiro and his mother Tina for their hospitality at their lovely guesthouse, and to Garrett and Nicole McNamara as the trailblazers of this place. There are countless others to whom I am hugely grateful in the town: Pedro Pisco, Paulo Salvador, Paulo Caldeira, Dino Casmiro, Joaquim Zarro, Al Mennie, Walter Chiccharo, C.J. Macias, Lucas Chianca, Alemao de Maresias, Lino Bogalho, Jorge Leal, Tim Bonython, Pablo Garcia, Laurent Pujol, Sandra Marina Lopes, Tom Butler, Nuno Oliveira and Axel Haber. Further afield, my gratitude goes to both Derek Dunfee and Shawn Dollar for reliving their traumas and to João Cruz and Falk Feddersen for explaining how waves work.

This book wouldn't have reached the light of day without my literary agent David Luxton or all those at Welbeck Publishing, who believed in this tale from the outset. Thank you Ross Hamilton in the early days, Beth Bishop for guiding a book-writing novice so brilliantly and Meredith Olson for your remarkable attention to detail. I'd also like to thank my boss at the *Evening Standard*, James Major, for allowing some last-minute escapes to Portugal.

My final mention goes to my wife and our boys for putting up with my disappearances, and for all your love and support.

PICTURE CREDITS

The publisher and author would like to thank the following sources for their kind permission to reproduce the pictures in this book.

1 (top, bottom); 2 (top, middle, bottom); 3 (top, bottom); 4 (top, bottom) Vitor Estrelinha; 5 (top, middle) Konstantin Reyer, (bottom) Vitor Estrelinha; 6 (top, middle) Andrew Cotton, (bottom) Vitor Estrelinha; 7 (top, bottom) Joerg Mitter; 8 (top, middle) Shutterstock, (bottom) Matt Majendie.

Every effort has been made to acknowledge correctly and contact the source and/or copyright holder of each picture and Welbeck Publishing Group apologises for any unintentional errors or omissions, which will be corrected in future editions of this book.

INDEX